THE GLASGOW ACADEMY

150 years

Iain MacLeod

Author's Note

In writing the history of The Glasgow Academy I have been fortunate enough to have had access to a complete set of Directors' and Governors' Minutes, to every prospectus for the school which has been issued and to an uninterrupted run of school magazines. These have formed the principal source for the story told in these pages, though I have also consulted local newspapers, principally for the early years. Some anecdotes have been drawn from *The Glasgow Academy 1846 - 1946*, published to mark the school's centenary.

I am grateful that I have been encouraged to draw on David Humberstone's study of the Academy roll as a source of information on changes of location and commuting patterns, 1846 - 1996.

I am grateful, too, to a number of Academicals who have taken an interest in this project and I thank in particular W M Mann, J W Dallachy, R N W Smith, A M W Thomson, D J Guthrie, A T W Liddell and G G Bannerman. The illustrations on pages 2, 6, 28 and 31 are reproduced by courtesy of the Mitchell Library, Glasgow, on page 4 by courtesy of the National Monuments Record of Scotland, on page 95 by courtesy of Midland Bluebird Company and Western Buses Ltd and on pages 147, 148, 162, 171, 173, 174, 176 and 179 by courtesy of the *Scottish Field*. The cover photograph was taken by James and Mark Gilchrist, an Academical and his son, a Sixth Year pupil.

This book is dedicated to the memory of those former members of The Glasgow Academy who 'left all that was dear to them, endured hardship, faced danger, and finally passed out of the sight of man by the path of duty and self sacrifice, giving up their lives that others might live in freedom'.

© Iain MacLeod 1997

Published 1997

ISBN   0 9530515 0 1

Published by   The Glasgow Academicals' War Memorial Trust
Colebrooke Street
Glasgow G12 8HE

Printed by   Lawn and Miller Ltd
21 Summerlee Street
Glasgow G33 4DB

Foreword

As other Glasgow schools might be tempted to remind us, 150 years is not really old as schools go – but 150 years of The Glasgow Academy is certainly a milestone well worth marking, and that has been done splendidly in this excellent book by Iain MacLeod, Deputy Rector of The Academy.

His book paints a detailed picture of both The Academy and many of those who have played a part in its story over the past century and a half. To produce such an account is no mean task and we thank Iain MacLeod for the patience, perseverance and many hours of painstaking work which he has brought to this project.

In this modern day and age and in such a swiftly changing world this history offers a pleasant opportunity to reflect on what has gone before and particularly to bring to mind teachers who have devoted their professional lives to The Academy and to whom so many of us are so grateful – in retrospect – for the influence they have had, and still have, on our lives.

Having reached its 150th birthday, The Academy, surely, is growing up. But far from feeling its age, the school is just as forward-looking and energetic as ever it was : indeed some might say that it is reaching new heights of prosperity. Of course it is not the same school that it was in the past – it was ever so – but I do hope that Academicals, parents and friends of the school who read this book will feel that The Academy is in good heart and that we can be justly proud of the school of which we are members.

That this is so is due in very large part to the excellence of the Rectors who have guided the school over the years and to the strengths of the teachers whom they have appointed: but it is due also to the quality of the pupils, now girls as well as boys. The current generation of pupils are at least the equal of their predecessors. They are bright and enthusiastic boys and girls, and they leave The Glasgow Academy as fine young men and women. Some will become household names and leaders in business, commerce and the professions, as have over the years many Academicals, some of whose achievements are reflected in this book. Most will in one way or another serve the communities in which they live, both in and furth of Scotland. I vaguely remember several decades ago being told that if one kicked a rugby ball or threw a cricket ball almost anywhere in the world it would probably land near an Academical. That remains true. Today, the ball might even be caught!

We embark on our second 150 years in the certain knowledge that the first 150 years, recalled in this history, have provided a strong foundation for The Glasgow Academy to maintain its leading position among Scotland's schools in the years ahead.

Bill Mann
Chairman
The Glasgow Academicals' War Memorial Trust

Contents

1845-1851

The earliest years

In 1844, the Crown Prince of Denmark paid the first royal visit to Glasgow for many years. If he had been allowed to, he would quickly have discovered that he was in a place of the most appalling contrasts. It was perhaps the dirtiest and most unhealthy town in Britain, with the poorest housing and social conditions. There was squalor at its very heart : masses of decaying vegetable matter lying in the streets and lanes of Blythswood Hill, manure spread in the roads close to the livery stables in Renfield Street.

Disease was rife : cholera and typhus took a heavy toll and half of all the children born in the city died before they reached the age of five. At the same time, the population was expanding hugely, quadrupling to 300000 in the first half of the century. The newcomers had to be housed, quickly and cheaply, and further overcrowding was the consequence. Slums had grown up where once the prosperous had lived. Another visitor wrote that he 'did not believe until [he] visited the wynds of Glasgow that so large an amount of filth, crime, misery and disease existed in one spot in any civilised country'.

Yet at the same time there was within Glasgow another city, growing richer and more splendid, enjoying ever better amenities. This city promenaded in the Botanic Gardens, laid out in 1841, and marvelled at the railway to Edinburgh which had opened in 1842. This was a city of splendid new buildings, built to meet the needs of the merchants and the manufacturers : the Western Club, the Linen Bank, the Western Bank, the Union Bank, the Glasgow and Ship Bank, the Merchants' House, the Corn Exchange, the City Hall and over a dozen churches put up in the early 1840s.

It was this city which the Crown Prince visited. He stayed at the Wellington Hotel in George Square and after going to the Cathedral, the Bridewell and the University he called next at the substantial premises in the Candleriggs of J and W Campbell and Company. This firm had been founded in 1817 by two young farmers from Stirlingshire, James and William Campbell, and was at first a small drapery business in the Saltmarket supplying handkerchiefs and pinafores to basket women and hawkers. Trade grew and soon the brothers were able to open the retail and wholesale store in Candleriggs at which the Prince called. It was a firm known for its fair dealing : every article was clearly priced and that was the price which all the customers were expected to pay. There was no risk that anyone dealing with the Campbells would be overcharged. They kept faith with their customers.

The brothers were pioneers and had done well. James had been knighted and had served the city as Lord Provost. William, the younger of the two, had his town house in Bath Street and his country home at Tullichewan Castle near Balloch. He quickly became known after the Disruption of 1843 as a generous benefactor of the Free Church of Scotland which had then come into being and on 8 May 1845 he took the chair at a meeting which was intended to extend the activities of the new church in the sphere of education. A number of gentlemen connected with the Free Church made their way that day to the Star Hotel in the corner of George Square, where they were joined by ministers of the Church : the most active in the scheme which unfolded as a result of the meeting were Dr John Forbes of St Paul's, the Outer High Church, and Dr Robert Buchanan, of the Tron, a particularly prominent 'Disruption worthy'.

William Campbell of Tullichewan had
convened the meeting so that the possibility
might be aired of establishing 'an Academic
Institution in this City'. The original minute goes
on to add that it was to be a school 'for the
children of the better classes' but the words were
later deleted. Dr Buchanan proposed, and it was
unanimously agreed, 'that an academic institution shall be established for the purpose of
teaching youth the various branches of secular
knowledge, based upon strictly evangelical
religious principles and pervaded by religious
instruction' and practical steps were at once
taken to put the resolution into practice. Henry
Dunlop of Craigton was chosen as President of
the new undertaking : he was a leading citizen
who had served a term as Lord Provost and who
was also Deputy Chairman of the Edinburgh and
Glasgow Railway and a prominent member of St
Enoch's Free Church. The family firm of James
Dunlop and Company were cotton-spinners,
with premises in Miller Street, Virginia Street, the
Calton and Barrhead, where Henry Dunlop also
lived, in a mansion 'situate on a beautifully

sloping lawn and adorned with fine old woods
and stripes of young thriving plantations'.

There was a real sense of urgency : a
committee was set up to look out for a site and, if
possible, find temporary accommodation so that
the Academy (as it was already being called)
could open after the summer holidays that year,
just five months or so later. That ambition
remained unfulfilled, but the committee did
quickly identify a site in Elm Bank which it was
hoped to acquire as the home of the new school.

Another committee was charged with
the task of finding a suitable Head Master and
staff, whilst a third considered matters of finance
and came to the conclusion that the costs of
establishing the Academy, estimated at £8000,
should be met by issuing 200 shares of £40.

In July 1845 it was decided to proceed
with the purchase of ground and the construction of buildings once 100 shares had been
subscribed for. By October, 82 had been taken
up, with the probability of more being accounted
for soon, but it was then resolved not to proceed
immediately but instead to approach the North
Albion Street and Wellington Street congrega-
tions of the United Secession Church and to go
ahead once 150 shares had been spoken for.
This was achieved by mid December and negotiations then began in earnest to buy the ground
at Elm Bank.

In January 1846 a further meeting was
held, at which far-reaching decisions were taken.
A school of 400 pupils was envisaged but it had
to be established whether or not the Academy
should cater exclusively for boys. The prospect
of admitting girls was one which found favour
with some members of the governing committee
but clearly not with enough. The minute of the
meeting records that it was to be left an open

question, and that the architect's plans for the Academy should allow the possibility of adding later, and without injuring the appearance of the building, the accommodation which would be needed if it were 'found advisable to admit girls'. It was not 'found advisable to admit girls' for almost 150 years.

James Cumming, ten years or so after he left the Academy

The meeting of January 1846 also appointed the Academy's first Head. At the very end of December Dr Buchanan had written to the man he and his committee wanted, James Cumming. Cumming had been born on 23 August 1799, the eldest son of the last Rector of the Canongate High School. He himself attended the Edinburgh High School and then Edinburgh University, where he was a prizeman. In February 1823 he had been appointed head classical teacher in the Quaker Academy at Darlington, and it was from there that in September 1826 he had moved back to Edinburgh to succeed William Henry Marriott, one of the original Classical Masters at the Edinburgh Academy. Cumming remained for twenty years before being tempted westwards. He was fondly remembered by his former pupils and those whom he taught during his final years at Edinburgh Academy formed themselves into a 'Cumming Club' : the *Chronicles of the Cumming Club* record that the master 'had secured for himself the reputation of a high-minded honour-able gentleman of large attainments and wide sympathies, which took the form of the most genial and kindly bearing towards his boys'. Cumming's appointment to Glasgow Academy, at a salary of £500 guaranteed for three years, was confirmed on 9 January 1846 and within a month his title had also been agreed – he was to be the first Rector of Glasgow Academy. On his move to Glasgow, Cumming took up residence in Clarendon Place and, as a Licentiate of the Free Church, became an elder and occasional preacher in St Andrew's Free Church.

The process of making further appoint-ments to the staff was a gradual one. Thomas Wilson was appointed Mathematical Master in February, at a salary of £250, having been for ten years resident Head Mathematical Master in the Grange School, Sunderland. One of the two Classical Masters also came from the Grange. Isaiah McBurney had graduated BA from the University of Glasgow in 1838. Now 32, he was appointed to the Academy at a salary of £200 after Cumming had satisfied himself on one or two points, as there seemed to be a 'want or blank in the testimonials'. His classical colleague was Robert Nelson, formerly Head of the Western Academy in Glasgow, and the Head Master of the Junior or English Department was Alexander Sinclair, whose salary was to be £250 and who had been Head of the Lower Ormond Quay Academy in Dublin.

The Writing and Book-keeping Master was John Macpherson whose salary was to be £200 and who was also to help out with some elementary Arithmetic. Macpherson was an established teacher in Glasgow and a press advertisement in mid August invited parents who intended their children to take up places at the new school to send them to him at 280 George Street until the Academy opened its doors. Alexander Finlay was appointed French and German Master on a part-time basis. The boys nicknamed him 'Mooshie' as he was the only master who wore a moustache. His ability to maintain discipline suffered from the fact that he was so extremely short-sighted that a ball could be rolled across the floor under his spectacles without his noticing.

A part-time Drawing Master was chosen and Donald McDonald was appointed Janitor : his wife was also engaged, 'upon the understanding that she gives her exclusive attention to the cleaning of the Academy, keeping on the fires and looking after the junior children'. A Lodge was to be built for them at Elm Bank, which they would occupy rent free.

This staff was supplemented by a number of assistants, engaged either by the Directors or by the masters themselves to help with the work of teaching, though in the early years at least, these men came and went quite regularly.

While the staff was being assembled, progress was also being made with plans for the building. Six rooms, each thirty feet by forty, would be needed for the Classical Department – four for Classics, one for Writing and one for Mathematics, together with a consulting room for the masters and Directors which, it was thought,

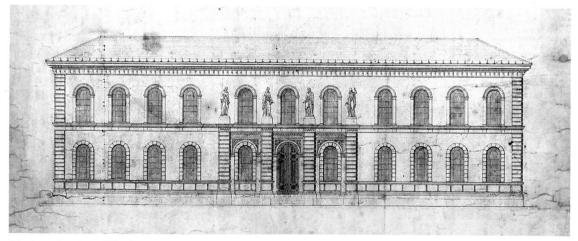

The front elevation of Charles Wilson's building, including the statues not fitted during the Academy's time in Elmbank Street

could also accommodate the Library. The Junior Department, too, would require six classrooms.

Charles Wilson was appointed architect in January 1846 : a young man in his mid thirties, he had recently been responsible for the hospital which later became known as Gartnavel Royal and for the houses in Kirklee Terrace, off Great Western Road. As one of the leading architects of his day, he was later to complete what has been described as 'the finest piece of town design in Glasgow', Woodlands Hill, part of which was the most striking Free Church College in Lynedoch Street.

In February 1846, that lay some ten years in the future and Wilson concentrated on producing plans of the Academy which were soon displayed to shareholders. In April, estimates for the mason work were considered and attempts were made to cut costs by deleting a number of items, with the result that the projected cost of the building was computed as £5662/9/3. In the event this was considerably exceeded.

By early August it had become apparent that the new premises would not be ready for occupation at the start of the session, which was to be on 1 October. They must indeed have been far from ready but the Directors' attention was drawn to premises which would tide them over. A year earlier, on 1 October 1845, F A Wolski, who taught Modern Languages in the High School, had opened the Glasgow Institution for the Education of Young Ladies at 15 and 17 Renfield Street. Within a few yards of St Vincent Street, these were two self-contained houses, though it was possible to move from one to the other without having to go outside. There were four large classrooms and ten other apartments. Wolski had moved to larger premises, and the

Directors of the Academy were able to rent the Renfield Street houses until the following Whitsunday.

Considerable alterations had to be undertaken, and even then the accommodation was really too cramped and on the whole not particularly suitable, but it was there, on 1 October 1846, that the Academy began its life. The first three pupils to be enrolled were Henry Dunlop, aged 12, and his two younger brothers, the sons of Henry Dunlop of Craigton.

Many of the first Academy families, like the Dunlops, were connected with the textile industry, so crucial to the economy of the city in the mid nineteenth century. The Dunlops were cotton spinners and power-loom cloth manufacturers, but there were also calico printers, turkey-red dyers, sewed-muslin manufacturers, woollen and linen drapers, silk mercers, gingham, pullicate and muslin manufacturers, silk merchants and throwsters, lace manufacturers and a 'calenderer and packer' among the fathers who sent their sons to the Academy in 1846. There were numerous merchants and warehousemen, too, and several men whose interests were in the financial sector : high-ranking officials of the Royal Bank, the Clydesdale Bank, the National Bank and the Union Exchange Bank, for example. There were writers, as solicitors were known at the time, including the Clerk to the sub-division of the Lieutenancy; there were steam packet agents, the managing partner of the Patent Rivet Company, a bookseller and stationer, the agent for William Younger and Company, brewers, an iron merchant, the printer and publisher of the *Glasgow Courier*, a patent brick and tile maker, a barracks-master, a plane-maker and a candle-maker. The minister of Free St Enoch's sent his three sons to the school and the pupil enrolled next after the Dunlop boys was the son of a goldsmith and jeweller who was 'watchmaker to Her Majesty'. Another pupil was William Lochhead, whose father was also William Lochhead, of Wylie and Lochhead who at that time advertised themselves as 'upholstery manufacturers, carpet, paper-hanging, down, feather, curled hair, and floor-cloth merchants, funeral undertakers, and post-horse and carriage hirers'.

The Directors had chosen for their school a site which was at the western edge of the city's built-up area. The middle classes of Glasgow had been moving steadily westwards, away from the smoke and grime of industry and the 'numerous and rather turbulent population' living in the lanes and closes off streets like the Bridgegate. Pupils came to the Academy from houses relatively close by, with addresses such as Lynedoch Crescent, West Regent Street, St Vincent Street, Hope Street, Hill Street, Elmbank Terrace and Clarendon Place, where four families had the Rector as neighbour.

Boys could enter the English Department of the Academy at the age of 6 and embark upon a three year elementary education to equip them for the work of the Classical Department to which they would progress at about the age of 9. There were five classes in the Classical Department and the course of study was designed very much as preparation for further work at college. The First and Second Classes studied Latin, History, Chronology, Modern Geography, English Composition, Writing and Arithmetic. Greek, the first principles of Algebra and French were added in the Third Class. In the Fifth, Astronomy, Physical Geography, Geometry, Trigonometry, Elementary Mechanics, Book-keeping and German were also offered.

It must have been with some sense of relief that Cumming, his staff and the Academy's first pupils moved into the school's own buildings in Elmbank Place during the spring of 1847. The formal opening ceremony was held on Wednesday 5 May 1847. The pupils were addressed by Dr Buchanan and press reports stressed the underlying principle of the Academy in giving religious along with secular instruction. Care was taken, though, to add that there was 'as little of a sectarian description as possible'.

Dr Robert Buchanan

The Academy's first session came to an end just over three weeks later. First, there was a public examination of the pupils within the new premises. At ten o'clock on Wednesday 26 May they were examined in English, Mathematics, Writing, French and German. The following day was the Queen's Birthday, so it was not until the Friday morning that the examination of Classics, History, Astronomy and Geography took place. This really was a *public* examination : parents and friends of the pupils were invited to attend, together with clergymen 'of every evangelical denomination'.

The proceedings on the Friday were wound up by William Ramsay, Professor of

Humanity in the University of Glasgow, who delivered what was described as a 'cordial eulogium' on the school and the display which had been given of the professional efficiency of the Rector and his staff. With that, a company of sixty repaired to the Tontine Hotel for a celebratory dinner.

No trace has been found of a prize list for the 1846/47 session but at the end of the Academy's second year John Hervey Wilson headed an extensive list as winner of the first prize for Scholarship in the Fifth Class, the Academy's first Dux. One or two slight changes had been made at the beginning of that second session. Instead of opening on 1 October, classes in the Academy began on 1 August 1847. Fees remained unchanged, from 3 guineas annually in the Initiatory Class of the English Department up to 15 guineas in the Fifth Class of the Classical Department, but instead of being collected every half session were now to be paid quarterly – presumably in an attempt to improve the school's fledgling cash flow.

There were also changes in the staff during the Academy's early years. Robert Nelson had clearly proved unsatisfactory, despite the 'long-tried skill and warm sympathy' of the Rector which had 'helped me over many a steep, when my unaided energies must have sunk in despair'.

Other resignations followed which perturbed the Directors more, as they meant the loss of successful teachers. In August 1849, Thomas Wilson, 'one of the Academy's most popular teachers, upon whose energies and professional character the Directors confidently relied as giving in his own department a name to the Institution', took over a boarding school near Kilwinning. At the same time, Alexander Sinclair and John Macpherson moved to the Collegiate and Commercial Academy, Garnethill, 'to which many of the pupils of the Glasgow Academy were in consequence attracted'. The Mathematical, English and Writing Departments all had new Masters in James Reid, James Bell and John Gow.

John Gow had previously taught in the High School and Mechanics' Institute, Liverpool : one of the conditions of his appointment was that he should not teach Writing or Bookkeeping in any other institution or private family without the Directors' consent. Several of the masters did, in fact, teach other pupils at this time. Before he left for Ayrshire, Thomas Wilson had an establishment at North Woodside House where a number of Academy boys were lodging between 1846 and 1848. In July 1849 James Bell advertised, or rather 'respectfully intimated', that the following month he would commence an advanced class for young ladies, for Grammar, Composition, Geography and Religious Knowledge in the English Class Room of the Glasgow Academy. The class would be conducted entirely by Bell himself, who enjoyed a high reputation and had been able to negotiate for himself a salary at the Academy of £350. A number of other masters or assistants taught in one or other of the Institutions for the Education of Young Ladies which were to be found in the city, including the Western Collegiate Institution, the West of Scotland Institution and the Garnet Bank Institution.

Even in those very earliest days, some of the Academy's pupils lived too far away to be able to travel daily to and from school. A number therefore boarded with one or other of the masters. Isaiah McBurney, who lived near the Rector in Clarendon Place, advertised accommodation for boarders, who would attend the Academy and have their private and preparatory studies superintended by himself and a resident private tutor. James Bell also indicated that he would take boarders in his house at Kew Terrace : he stressed that 'particular attention would be paid to their moral and religious

improvement'. As many as fourteen Academy boys were lodging with Bell during 1858/59, which was his last session as a master at the Academy. The arrangement must have been well thought of, for at one time Bell numbered among his lodgers two sons of Henry Dunlop himself.

When the Academy opened, it had been expected that all boys enrolling would follow the same course of study, but after three sessions a rather more flexible approach was adopted. It was strongly recommended that pupils in the Classical Department should adhere strictly to the regular course and there were financial incentives for doing so, but they did not have to, and those who wanted their sons to have a commercial education rather than a classical one found that the Academy now offered a suitable course and unlimited freedom to choose for their children whatever classes seemed best fitted to prepare them for their future professions. The Prospectus stood firm on one point, however: 'It is a standing Rule that no Pupil shall, at the same time, attend any other Seminary, for instruction in any of the branches taught in the Academy, except Drawing, Dancing, and Vocal Music'.

This adjustment was a response to the demands of the market. As an independent commentator put it, some years later, 'The original system was better adapted for Edinburgh than Glasgow. It was found necessary to make more adequate provision for the requirements of the purely commercial class of pupils, many of whom were not disposed to put a very high value upon a classical course extending over five years.'

It is clear that in its earliest years the Academy faced another difficulty in that it was widely perceived to be a uniquely Free Church institution. This did not help the school in its struggle to become established. Indeed, the Directors later reported that 'the original promoters would have abandoned the scheme, in despair, but from a conviction of its great importance, and the hope that time and their mode of conducting the Institution would gradually dispel' the belief that the school was to be 'sectarian in its principles and proselytising in its object'. Even after the prejudice against it had begun to recede, the Academy's early years were not easy ones, financially. It took great determination and courage on the part of the Directors to persist with their scheme.

The site in Elm Bank, extending to almost six thousand square yards, cost over £5300. Putting up the school building cost a further £7600, to which was added the cost of an additional plot of ground, acquired for sheds and the Janitor's house. Apart from this initial capital expenditure, running costs were incurred from the outset, most notably the masters' salaries. These were paid in full from the beginning, even when the number of boys on the roll really did not warrant the employment of a complete staff. During the first four sessions there were respectively 170 pupils, 305, 330 and 357. The Directors, however, had 'started upon the principle of getting the best men, and paying in proportion, even at the risk of the Institution getting for a time into difficulties'.

To meet these early costs, the Directors were of course able to draw on the funds raised from shares, which amounted to just under £7000. This was far from enough and as early as August 1846 a loan of £5000 was negotiated. As time went by, it became clear that a further injection of capital was necessary and £2000 was borrowed from the Royal Bank of Scotland, seven of the Directors acting as guarantors.

Strenuous efforts were made to attract further shareholders and £560 was raised in this way but the financial position was weakened by the fact that the school did not produce enough income from fees to cover its costs. At the end of the financial years in both 1850 and 1851, well over £400 was owed to the bank as a floating debt, over and above the other loans.

In February 1851, however, an opportunity arose which allowed the masters to approach the Directors with a plan which they felt confident would save money.

Ten years without a Rector

The Directors had reason to be grateful to James Cumming. He had responded to their financial embarrassment by foregoing £100 of his salary during the 1849/50 session, but it was perhaps of greater importance that he was clearly a distinguished man whose standing, and with it that of the school which he headed, had been acknowledged in several different ways since his arrival in Glasgow. In 1847 he had been appointed as one of the Directors of the newly-established Athenaeum, while in the following year he had become President of the Educational Institute of Scotland. In November 1849 he had been elected a member of the Philosophical Society of Glasgow and in January 1850 the University of Glasgow had conferred upon him the degree of Doctor of Laws, at the instigation of Professor Ramsay.

Cumming's eminence was recognised further afield, and on 5 February 1851 he was appointed one of Her Majesty's Inspectors of Schools in Scotland, sending in his resignation from the Academy two days later. In these earliest days of the Inspectorate, responsibilities were assigned on a religious and indeed a denominational basis and James Cumming was in fact the first and for some time the only Inspector of Free Church schools. The Directors recorded their sense of the 'zeal, ability and discretion' with which he had carried out his duties at the Academy and presented him with a tea and coffee service.

The news of Cumming's imminent departure had also reached the masters, and as soon as the Directors had dealt with the Rector's letter of resignation and their response to it, they turned to another letter, this one bearing the signatures of the six Masters of the various departments in the school. They had lost no

---

GLASGOW ACADEMY.

President.
HENRY DUNLOP, ESQ.

Vice-Presidents.
MICHAEL ROWAND, ESQ.
WILLIAM CAMPBELL, ESQ.
ALEXANDER DUNN, ESQ.

Directors.

JOHN BAIN, ESQ.	WILLIAM DAVIE, ESQ.
ROBERT BELL, ESQ.	ANDREW GALBRAITH, ESQ.
JOHN BLACKIE, SEN., ESQ.	RICHARD KIDSTON, ESQ.
HENRY BROCK, ESQ.	LAWRENCE ROBERTSON, ESQ.
HUGH BROWN, ESQ.	JAMES SCOTT, ESQ.
WILLIAM BROWN, ESQ.	WILLIAM W. WATSON, ESQ.
CHARLES CUNNINGHAM, ESQ.	JAMES WRIGHT, ESQ.

ROBERT THOMSON, ESQ., *Secretary.* | JAMES BUCHANAN, ESQ., *Treasurer.*

CLASSICAL DEPARTMENT.
MASTERS—MR. ISAIAH M'BURNEY, B.A.—MR. CHARLES E. WILSON, M.A.
ASSISTANT—MR. DAVID BONNAR.

FRENCH AND GERMAN DEPARTMENT.
MASTER—MR. ALEXANDER L. FINLAY.

ENGLISH DEPARTMENT.
HEAD-MASTER—MR. JAMES BELL.
ASSISTANTS—MESSRS. DONALD M'GREGOR AND WILLIAM BENNETT.

MATHEMATICAL DEPARTMENT.
HEAD-MASTER—MR. JAMES REID.
ASSISTANT—MR. THOMAS MILLER.

WRITING AND BOOK-KEEPING DEPARTMENT.
HEAD-MASTER—MR. JOHN GOW.
ASSISTANT—MR. JOHN FRASER.

DRAWING DEPARTMENT.
MASTER—MR. CHARLES WOOLNOTH.

Janitor—DONALD M'DONALD.

---

time in putting together a detailed proposal – to run the Academy themselves, on a collegiate basis without a Rector, a move which they estimated would save £200 annually.

Each of the masters in turn, according to seniority of appointment, would for a whole session look after the books, see to the enrolment of pupils, receive the fees and pay the bills. That was as far as the notion of seniority would extend, however. All the masters would attend on the Quarter Days in August, October, January and March to assist with enrolment and payment of fees, there was to be consultation of each master when it was proposed to place a pupil in his class and, in particular, both the Classical Masters would be consulted about the placing of boys in their Department. One of the Classical Masters would take charge of the First, Third and Fifth classes one year and of the Second and Fourth the next. This practice was defended in the prospectus by the assertion that it would mean that 'the loss of time, and other inconveniences arising from a change of teachers, [would be] avoided'. There was a precedent within Glasgow for the proposal to do without a Rector since the Academy would in fact be following the example of the High School, which had had no Rector for many years. There was nevertheless some disquiet among friends of the school when the Directors decided to adopt the masters' proposal. As it turned out, their course of action seemed at first to be have been vindicated, as the school's fortunes began to improve. The financial results which the masters had predicted were, in fact, achieved in the first year of the new régime, a fact which must have augured well for the future prosperity of the school.

In May 1851 the masters drew up their first prospectus for the Academy. It was, they announced, a school instituted with the intention of providing a sound education to pupils of all ages, from six to sixteen. Although most pupils progressed from the Third English Class to the Classical Department, the English Department did provide an extra class in which the education

of the senior pupils in the 'Higher Branches of English' was completed, pupils who required a 'complete Commercial Education' and who did not wish to study Latin or Greek,

By and large at this time boys moved up through the school more or less automatically, though by 1857 the Mathematical Department was insisting on its right to classify boys separately, according to the progress which they had made in that part of the curriculum and without being bound by their standing in other Departments.

Before the new system of administering the Academy had long been in place, another of the masters left his post. Charles Wilson, who had succeeded Robert Nelson, joined James Cumming in the Inspectorate, as one of Her Majesty's Assistant Inspectors of Schools, and a replacement had to be found quickly. So it was that in March 1852 Joseph Currie was appointed as a Classical Master, taking it turn and turn about with McBurney to have charge of the First Latin Class. Currie was remembered as a painstaking and rather plodding teacher. He was conscientious, austere in discipline though kindly towards those who were doing their best, moody and modest. He had prepared editions of extracts from Horace and Caesar, with original notes, which the University Press had published.

McBurney was quite different and altogether a much more colourful and showy character, perhaps the most colourful in the Academy's early history. Rather a vain man, he too had published a textbook, of extracts from Ovid. He preached on Sundays to a small congregation of the sect of the Scottish Church known as the Cameronians. Distinctive in appearance, he was somewhat plump, had clean-shaven rosy cheeks and usually wore a swallow-tailed coat. He wore glasses, was fond of taking snuff and bore a striking resemblance to Charles Dickens' Mr Pickwick. He enlivened his teaching by adding to it various snippets of general knowledge and from time to time would put forward for translation into Latin some sentence like, 'I say that Isaiah McBurney is a better master than Joseph Currie'.

The improvement in the Academy's fortunes which followed the new scheme of management meant that some salaries could be increased and essential maintenance could be carried out – painting the interior walls and ceilings and oiling the exterior of the building to save the stonework from decay. Decisive steps were also taken to remove a cause of complaint during the winter months : the heating equipment had proved ineffective and inadequate and an additional boiler had been fitted, but still more radical steps were required. Two of the openings at each end of the portico were filled in partly with stone and partly with glass, 'so as to stop the great current of air introduced into the Class Rooms particularly during easterly winds'. The work cost nearly £100.

The Academy could not afford to rest on its laurels and the keen wind of competition was felt from time to time. The Directors noted in August 1855 that the Collegiate Institution had recently been 'remodelled under new and respectable auspices' and that one of its attractions was a gymnasium. The Academy had gone a little way towards meeting the demand from parents for gymnastics by authorising Messrs Foucart and Son to give lessons in fencing in one of the classrooms, but the suggestion had now been made – by the teachers, voicing the views of parents – that a separate gymnasium should be constructed, and this important development was undertaken during the next session. As his

name suggests, the older M Foucart was French. 'A very big man and a kindly soul,' he had been present at the Battle of Waterloo and a no doubt apocryphal legend amongst the boys had it that he and the Janitor had met and fought with each other on the battlefield.

Certain fees were reduced for the session 1855/56, presumably in order to dissuade parents from sending their boys to cheaper schools. The financial situation was not helped by the fact that there were some parents who persistently allowed themselves to fall into arrears with their fees. Nevertheless, it did prove possible to pay off the final remnant of the £2000 borrowed from the Royal Bank and to replace it with a manageable overdraft. The following year, though, income fell again and the Directors did not feel justified in spending money to comply with the wishes of Charles Wilson, their architect: he had provided four piers at the front of the building on which it had been intended that statues should be placed – but no statues had yet been prepared. Wilson felt that the time had come for this omission to be rectified, but the Directors did not share his point of view and in fact the piers did not carry statues as long as the building belonged to the Academy.

It was at about this time that Robert Somers, a campaigning Victorian journalist, carried out a survey of the state of education in Glasgow. He reported approvingly on what he found at the Academy, describing it as a high-class Upper School in the West End and noting that the religious element at its core had never been the cause of the slightest jarring or unpleasantness. He described the course of study and the amendments which had been made to it, so as to provide in effect two branches in the Fourth and Fifth years of the Senior Department. Boys who intended to proceed to the University continued with the Classical course whilst those who were being prepared for business could opt instead for a course which concentrated on English, Writing and Book-keeping, French, Arithmetic and Mathematics.

He noted, however, that the Academy had to contend with the prevailing practice of taking young men away from school and sending them to business or indeed to University before they had had the opportunity to complete the full curriculum. It was, he argued, too easy to enter the University, since there was no entrance examination. Many pupils were sent there after their fourth year in the Classical Department of the Academy whereas it had been the intention of the school's founders to provide a sixth class – and in the upper schools of Edinburgh there was even a seventh. Since there were clearly parents who felt that their sons were ready at the age of 15 or 16 to progress from the Academy to the more testing studies of the University, it was not surprising to find that there were others who felt that their boys were fully qualified for work in a counting-house after an even shorter school course. The complaint that boys were not allowed to benefit from all the opportunities which the Academy had to offer before being moved on to the next step in their careers was one which was to persist for many years.

Somers felt that one of the advantages for parents who sent their children to the Academy was that the boys were instructed in all branches of education under the same roof. That enabled the masters to ensure that boys were neither left idle on the one hand nor worked too hard on the other. It was an aid also to what he called 'moral discipline' in that a boy's behaviour throughout the day was known, and misconduct in the playground or in any one department could be checked by the combined authority of all the masters. Somers' comments on these matters chimed well with the wish of the Academy authorities that it should be the norm for the pupils all to follow the full course provided for them.

In the autumn of 1857 James Reid, the Head Mathematical Master, was absent from duty through illness. His Junior Assistant, William Reid, had intended to leave and go to college – an interesting reflection on the qualifications of the assistants in the Academy – but instead stayed on until the end of the session. Mr Reid the assistant was known as 'Wee Reid' – and in one of the Academy jokes that has passed down over the years this nickname became translated as 'Nos legimus'. James Reid in fact died during November and was greatly missed : nearly every boy in the school attended his funeral and, after the fashion of the time, they all wore crepe bands in their hats and white 'weepers' on the sleeves of their coats. In January 1858 William Marr was appointed as James Reid's successor, since it was he who seemed best to satisfy the Directors' criteria : 'a preference should be given to those candidates who combined high mathematical attainments with the power of communicating easily and earnestly their knowledge to boys, and with the experience of managing large mathematical classes of boys'. 'Billy' Marr, who came to the Academy from George Heriot's Hospital, Edinburgh, certainly had high mathematical attainments but he did not find controlling the boys easy, perhaps because he was too kind-hearted and too easily imposed on.

James Buchanan, who had served as Treasurer since the earliest days of the school, died, ironically, only months before the meeting in June 1858 at which, for the first time in the Academy's history, all debts cleared, the Directors were able to recommend payment to shareholders of a dividend. It looked as if a new dawn was breaking : but in fact it proved to be a false dawn, since further financial difficulties lay not too far ahead.

In May 1859 the Directors considered the position of drill in the school, since it was 'now considered an important matter connected with education and desired by many of the parents'. They had to decide whether or not to appoint a Drill Sergeant, but resolved to continue with the arrangement whereby Sergeant Major Brown, who had become Janitor the previous year, drilled the boys himself. In July 1860 Brown died and the Directors appointed in his place another man who could act as both Janitor and Drill Sergeant. Samuel Boyd, recently of the 26th or Cameronian Regiment, was eminently well qualified since he was 'acquainted with the system of drilling recently introduced at Hythe' and would drill all the pupils 'at suitable intervals between half past nine and half past four o'clock'. He would also supply 'plain bread or biscuits and milk or coffee'. The Janitor's house had been extended to provide more space for serving luncheon.

Another addition to the curriculum introduced for the session of 1860/61 was vocal sacred music, which was offered on three days a week, half an hour in the morning and another half an hour in the afternoon.

Just before the start of the previous session, in July 1859, the Directors learned that they had lost the services of James Bell, who had gone as English Master to the High School. He had the reputation of being a first-rate English master, a brisk man, and occasionally brusque : but younger boys knew that on examination days he would toss them a sweetie from his back pocket if they gave him a correct answer. He was connected with the Foundry Boys Society, a prominent charitable institution in the city.

Bell had given the Directors fair warning and had asked for an increase in salary if he stayed, but the Directors had felt unable to agree, anxious not to set a precedent. Despite the difficult financial times – there was a 'commercial crisis' in the city and numbers at the school were falling a little – the Directors decided that they would take this opportunity to strengthen the English Department, even though this involved an increase in the salaries to be paid. They resolved to engage two masters with just one assistant, rather than have a master and two assistants, and their choices were William Moyes, Headmaster of the Circus Place School, Edinburgh, and David Pryde, also of Edinburgh.

GLASGOW ACADEMY.

THE regular Curriculum of the GLASGOW ACADEMY, in addition to the ordinary Branches of an English Education, embraces a Five years' course of Classics, Mathematics, French, and German.

Provision is also made for giving a complete Commercial Education to such Pupils as do not wish to study Latin or Greek.

As respects Pupils attending the Classical Department, while a strict adherence to the regular course is strongly recommended, attendance upon some of the classes may, in particular cases, be dispensed with ; and, as respects other Pupils, parents have unlimited freedom of choosing for them such classes as may seem best fitted to prepare them for their future professions. It is, however, a standing Rule, *that no Pupil shall, at the same time, attend any other Seminary for instruction in any of the Branches taught in the Academy, except Drawing.*

The Session extends over Ten Months—from the 1st of August to the end of May. As the Business of the Classes proceeds from the first in a systematic manner, it is particularly desirable that Pupils should attend from the very commencement of the Session.

The hours of teaching are from 10 A.M. to 4 P.M. The Junior English Pupils, however, attend 2, 3, or 4 hours daily, according to age.

All the Classes are opened with Prayer, and in all of them Religious Instruction is systematically given.

In the absence of the Masters, the Play-ground is under the superintendence of the Janitor ; and care is taken to prevent the Junior and Senior Classes from mixing in the Play-ground, during their intervals. The youngest English Classes are, while in the Play-ground, always under the care of one of the Masters.

Quarter Days.

1ST AUGUST, 16TH OCTOBER, 1ST JANUARY, AND 16TH MARCH.

On these days *all the Masters* attend to enrol Pupils, and give explanations to Parents regarding the Classes. In order to save the time both of Masters and Pupils, it is particularly requested that, as far as possible, the Accounts be paid on the Quarter Days.

Moyes was remembered for a stentorian voice and short temper and Pryde for a glossy silk hat and an ability to inspire a real interest in English literature.

Before long, the Directors were forced to confront the possibility that the deteriorating financial position of the Academy was not altogether to be blamed on prevailing economic circumstances. In September 1860 they received the alarming news that a recent pupil of the Academy had been entered for a school in England, but had been refused admission 'on the ground of ignorance of the elements of the languages he had been taught'. Clearly very worried that if such knowledge became widely known the Academy's reputation would suffer and numbers would fall still further, the Directors decided to ask a 'competent person' to examine the system of teaching in the school. The 'competent person' they had in mind was James Cumming, and the former Rector began an inspection of his old school on 24 September. Details of what he found have not been preserved, but a dramatic development which would affect the whole future of the Academy was just around the corner.

The Directors had a whole range of other matters to discuss, besides the academic standing of their school. They had, for example, been approached by Sir Islay Campbell, who wanted to see whether the boys would be interested in forming a Cadet Corps of Volunteers, but they decided to take no action. This would not be the last occasion on which the question of forming such a body within the school would be raised without result. There were also matters of house-keeping to be considered : the heating apparatus, which had continued to give great trouble, was greatly damaged by frost during the winter of 1860/61 and had to be renewed. The old system, combining hot air and hot water heating, was taken away and replaced by a warm air system alone.

The Directors must sometimes have felt that, despite the costs involved and the school's precarious financial standing, the damaged heating system was a much easier matter to deal with than the other major issue which confronted them that winter. Isaiah McBurney, who had been with the school from its very beginning, had become the subject of complaint and public talk as a result of his 'unsteady habits' and style of teaching : the implication was that Dr McBurney (as he had become some three years earlier) was coming to school the worse for drink. He was seen by some of the Directors, warned and put on probation, but it was to no avail. In February 1861 William Marr, who that session was the master on whom such responsibilities fell, had the unenviable task of delivering to the Directors a damning report about a senior colleague. Boys were being withdrawn from McBurney's classes and indeed from the Academy altogether. The 'resignation' which Dr McBurney had offered the Directors when he was first warned had, therefore, to be accepted. McBurney left Glasgow to take over the Athol Academy in Douglas, Isle of Man : but clearly he did not feel that his reputation had suffered too greatly, since he advertised for pupils in the *Glasgow Herald*. Eventually he emigrated to Australia and died in Melbourne in the summer of 1896, at 82 years of age.

Donald Morrison

The departure of McBurney must have been an embarrassment to the Directors, but it happened at a time when it had become clear that decisive action was needed if the Academy was ever to recover and sustain the standing in the city which its founders and supporters had anticipated for it. In filling the vacancy which had been created by McBurney's dismissal, the Directors were clear that they needed not just a master who would lead the Classical Department but a man whose remit would be to superintend all the classes in the Academy – in other words, a Rector.

On 16 February 1861 the Secretary wrote to William Marr, informing the staff that the change was to be made. Advertisements were soon placed in several newspapers both south and north of the border and on the afternoon of 29 April Donald Morrison was elected Rector of Glasgow Academy.

Morrison had been born in 1822 at Edinkillie in Aberdeenshire, on the banks of the River Findhorn, and had attended first the parish school of Forres and then Forres Academy before going on to Aberdeen University. At King's College he had a distinguished career, winning both the Hutton Prize, given to the best all-round student of the year, and the Simpson Prize for the best mathematician and then graduating Master of Arts in March 1843. Morrison then became a teacher, taking up first a post as Classical Master in a college in London connected with the Society of Friends, but later returning north to do similar work at Elgin Academy.

Morrison was a married man, with four sons and two daughters when he came to Glasgow : another daughter was born soon afterwards. He had three distinguished brothers, who like him were recipients of the honorary degree of Doctor of Laws, conferred upon him by the University of Aberdeen in 1868. Thomas Morrison was Rector of the Free Church Training College in Glasgow, Alexander Morrison was Principal of the Scotch College in Melbourne, and George Morrison was the Free Church minister at Urquhart.

Anderson Kirkwood, who was acting at the time as Secretary, wrote to Morrison on his appointment, asking when it would be convenient for him to take up his duties and, perhaps rather shamefacedly, offering an annual salary of £400, the minimum figure which had been

D. Morrison

mentioned in the advertisements. He added in a rather tortuous way that the Directors hoped that under Morrison's guidance the Academy would soon regain its former popularity : when that happened, and numbers increased once more, they would be able 'to render the situation more advantageous to you in point of emolument'.

Morrison replied, of course, that he was honoured to have been appointed. He would not be able to start his duties until the beginning of August, but he did attend a Directors' committee meeting on 28 May, together with Joseph Currie, the remaining Classical Master. No doubt the two men took the opportunity to weigh one another up, but at the time Currie probably hoped that he would never actually find himself working under the new Rector, since he had applied for a job at Edinburgh Academy. He was not successful, however, and two weeks later the same committee found that the two men were already in disagreement. The Directors seem to have taken Currie's part, for they decided to let Morrison know that, for the year ahead, they did not wish to see any changes made in the arrangements of the Classical Department.

Morrison had a bushy head of hair and a full beard, both as black as a raven, and he seems instantly to have acquired the nickname 'Beetle', which may also have owed something to his appearance when seen from behind, his dark clothing offering nothing to relieve the overall impression of blackness. Perhaps, too, his slow and silent mode of movement had something to do with the name, which stayed with him throughout his many years of service at the Academy.

The Directors took other decisions about staffing at this time. The employment of two English Masters no longer seemed justifiable

and David Pryde was told that his services would not be required after the end of the session. He went on to a successful career as Principal of a large Ladies' College in Edinburgh and eventually had the honorary degree of Doctor of Laws conferred upon him.

Another man who received notice of dismissal at this time was John Gow, the Writing Master. He was an expert penman, thin and pale, but he was excitable too, and when he

The Academy's Elmbank Street home as enlarged, seen from the playground

thought that the noise of conversation in the long Writing Room had grown too loud he would suddenly spring from his desk and dart down the centre passage, his coat tails flying behind him, whacking with his tawse to right and to left, more or less indiscriminately, the end of every desk from which he thought the noise was coming. Such impetuosity did not make for good order in the classroom and there had been complaints, so the Directors wished to be rid of an embarrassment. In this case, though, they agreed to offer a second chance : but Gow's discipline did not improve and his reprieve lasted only one session, until the summer of 1862.

When, half a century on, John William Arthur looked back to his schooldays at the Academy, he recalled that although the strap was ably wielded, discipline in Elmbank Street was somewhat lax. The code of rules was carefully read to each class at the beginning of the session, but comparatively little heed was paid to it. One rule which he recalled with wry amusement stipulated that any boy over-heating himself during the play hour was liable to punishment.

He remembered large classes and he remembered the so-called 'examination' conducted over two days at the end of the session. The boys, who had been thoroughly coached for the occasion, wore their Sunday best, with bows of red or bright blue, and flowers decorated the classrooms as parents and families passed proudly through. After the Prize Giving in the Merchants' Hall, the only occasion on which the school met together, there were the two months of holidays, to which were added only a week at Christmas and three days each in October and April at the times of the Autumn and Spring Fast Days.

There were scones, cookies and milk on sale, but no evidence of soap or towels, just a trickling pipe. Football in the playground was played in long trousers and shirt sleeves, with coats piled up to make goals. Occasionally a match would be played between Fourth Latin and Fifth Latin. There was also a bat and ball game against a blank wall, there was rounders and there was 'Creesh a", in which boys tried to hit one another as hard as they could with a hard ball. Other games included 'Steamers and Pirates' and 'Foot-and-a-half'.

Although Arthur recalled that there was little esprit de corps in the Academy of those times, a group of young men, many of them former pupils, did band together in May 1861 to ask the Directors if they might be allowed use of the gymnasium. The Secretary wrote back, telling the applicants that if the gymnastics master was present to superintend their use of the gymnasium they could have it without any charge. Kirkwood added how pleased the Directors had been to receive such a request from so many former pupils of the school. Within five years a more formal association of Academicals had come into being with the establishment of the Academical Club.

Of much more pressing importance at the meeting in May was the need to arrange a cash credit from the bank so that the masters could be paid their quarterly salaries the following day. The Treasurer, Charles Cunningham, arranged an overdraft and gave his own personal guarantee for its repayment. It was agreed later in the month that it was important to deal promptly and effectively with arrears in school fees, since this would help to keep the need for cash credits to a minimum.

Despite Donald Morrison's appointment, the Directors were pessimistic. Financial anxieties continued to exercise their minds during the summer, while they waited for Morrison to begin the task of re-establishing the Academy's reputation. They wondered whether it might not be sensible to introduce a scheme which would mean that the masters had a financial interest in the success of the school, by receiving a proportion of the fees of their respective classes, but nothing came of it.

Uneasy and restless, the Directors decided to take a closer interest in the day-to-day work of the school and perhaps to exercise a little more control over the masters. Two of them would visit the school each month by rotation, reviving a previous practice, and they would meet quarterly in order to discuss the visitors' reports and the state of the Academy. The Board also wanted to ensure that all the energy of the masters would be devoted to their work in the school. In April they had agreed to tell Joseph Currie that in future masters would not be allowed to teach extra classes in the Academy and now, when they heard that William Moyes had arranged to teach classes in a Ladies' School, they agreed to make it clear that extra tuition of this sort, too, would be prohibited. Moyes did in fact persuade the Board to allow him to continue his extra work : it was valuable to him, as it added £60 a year to his salary.

The masters had drawn up a Prospectus for the Academy's first session under Morrison, giving prominence to the Academy's religious tone and emphasising the rule that pupils were not allowed to attend any other institution : 'it has a tendency to prevent misconduct and to encourage propriety of behaviour in all the Classes, as each Pupil feels that what is known to one of the Masters is likely to become known to all'. Most boys did follow the complete course and paid a composite fee for all their classes but each year there were a few 'extra pupils' who did not.

The Rector would enrol pupils and receive fees on Quarter Days. He would also be available every day between 12 and 1 o'clock so that parents could see him on any matter concerning their children. The intention was that this would prevent the business of the school from being interrupted at any other time but experience was soon to prove that this was an unrealisable dream. The Rector quickly became known as a man who always had time for parents and his teaching seemed constantly to be interrupted by their visits.

In November 1861 pupil numbers and income were both reported to be fractionally higher than they had been a year before, but the financial position remained exceedingly grave and during the summer of 1862, with bills of over £2000 to meet, the Directors agreed to arrange a cash credit on their personal security.

In the midst of such financial uncertainty, Morrison had had to wait for a year before being allowed to do anything to steer the curriculum of the Academy in the direction he wanted, but in April 1862 he was at last able to put forward his proposals. There would, he knew, be no opposition now from Joseph Currie: there had been complaints about his inefficiency and it was soon arranged that he should be asked to retire, taking with him a handsome allowance of £250.

The Rector outlined for the Board changes which he wished to make. After the Second Latin year, when boys were about twelve, they spent no more time with the English Master:

Morrison wished to remedy this, on the grounds that pupils in the Third, Fourth and Fifth Latin classes would benefit from regular instruction in English Composition and from critically examining worthwhile passages from Milton, Shakespeare, Macaulay and other authors. More time should be devoted to Mathematics in Fourth Latin and to Latin in Fifth Latin, to be provided at the expense of Writing. More radically, the Fourth Latin class would be divided: a so-called Modern Side would take an hour a day of English while the Classical Side continued to do Latin.

Other preparations for the new session included the appointment of staff. John Maclaren from Hamilton Place Academy was appointed as the new Writing Master, in succession to John Gow, and thus began a very lengthy association with the Academy. Morrison also looked hard for a new Classical Master, to the extent of visiting Belfast to enquire about a candidate there. Finally, though, the position went to Alexander Watson, after he had produced a certificate from his doctor describing him as not 'a very robust person [but] sufficiently healthy and strong to discharge the duties of the office'. It was made very clear that the Rector was to be the chief Classical Master. Watson's salary reflected this : he was to be paid £180 a year, compared with Maclaren's £250.

The Prospectus for 1862/63 was the Rector's own. He laid special stress on the study of Classics and Mathematics being combined at the Academy more fully than was usual elsewhere with instruction in the English, French and German languages and what he called 'other useful branches of knowledge'. Parents were always welcome, but were specially invited to visit the classes every Friday. Attention was

TIME TABLE—SESSION 1862–63.

ENGLISH DEPARTMENT.

FIRST CLASS.

From 10 to 1,	... ...	English.
— 1 — 2,	... ...	Writing or Arithmetic.

SECOND CLASS.

From 10 to 1,	... ...	English.
— 1 — 3,	... ...	Writing and Arithmetic.

THIRD CLASS.

From 10 to 11,	... ...	Writing.
— 11 — 12,	... ...	English.
— 12 — 1,	... ...	Arithmetic.
— 1 — 3,	... ...	English.

CLASSICAL DEPARTMENT.

FIRST CLASS. (THE RECTOR AND ASSISTANT.)

From 10 to 11,	... ...	Classics—Latin.
— 11 — 12,	.. ...	Writing,
— 12 — 1,	... ...	Classics—History, Geography, &c.
— 1 — 2,	... ...	English.
— 2 — 3,	... ...	Classics—Latin.
— 3 — 4,	... ...	Arithmetic.

SECOND CLASS.

From 10 to 11,	... ...	Arithmetic.
— 11 — 12,	... ...	Classics—Latin.
— 12 — 1,	... ...	Writing.
— 1 — 2,	... ...	Classics, History, Geography, &c.
— 2 — 3,	... ...	English.
— 3 — 4,	... ...	Classics—Latin.

drawn particularly to the religious spirit which pervaded everything undertaken in the school. Classes began each morning with Scripture reading and prayer and there was a complete course of Religious Instruction, designed so that every boy would develop an extensive and correct knowledge of the historical portions of the Old and New Testaments. Pupils in advanced classes would have their attention directed to 'the Types in the Old Testament, their fulfilment in the New and the evidences of Christianity'.

The new session began well : the attendance rose to 407 boys, an increase over the previous year of 62. A vacancy arose in the Classical Department and the Rector again urged the Directors to appoint William Murphy, whom he had seen in Belfast : this time he had his way.

In November 1862 Foucart, the fencing master, protested that there were so few boys attending his gymnastics class that it was not worth his while attending the Academy. Perhaps the Directors had had some inkling that he was dissatisfied, for when Samuel Boyd, the Janitor, had died early in 1862, they had appointed as his successor Thomas Smeaton, formerly a Colour Sergeant of the Royal Engineers, and told him that he was to act as drill instructor and, if required, to qualify himself to teach gymnastics.

It did not come to that, however. The Rector took the opportunity to lay before the Directors his thoughts on physical training. He had felt for a long time that gymnastics should take a prominent place in the education of the young : it was too much to expect boys to sit in class with what he called watchful and devoted attention for six hours a day, with only brief intervals. If at all possible, there should be a lesson in the gymnasium at about the middle of the teaching day, since the exercise would refresh both mind and body, and boys would return to their classes with all their powers invigorated. The Directors sympathised with this vision of what could be achieved in the gymnasium and Morrison was authorised to approach Charles Long, who took over the teaching of fencing and gymnastics and who was soon supplied with carbines for the use of boys in the gymnasium.

In May 1863 the Rector reflected on the state of his school. Things seemed to be going well : 'in every Department there has been maintained a system of almost perfect discipline, without severity; and all the Class-rooms have uniformly presented an appearance of the greatest order, energy, and intelligent devotedness to work.' The Rector had a recommendation to make about the future management of classes. He reported that during the session he had taught the elementary Latin class himself, specifically so that he could judge how many boys could be taught efficiently in one room. He had come to the conclusion that a class of eighty ought to be divided, so that particular help could be given to boys whose progress had suffered through either absence or what Morrison called 'inferiority of talent'. If this were done, and the strengthening of the Classical Department through Murphy's appointment meant that it was indeed possible, it would also be possible to devote more attention to Latin Composition, which would be useful not only for obtaining a thorough knowledge of the language but also for promoting habits of accuracy in thought and precision in expression. The advantages to be gained by sub-dividing classes were close to Morrison's heart and the whole matter was a question to which his thoughts often turned.

The Rector was also eager to stress the benefits which everyone concerned with a boy's education would enjoy if parents were to visit the classroom. There they could give 'valuable hints to the faithful instructor' and help him to distinguish between boys who were habitually indolent and those who were naturally slow. Such co-operation between teacher and parent would do more than anything else to remove difficulties and to banish for ever, as far as lessons were concerned, any need for corporal punishment. That was a goal, the Rector main-tained, which had already been almost attained in some Departments in the school.

One of Morrison's regrets, which he was to express often, was that so few pupils went on from the Academy to the University. In 1864 he made it possible for students to return to the Academy for special classes during the two sessions after they had left school, to occupy the time which might otherwise be lost because of the long university vacations which some parents felt represented a significant waste of time. The scheme would also go some way towards redressing a considerable disadvantage felt by those who had been educated in Glasgow and who had studied Classics for five or sometimes only four years, and who then came into competition at college with others who had devoted six if not seven years to their classical studies. The scheme was not a success : one commentator remarked that 'very few have been found to take advantage of this boon'.

Another complaint to which Morrison was often to give voice during his early years in Glasgow arose from the habit of sending boys back to school well after the beginning of the session. The Rector even went so far as to describe the practice as 'the greatest of all educational difficulties in Glasgow' and he urged parents to consider whether 'the highest interests of their families would not be promoted by some change in their usual arrangements in this respect'.

Morrison was confident that he had made a start of which he could feel proud and he therefore brought before the Directors a detailed financial statement, showing that since his appointment the income from fees had increased considerably whilst expenditure on salaries had decreased. The Directors took the hint and increased his salary to £500, keeping the promise

they had made to him on his appointment. They also endorsed his wish to develop the curriculum by agreeing that in 1864 William Keddie, of the Free Church College, should deliver a course of lectures on Natural Science which it was hoped that all senior pupils would attend, since the lectures would offer them the opportunity to study subjects 'so inviting and tending so directly to cultivate the taste, to open up sources of enjoyment in every locality and to encourage habits of observation and methodical arrangement'. One boy remembered Keddie years later as 'a dear old man, who discoursed upon fossils and was willing on Saturdays to lead us to quarries where the calamites and coniferae of the coal measures could be found'.

During the summer of 1864 a General Meeting of shareholders was held at which the Directors were at last able to present a much more optimistic report on the financial state of affairs. In the eighteen years since the Academy had been founded, income had exceeded expenditure nine times : an overall surplus of £960 had been earned, of which £680 had been paid out in dividends. During the current session income had exceeded expenditure by over £500 and it had been possible to reduce the Academy's indebtedness : the £5000 bond had been reduced to £4000, with a floating debt of just over £1500.

The financial storm had been weathered, but another crisis was about to break.

1864-1877

The last years at Elmbank

At the beginning of October 1864, six of the masters wrote to the Directors explaining that, since they had a number of complaints against the Rector, they had stopped co-operating with him in the enforcement of school discipline. It was left to the Rector to explain what had happened : at the last moment, and after a number of the boys had been assembled, the masters had told him that they would not be present at the annual reading of the playground regulations. It had then been necessary to dismiss the boys, which was not, in the Rector's view, consistent with good discipline.

At the heart of this serious challenge to the Rector's authority was the masters' contention that Morrison wished to be seen as the only power in the Academy and to reduce the standing of the masters to that of assistants. He had not held meetings to discuss matters of discipline and the general business of the school; the prospectus and advertisements did not pay due regard to the masters' position; a room formerly used as the Masters' Room had been changed to a Visitors' Room, used by the Rector to the exclusion of the masters.

The Directors had little sympathy with the masters' complaints. They had decided to return to a system of rectorial administration and they held the Rector alone responsible to them for the internal management of the school. The masters were his advisers and counsellors, but the Rector must have 'authority to enforce due administration in the several departments'. The Directors were able to cite James Cumming, whose view was that the Rector of a school 'ought to have the entire direction of its literary management, every other master being directly responsible to him, as he himself must also be to the Committee by whom he is appointed. It is surely possible to have the subordination recognised without exciting feelings in any quarter unworthy of gentlemen.'

There were concessions to the masters : they were to have the opportunity to consider the proofs of the prospectus; the Masters' Room was to be furnished in a suitable manner for their comfort and the Directors regretted that this had previously been overlooked; Quarter Days were to be observed as holidays and the masters should be on hand to meet any parents who wished to confer with them when they came to pay the fees. Overall, though, the Rector's authority was asserted.

Morrison was able to use his annual Reports to the Directors in the mid sixties to give wider circulation to some of his views about the way in which the Academy should be conducted and indeed was being conducted under his leadership. He was anxious, for example, that parents should not engage tutors to assist their sons, since the masters set for homework only tasks which most boys could undertake without assistance and if help was on hand, indolence would be the result. Attention was drawn each day to the principal points of the work to be covered the following day. The principles behind it were explained and points requiring special study were carefully marked. The amount of new material covered at school in any one day was never great – in fact it could be repeated by an intelligent boy in a few minutes – but it was only after it had been expounded that there came into play what Morrison described as 'the true business of school education and the skill of the teacher'. The subject of the lesson was examined in all sorts of different ways which would test not only the memory but also 'and especially' the pupils' logical faculties.

Morrison was also at pains to explain that the Masters of English, French, Latin and Greek all used the same terms in grammar and analysis and as far as possible the same methods of instruction, so that the work of the various departments formed part of a 'combined and harmonious whole'. The staff consulted and co-operated with one another in deciding how best to deal with pupils who were having difficulty. The ablest Academy boys went on to do well at the University and to equip them still better for their time there, the time devoted by boys in the Fifth Latin to Latin and Greek was increased.

Morrison was pleased that he seldom encountered the utilitarian argument, that a boy ought to learn only what would turn out to be of practical use to him in the business of life, but he continued to be exercised by the question of class size. On the one hand, he saw educational advantages in large classes, foremost among them the principle of emulation which he regarded as one of the most powerful in the work of education : it was good for the less clever to have in front of them an example of high attainment and to be able to 'measure themselves by a standard more perfect than their own'. Talented boys could also profit from the reminders of first principles which had often to be brought into play to remedy the mistakes of others. Morrison was convinced that there was a valuable liveliness in a large class and he maintained that under the guidance of an experienced and enthusiastic master progress would not depend to any perceptible degree on the number of boys being taught together.

On the other hand, for a number of years extra time had been devoted to boys who for some reason had needed special assistance and this system had clearly been beneficial. It would in future be extended and each of the larger classes would for part of each day be divided into two, thus allowing every boy more easily to be given individual attention. The classes would remain large enough to permit the spirit of emulation to have its effect, but not so large that the numbers ceased to be a blessing and became only a drag.

TABULAR VIEW OF THE

COURSE OF STUDY.

PREPARATORY ENGLISH DEPARTMENT.

FIRST CLASS.

Constable's First, Second, and Third Reading Books—Reid's Outlines of Geography—Oral Lessons in Scripture History.
Writing or Arithmetic.

SECOND CLASS.

Constable's Fourth Reading Book—Reid's Outlines of Geography—Lennie's Grammar—Bible—Catechism.
Writing or Arithmetic.

THIRD CLASS.

Constable's Fifth Reading Book—Reid's Geography—Lennie's Grammar—Collier's Pictures of English History—Coutie's Spelling Guide—Bible—Catechism.
Writing and Arithmetic.

CLASSICAL DEPARTMENT.

FIRST CLASS.

English.—Scott's Lady of the Lake, Cantos I. II.—Collier's Pictures of English History—Lennie's Grammar—Spelling Guide.
Latin.—Edinburgh Academy Rudiments and Delectus—Reid's Geography—Bible.
Writing and Arithmetic.

Morrison was quite specific about the arrangements which he thought feasible at each stage. The First English class was really an Infant School of 120 boys in five or six separate groups at different stages of learning but it could be taught thoroughly by one master if for part of the morning he had the assistance of another master. This would enable him to devote special time to boys almost ready to be promoted to Second English, a class which – like Third English – should not exceed 60. Provision should be made for 120 pupils at each of these stages, generally formed into two classes but occasionally united for examination or for the teaching of subjects such as elementary grammar or history.

The First and Second Latin classes should not exceed 50 or 60 each and even then an hour's separate drill would often be necessary for a few pupils. Classes above the Second Latin should not exceed 40 and indeed the number in Fifth Latin should be reduced to 30 or 35.

Morrison wanted to be able to divide the first three Latin classes and to ensure that even when the larger classes attended the Writing and Arithmetical Departments they had the attention of two or even three masters. He was able to put forward ambitious plans to meet these objectives during the session beginning in August 1867, secure in the knowledge that a much healthier financial situation allowed the Directors to commission the building work which would be needed to accommodate the extra classes.

Some work had already been done. In May 1865, when 575 boys were on the roll, the floating debt had been reduced and a bonus of 10% of their salaries paid to the Rector, the masters and the assistants. The following year, with numbers up to 633, the results had been even better, so a further sum had been paid off, a bonus of 15% paid to the staff and an additional classroom for the English Department added to the south of the existing building.

The Directors' first thought in 1867 was to put up another addition to the buildings, this time to the north, two storeys in height and providing two extra classrooms. The new room to the south would be retained, but used in the meantime as a cloakroom. Before long, though, it was decided that each master should have his own room and that the extension should provide four extra classrooms. An overdraft was authorised, to finance this building work.

It was not only in the classroom that Morrison wanted to improve the facilities and opportunities which the Academy offered boys and their parents. He had emphasised the importance of physical training and gymnastics soon after he had taken up his post and now he turned his attention to outdoor activities. Convinced that the boys should have every opportunity of enjoying active and invigorating exercise, it was his practice on hearing a good report about a class from its master to release the boys from their work for an hour or two, so that they could play football : in suitable weather, he granted skating holidays for the same reason. But Morrison felt that more should be done and that it would be a considerable asset to the school if a field of eight or ten acres could be obtained. The Edinburgh Academy and the great English schools had such a field and he was confident that parents would happily support such a development.

By 1866, the Directors had obtained and enclosed a field known as the Burnbank Coup, between Great Western Road and Woodlands Road, in the area of what are now Barrington Drive and Rupert Street and extending as far west as Park Road. Part of the eighteen acres was quickly levelled for cricket. The Rector looked forward to the beneficial influence which the field would exert on the boys : 'generous competition, a high standard of honour, self-restraint, mutual respect and forbearance, independence of character and habits of self-reliance can nowhere better be acquired than in such a sphere'. The field would also provide a valuable link between the Academy and its former pupils, who had recently formed themselves into a Club which had in mind various ideas to encourage both the sporting and academic pursuits of the boys still at school. On 2 May 1868 the first Sports Day was held at Burnbank, organised by the Club but including events for boys still at school. Sports Day has been a part of the Academy's annual calendar ever since, uninterrupted even by two world wars, though the Club's active participation did eventually come to an end.

The Rector had a clear and lofty vision of what the Academy could achieve : members of the school, 'guarded from evil influences under the parental roof, with its sacred associations, and actively engaged during the day in the intellectual competition of the classroom and the athletic exercises of the gymnasium and play-ground are placed in the best possible, because the most natural, circumstances for growing in all that is great, and noble, and true'.

Beneath the surface, though, all was not well. The masters still had reservations about the rectorial system, though most had said that they would do their best to co-operate with the Rector and the Board. The two exceptions had been the Classical Masters. Alexander Watson in particular had made repeatedly clear his disagreement with the Board, suggesting specifically that undertakings about salary had not been honoured. He had written slightingly about both the work of the Rector and the standard of classical education which was being attempted under him at

the Academy and the Board had only been prevented from dismissing him by Morrison himself, who on that and other occasions had spoken up for him.

In October 1866, however, he went too far, dismissing a boy from his class with the advice that he should 'go and learn something useful' : he had been studying Greek for seven months and still did not know his alphabet. The boy's father objected to the humiliation that his son had suffered and maintained that he and the Rector ought to have been consulted before any action was taken.

The Directors recognised the 'harassing and trying nature' of the teacher's duties and could sympathise with any sudden outburst of temper, but all boys were not clever and the dullest boys had special claims on the teacher's care and patience which Watson did not seem inclined to fulfil. He was dismissed.

There was a swift reaction : a meeting of shareholders was mooted, to discuss the direction of the Academy and the duties, qualifications and emoluments of the teachers. The Directors took this as a threat and responded in a mood of indignation. They were trying to protect from disaster an institution which they had for years attempted to foster and on behalf of which they had accepted individual financial liability. If the shareholders declined to support them, they would 'with great pleasure and with a sense of relief from a very troublesome and delicate task devolve the management of the Academy on those who may be selected as the exponents of the more enlightened and liberal policy which your constituents desiderate'.

The matter was resolved only when Watson apologised in writing and undertook to defer in future to the Rector. His letter was shown to Morrison, who had taken no part in what had been going on but who now accepted the apology and explained that it would give him great personal satisfaction if the Directors would retain Watson's services. The Board agreed to do so, but emphasised to Watson and also to William Murphy that the Rector was also the Head Master of the Classical Department.

There were still problems : towards the end of the year, Morrison reported that Watson

The Staff in 1866

was frequently absent and Murphy totally absent, both through illness. The Directors took the view that, illness apart, a larger staff was now needed and an additional appointment was made to the Classical staff. Murphy resigned soon afterwards, on the orders of his doctor, who had told him to live somewhere warmer. The Directors presented him with £100 and their best wishes for his restoration to health. Further changes to the Classical staff in September 1867 brought Alexander Ogilvie Barrie of Bothwell to the Academy and with him, as a pupil, his brother James. As the author of *Peter Pan*, James Barrie would eventually become one of the most famous of all Academicals.

James McRaith, one of the English Assistants, advised the Directors in 1868 that he planned to take over the school run by William Munzie in Sauchiehall Street : he had been told it would pay him £200 a year, compared with his present salary of £100. The Directors wished him well : they valued his services but could not raise his salary enough to make him reconsider his proposal. McRaith's school became the Albany Academy. In 1876 it moved to West Cumberland Street and in 1895 it was taken over by the School Board whose Woodside School occupied the buildings. It continued to enjoy a long association with Glasgow Academy since in November 1906 the offer was made by the Albany Academical Club of a gold medal, to be awarded annually in memory of McRaith to the best boy in the Sixth Class, unless he was also the Dux, in which case it would go to the next best.

Another master who left at this time was Alexander Finlay. Many parents believed that French and German should be taught by native speakers and in any case Finlay's discipline was not good. In August 1865, he had been a candidate for the chair of Modern Languages and Literature at Queen's College, Belfast, and the Directors had praised the 'enthusiasm and refined taste which he displays in his prelections to the more advanced' and 'the purity of accent' with which he spoke the Modern Languages. In April 1869, however, he was told that he must feel free to employ his services elsewhere and he took with him a year's salary.

Successors were quickly found. Jules Amours was appointed as French Master and Clemens Schlomka, from Culloden House, Inverness-shire, as German Master. Both men were to be allowed to teach elsewhere, since they were not required full time at the Academy. Boys would now take up French at the beginning of Second Latin and German at the beginning of Fourth Latin.

Other matters of an administrative nature had been concerning the Directors. In order that the Academy should register as a Company under the Companies Act of 1862, the Board drew up in December 1866 proposed articles of association which included provision for appointing as Directors four gentlemen each year who had boys in attendance at the school. Although the legal stipulation that this should be the case was eventually to disappear, the importance of having parental representation on the Board was recognised afresh in later years and became definite, though unwritten, policy.

On 10 May 1867 Henry Dunlop of Craigton died. He had been Chairman of the Directors since the Company's inception and was succeeded in that post by Dr Anderson Kirkwood, a writer with Bannatyne, Kirkwood and McJannet.

The buildings and their upkeep continued to be at the forefront of the Directors' minds.

Henry Dunlop

They had spent £2700 on the new accommodation to enable classes to be subdivided and all this had been met, with the exception of some £600 owed to the Clydesdale Bank. Thanks to increasing income from fees, the debt was repaid within a year. The Gymnastics Master suggested to the Directors in 1868 that they should build a new Gymnasium, but at that stage the Board had other priorities. They attended to the ventilation of the rooms, they put up a lavatory, they improved the playground, and they provided a large new porch which offered welcome additional protection from the rain. In August they opened a new Dining Hall, which was a particular boon to boys who lived some distance away from the school.

Charles Long continued to urge that the Gymnasium should be improved and the Directors took his promptings seriously until the Rector brought to their attention rumours which had been circulating about Long's moral character and which made his continued employment at the Academy impossible. He admitted that relations between him and his family were 'such that they might create a public scandal', that he was in serious debt and that he had had to give up his positions in other schools.

In April 1870 the Directors accepted the proposal of Captain George Roland, who taught boys at Fettes and Loretto, that he and his son would travel twice weekly from Edinburgh to give tuition in Fencing and Gymnastics between eleven and two and again at the close of school but they decided to wait until they saw how the new arrangements worked before committing themselves to building a new Gymnasium, even though John Burnet had already drawn up plans for one. The plans did in fact go ahead in 1871 and a brick building was put up, cemented on the outside in imitation of stone work. Burnet had already designed a number of banks in Glasgow and in 1874 was responsible for the Merchants' House in George Square. A year later he built the Glasgow Stock Exchange.

Another alteration to the Academy's curriculum made at this time was the introduction of phonography under William Silver on Tuesday and Thursday mornings before the regular classes started : the study of Pitman's phonetic shorthand remained in the Prospectus until 1894.

The Janitor's conditions of work were reviewed early in 1868 and Thomas Smeaton declined to accept the new regulations. He was dismissed and replaced by Henry Hogben whose salary was fixed at £100. His day-to-day work was to see to it that the Academy was swept and dusted every day and enough floors washed every Saturday to ensure that the whole school was attended to once a month. He was to watch the boys in the playground and report any breach of the rules either to a boy's master or to the Rector. The 'No football' sign was to be displayed when it rained or when there was a risk that the boys' clothes might become dirty. He was to ring the bell at exactly the right times.

After the school had been dismissed, he was to go round all the classrooms, opening the windows and leaving them open for two hours. On his rounds, he was to collect all 'books, cloaks, umbrellas and other articles' left by the boys and keep them until eleven next morning when he was to go round the rooms again, levying a fine of one halfpenny for each article claimed. The money was to be left with the master and put towards the library, of which the Janitor also had charge.

Stoves were to be kindled on the Tuesday after the October Communion and kept alight during the week until the Communion in April unless the state of the weather should require a longer period of heating. Windows were to be cleaned during the Christmas and Summer holidays and during the October and April Sacrament weeks, or when the Rector required it.

The Janitor was also responsible for supplying luncheon to the masters, but not at first to the boys : the Directors' view was that it might diminish the respect shown to him by the boys if he did so, and they gave the work to a baker and confectioner, Brownlie. Soon, Brownlie was being urged to pay particular attention to the tidiness of the rooms and to the quality and freshness of everything that he offered for sale, but complaints continued and it was eventually agreed that the Janitor should once again supply the boys with lunch.

The financial success of the school meant that in June 1869 it was possible for the first time in some ten years to pay a dividend to shareholders of 5% free of tax, together with a bonus of 2.5%. Similar payments were made over the years that the school remained in Elmbank Street. The masters also shared financially in the school's success and their bonus arrangements continued, though between 1872 and 1874 rather than being paid a percentage of their salaries they were awarded a proportion of the profit to divide amongst themselves. In 1875 the bonus was 25% but that was the last occasion on which it was paid : a large increase in salaries was awarded in 1876 and the practice of paying a bonus ceased.

By the summer of 1870 there were almost 700 boys in the school, distributed into eighteen classes. The average number in each class was therefore 39, which was invariably reduced by absence to something like 35. The following year Morrison reported that the largest classes, the First and Second Latin, contained as many as 44 boys : in future, though, First Latin would be divided into three, so that the maximum number would be 35, enough for healthy competition but not too many to preclude individual attention from the master.

In April 1870, reluctantly, the Rector had to draw the Directors' attention to Alexander Watson, whose attendance was so irregular that his classes were being neglected, a fact which had not escaped the notice of parents. The Directors decided that Watson should leave at the end of the session and awarded him a leaving allowance of £125. Watson went to Kelvinside Academy for a short time and then to a school at Hamilton. 'Always a keen critic of boys and their ways', he was nevertheless popular because of his interest in games and 'because of the entire absence of any conventional demeanour' : he had been enthusiastically involved in the foundation of the Academical Club. Other changes in the Classical Department included the departure of Barrie, who had been appointed one of Her Majesty's Inspectors of Schools. This meant still more work for the Rector, who had been already awarded an additional payment of £100 for extra duties during the illnesses of Watson and William Moyes.

The Rector had first urged in 1868 that independent examiners should test the pupils' attainments and the following year overtures were made with a view to such an examination being conducted by the Senate of Glasgow University, where more and more Academy boys were gaining honours, but it was not until 1871 that arrangements were finally concluded with the University of Cambridge Syndicate. Two examiners, Fellows of Cambridge Colleges, conducted the examination early in May. The Rector reported later that the boys 'entered heartily into the severe ordeal through which they had to pass and they exhibited, almost without exception, a happiness and an intelligence which I have seldom seen surpassed'. The results, however, disconcerted the Directors in two major areas.

The first of these was Mathematics, and William Marr, the Head Master, was warned that if there were not a decided improvement in the teaching of Mathematics there would have to be what they called a 'reconstruction' of the Department. Marr agreed that more written work would be set to the advanced classes and that trouble would be taken to encourage neatness and a methodical approach. He wanted more teaching time, but the Directors did not agree, suggesting that with careful organisation he would find that the number of hours available was quite sufficient.

Attention also had to be given to the position of Drawing. The existing classes were attended by only ten or at most twenty boys, perhaps because proper accommodation was not available. Now, though, the enlarged Gymnasium could be equipped with folding desks around the walls and pupils could attend for two hours each week, to be taken off the time allowed for Writing. Woolnoth could continue his present classes but an additional master would be employed for two days a week to implement the scheme used in the Government Schools of Design, Drawing days to alternate with Gymnasium days. James Greenlees, son of the Head Master of the Government School of Design in Glasgow, was appointed to this post and hopes were high that the Academy could to some extent at least emulate the schools in Germany, where Drawing was a central part of the curriculum for all boys from the age of 11 upwards.

William Whitelaw, who had been Classical Master in Dreghorn Castle, Edinburgh, and then Headmaster of the Proprietary School in Hexham, came to the Academy as a Classical Master in 1866. He left in 1870 to open the Park School in Lynedoch Street. Although from 1880 Park provided an education for girls, it was in fact established as a boys' school and as such represented direct competition for the Academy. Whitelaw's enterprise therefore dealt a serious blow to his former employers. In 1861 there had been just under 400 on the roll, which had almost doubled by 1868. Since then the number had fallen, first to 700 and then, with the opening of the rival school, to just under 600.

This slump in numbers naturally entailed a corresponding reduction in fee income but it nevertheless proved possible in February 1871 to repay £1000 of the Bond over the Academy. Further building work continued. During the summer of 1871, a separate entrance was provided for the youngest pupils so that they never had to come into contact with the older boys. From the front of the Academy they went to a door opening into their own rooms, on the south side of the building. Furthermore, part of the playground was railed off to be used only by the youngest pupils when the rest was occupied by other classes.

During 1871 the Directors had to find a successor to the Secretary, J S Fleming, who had held the position since 1861 but had now resigned. It was agreed that the office should continue to be combined with that of Treasurer and John Alexander Spens, a writer with Maclay, Murray and Spens, was appointed in July. At the same time Anderson Kirkwood resigned as President and as a Director and was succeeded by William Blackie, the publisher.

William Blackie

In March 1872, the Directors accepted with sadness the resignation of William Moyes who had continued to be absent, in Aberdeen, through ill health, voting him an annuity of £100 a year for five years, which was particularly to assist him in keeping up insurance policies which he had taken out as provision for his wife and family. Less than two months later, Moyes died. In his place was appointed James Colville, who was born in Leuchars, had graduated from Edinburgh in 1868 with First Class Honours in Classics and had already taught English at Madras College, Merchiston Castle School and George Watson's College. The Rector endorsed his appointment enthusiastically : 'under such a Master the English Department cannot fail to maintain that high place in public estimation which it has so long held'. Colville wished to see the study of English as highly regarded as that of Classics and worked hard to secure proper recognition of the Modern side of the school. He was connected with the Early English Texts Society and introduced the teaching of Middle English authors such as Chaucer.

In October 1871 the Directors decided not to alter the school's hour of opening from ten o'clock to nine. They did, however, agree to follow the example of the High School and arranged that the Academy's summer holiday should in future be taken in July and August, rather than June and July. This decision entailed an extra month's teaching, in June 1872, for which the masters were paid an extra month's salary and for which the parents were charged, and also led the Directors to decide that it would be inexpedient that year to have the school examined by the Cambridge Syndicate. There would instead be a private examination, which would complement the system of monthly or in some cases weekly written examinations which had recently been introduced for the whole of the Upper School. When masters were not satisfied with a boy's results, they communicated with his parents by means of a printed form.

Class sizes had been further reduced, so that by 1872 no class above First English exceeded 40. The Fourth and Fifth Classes were divided into a Classical and a Modern side and more time was to be devoted by senior boys to the study of French and German. At the beginning of that session Academy boys had been placed first, second, fourth and sixth in the Bursary Competition and University honours were growing more and more numerous. The Rector publicised such honours so as to 'stir up many of the boys, advancing at present step by step through the various Classes to increased diligence at work'. Other activities, perhaps not strictly academic, were also being encouraged, for example by the appointment of a Singing Master.

From Morrison's point of view, changing the dates of the session was a complete success : in the past 'not unfrequently two months, and sometimes even a whole quarter, passed before all the members of a Class were brought to such a degree of equality that they could effectively be taught together.' In 1872, though, the Academy had started on 2 September and on the third day of the session the number enrolled had been as large as at the end of the fourth week the previous year. It seemed to be the most 'effectual means of checking the growing tendency in Glasgow to extend School holidays to a degree unknown perhaps in any other city in the kingdom'.

All was not well with the teaching of Mathematics, though, and in April 1873 Marr was asked to resign : in view of his fifteen years' faithful service, the Directors voted him £100 a year for five years. Finlay Macrae was soon appointed to succeed him : he had taught at Merchiston Castle School and at Daniel Stewart's, and he was to assist with Chemistry and Physics if required.

In 1871 the Academical Club had proposed to move to a more suitable ground, an idea which had pleased the Directors, but at the end of the following year they were still at Burnbank and apparently in some difficulty. The Directors could not accept the proposition that all the school's pupils should pay a levy to assist in maintaining a field which it was clear could only be used by some of them. It would be better if the boys were asked to join the Club : if they did not do so, the Club would have to give up the field. The Directors did agree that if, in the year ahead, the boys' subscriptions did not amount to £25, they would make good the deficiency to the extent of ten guineas. The Club actually left Burnbank in 1874 and moved to a ground in North Kelvinside, close to Kelbourne Street and Garrioch Drive.

In July 1874 the Directors agreed to raise Macrae's salary to £400, to prevent him from becoming a candidate for the Head Mastership of the Mathematical Department in the High School, but they did lose the services of one of the Classical Masters. When this vacancy arose, the Directors asked the Rector to report to them on the work which he himself was doing. Morrison insisted that he would carry on the work for which he considered himself engaged 'at any amount of personal annoyance and consistent with the good of the school' : but he had clearly found it difficult over the years to carry out the duties of a Head Classical Master as well as those of a Rector.

When he first came to the Academy he had had to teach five hours a day and was able to examine the general working of the school only occasionally, by leaving his class with written work to do. His teaching was later reduced to four hours a day, but it was often still impossible to visit another class or consult a parent or see to a difficulty without leaving his class unsupervised. During the first few weeks of each session, in fact, he had to give up his class almost entirely to another master. He reckoned to lose one tenth of his teaching time altogether.

There were also tasks which he had always regarded as part of his duties but had not been able to perform adequately. He would like to be able to have some personal dealings with every boy who passed through the school, but as things were this was possible only in the case of those who entered the higher classes in the Classical Department.

He also felt that he should be in a position to inspect each classroom regularly, to ensure that there was thorough work, that there was uniformity of system and that each day the work set by the masters for one class was neither too great nor too little. He wished also to be able to relieve the Head English Master from time to time, so that Colville could inspect the work of his Department, and to have time to examine the masters' registers and thus to enquire into cases of irregular attendance.

Morrison would like the masters, under his superintendence, to conduct regular examinations which would enable him to know exactly how well each boy was doing. The results would stimulate indolent boys, would bring to light cases where boys excelled in one subject at the expense of another, and would provide evidence on which to recommend to parents a special course of study.

These were high ambitions, but the Directors wished to see them fulfilled and so agreed to look for a Head Classical Master whose appointment would allow Morrison the freedom to devote his time to 'imparting religious instruction' and to the 'proper Rectorial work of thoroughly superintending and examining all the work and all the details of the school'. It was not in fact until the following session that James Moir, who had been Rector of Banff Academy, took up the new post. When he did so, the salary paid to the Rector was £650, to Moir and Macrae £500 and to Colville £425.

In the meantime, the Directors had dismissed Greenlees from his post as Drawing Master on the grounds that his habits were irregular and dissipated. The man they found to succeed him, a Mr Douglas of Edinburgh, was well suited for the post 'except for his want of experience in teaching'. He was offered a six months' trial, which must have been successful since he continued at the school for some time.

The Directors and the Rector were working hard to improve still further the academic standing of the school. In the summer of 1875 the work of the boys was inspected by external examiners : such examinations eventually became annual affairs. In 1875 Morrison also undertook a project which had first been mooted four years earlier and on the afternoon of the Prize Giving, 24 June, set off to see for himself what was done in some of the schools of Germany.

A little over a month later, he reported on what he had found. He had visited the Kloster Gymnasium and the Friedrichs-Realschule in Berlin and then schools in Elberfeld and Cologne. A significant difference between the two countries was that boys left school in Scotland at an age three or four years younger than was the case in Germany : at the Academy, boys left for business or for College at an average age of little more than fifteen. One way of countering this tendency would be to make it quite clear that the Classical course lasted for six years.

TO PARENTS.

Parents will please to observe that boys will be promoted twice a year from one stage to another, and arranged not according to the <u>time</u> spent in any particular class, but according to the <u>progress</u> made during the previous half session in all the work of that class.

Morrison also proposed, and adopted, a radical alteration to the system of promotion from class to class. Boys should not move up simply on the basis of time spent in a particular class but instead should be promoted twice yearly from one stage to another, according to the progress they had made. In this way the consequences of even a few months' neglect or idleness would become apparent to all, while on the other hand boys who were diligent and careful would not be held back by those who had failed to make the most of the teaching available to them.

Changes were also to be made to the curriculum. A significant alteration was to be introduced in the teaching of science. Keddie's lectures should be discontinued and replaced by systematic lessons, in Zoology and Botany for junior classes and in Physical Science for the senior classes of both the Classical and Modern sides. Use would be made of 'Science Primers and appropriate Illustrations and Experiments'.

Drawing, of particular importance in a city such as Glasgow, should not remain optional but should be part of the course for all boys for at least three years, from Third English to Second Latin. Advanced classes in Landscape, Figure and Mechanical Drawing would continue to be available for those who wished them. Gymnastics should also become a compulsory part of the curriculum for all boys up to Third Latin or Fourth English.

Further developments took place in 1876. The fees were raised by ten per cent, in order to fund a large increase in teachers' salaries designed to do away with the bonus system. John Burnet was commissioned to produce designs for new buildings, and in June it was announced that these would include a Laboratory, with the first floor devoted to Drawing.

During the summer, the Rector visited a number of English public schools, Giggleswick, Manchester Grammar School, Rugby, Clifton College, Eton, Dulwich and Harrow. By and large what he found reassured him that the course of education offered by the Academy to the public was a sound one. In particular the new system of promotion should be maintained. He did, however, return with one or two new ideas.

A copy of the timetable should be sent to every parent, together with a note about the time that should be spent on homework. Parents would then know what their sons would miss if they were not sent to school. The Rector felt that in Glasgow 'with many parents any cause, however trifling, seems a sufficient excuse for absence or neglect of work'. Communication with parents should also be improved by sending home at least twice a year, at Christmas and at the end of the session, a report about the position in the class, the progress and the conduct of each boy.

Morrison also felt that every boy in the highest class, on the Classical Side and the Modern, should be examined with a view to receiving a Leaving Certificate if he proved to be qualified for it. The Directors did not feel ready to implement this proposal, which was somewhat ahead of its time.

The Academy now had a staff of twenty and a roll of 675 pupils and seemed poised to make still further advances. On 21 March 1877, however, the Directors learned that the School Board of Glasgow wished to buy the Academy. A committee was appointed to negotiate with the Board and two days later an offer to sell the school was signed by William Blackie, the Chairman. On 6 April an amended offer was accepted by the Board, which was prepared to pay £32000 for the school, with entry on 30 June 1878. A public meeting was held on 2 May at which the resolution to sell the school was passed : three weeks later a further meeting confirmed the decision, which was perhaps motivated by a mistaken belief that the Education Act of 1872 meant that there would soon be little need for such privately run schools as the Academy.

The Rector and the masters had been consulted about continuing the school until June 1878 : by mid June 1877 they knew that proposals were in hand which would enable them to continue their work elsewhere.

Donald Morrison had been Rector in Elmbank Street for sixteen years and could look back with some satisfaction at what had been achieved under his guidance. The financial

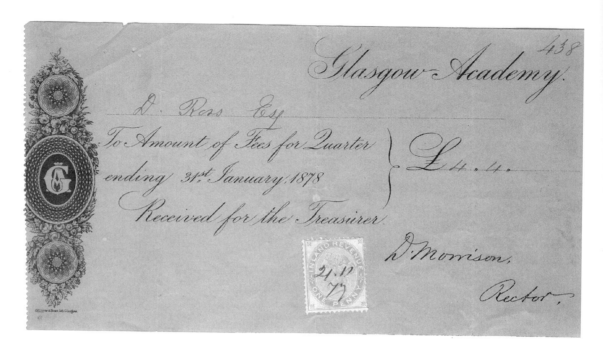

position had improved, difficulties with the staff had been overcome, competition had been met. The buildings had been improved, so that instead of nine classrooms there were now sixteen. The gymnasium had been enlarged. Class sizes had been limited by subdivision and boys were now arranged throughout the school according to merit, promoted only when they had mastered the work of each class.

English, including literature and the history of the language, was now taught throughout the school, whereas when he arrived, it had not been taught systematically to boys above the Second Latin class. Mathematics was taught for four years rather than one, French for five years rather than two, German for three years rather than one. Drawing, Music, Gymnastics and Science were all part of the regular curriculum.

As if to underline the effectiveness of all these reforms, Morrison was able to reflect that six young men from the Academy had been elected as Snell Exhibitioners at Oxford, where they were earning honour for themselves and for their school. The Rector was not alone in rejoicing that the Academy was not to be lost to Glasgow.

1877-1883

The move to Kelvinbridge

The first moves to ensure that the Academy did not die were made early in June 1877 by John Spens, Secretary to the Board of Directors. He circularised a number of gentlemen who then wrote collectively to Donald Morrison, requesting that he should call together some of those who might be interested in ensuring that the Academy continued, albeit on a different site. This he did, and on 14 June a meeting was held in the Religious Institution Rooms, Buchanan Street.

It was clear that although the present Directors and Shareholders were not prepared to continue the Academy, the Board would be entirely happy to hand over the name and whatever prestige that would carry with it to any new company that might be formed. Furthermore, a significant number of the Directors would willingly associate themselves with the new school, including William Blackie.

Donald Morrison explained that there was no adequate alternative provision in Glasgow for the education of the boys now attending the Academy and that the teaching staff would be willing to work for the new company, if one were formed. Sites for the new Academy had already been examined and at a further meeting next day Morrison was able to refer in detail to a plot of land which the Police Board had for sale close to Kelvingrove Park, at Eldon Street and Woodlands Road. He was even able to produce plans of buildings which would be suitable for the site.

It was agreed at once to appoint provisional Directors for the new Company and, from their number, Committees on Finance and Building. Efforts would be made without delay to have shares taken up at £10 each, so as to acquire capital of £30000. Negotiations would be entered into at once with the Police Board.

The price for Woodlands Road was greater than the Directors were willing to pay, and other sites were examined. There was one in the West End Park, close to the Museum, and another in University Avenue, opposite the University.

As June passed into July, talks were held with the School Board about delaying for a year their entry into the buildings of the existing Academy, and the decision was taken to organise a competition for the appointment of an architect.

On 5 July it was reported that the proprietors of some vacant ground near Belmont Crescent were willing to dispose of a plot lying to the east of an intended new street there. Architects had already been sounded out on the question of whether the ground was capable of holding buildings and the views of James Deas were also sought. The conclusion of the Engineer to the Clyde Navigation Trust was that there would be no difficulty, though the foundations needed would cost between £550 and £600.

The site was an extensive one of more than 23000 square yards, of which more than 15000 would be suitable for the building and playgrounds. The cost was just under £20000. Before a definite bargain was struck, however, further precautions were taken to ensure that the existence under the site of an old coal working would not mean considerable extra expense for piling.

At this time it was still hoped that, together, the old and the new Academy companies might persuade the School Board to delay until June 1879 its move into the existing buildings, though it was pointed out that the old company was to be wound up on 30 June 1878. On 14 August, however, with over a thousand

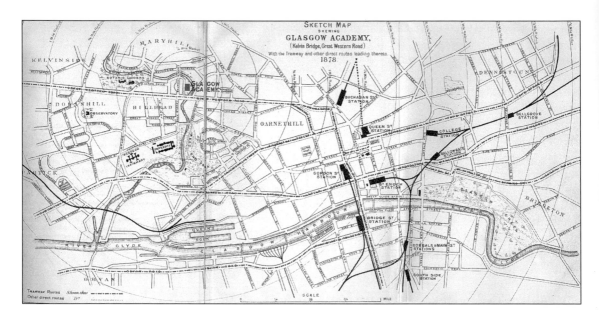

shares in the new company already taken up and paid for, it was decided to go ahead with the purchase of the Belmont Street site.

The ground which the company had bought had once been used as a coup, but latterly had been home to the Caledonian Cricket Club, which in 1875 had sought permission to put up a clubhouse there. The Club did not survive the loss of its ground, so the decision to sell must have been a difficult one, particularly for the President, H E Crum-Ewing, who was also a leading light in Academy circles, the first President of the Academical Club and a member of the committee charged with organising the financial arrangements of the new school.

The advantages of the site were numerous. It enjoyed a central location, with the large and expanding suburb of Kelvinside to the north, Hillhead to the west and south and the City to the east. It was on the line of the tramway cars

and the houses which had been built close by seemed certain to guarantee the respectability of the locality. Parts of the ground adjoining Great Western Road and at the north west boundary could be disposed of if that seemed appropriate. The site was in fact higher than Great Western Road, so the building would be conspicuous. Extensive playgrounds would be available. The River Kelvin, which flowed to the north and east, was comparatively pure and perhaps before long would be perfectly pure, and the banks leading down to it would be available for shrubbery. Finally, the cost was only one third of the cost of other sites which had been considered.

With the benefit of advice from John Burnet, the Directors resolved to appoint Messrs H and D Barclay as architects for the buildings and less than two weeks later Hugh Barclay produced plans of a square building about one hundred feet long. On his recommendation it was agreed that without finalising other plans, work should proceed at once with the foundations. The estimates for these were examined early in September, when Barclay had finally resolved they should be formed of hard-burned brick set in Portland cement and firmly bound together by means of timber and iron beams.

Hugh Barclay and David, his younger brother, were to become well known in Glasgow for the schools which they built. The new Academy building was among the first : others included Partick Academy, Abbotsford Public School, Pollokshields Secondary School, Rutland Crescent Public School, Govanhill Public School and – the Academy's closest neighbour – Hillhead High School.

Directors were formally elected on 6 September and eight days later Robert Young, a ship-broker, was appointed Chairman and William Ker Vice-Chairman. Gordon Smith was elected Secretary and Treasurer. The Articles of Association subscribed by the new Directors specifically stated that on reaching the end of the curriculum pupils of the Academy should be fit to enter the arts classes of Glasgow University. The New Glasgow Academy Company Limited was registered the following month. The shareholders, many of whom also sent their boys to the school, reflected the changing face of Glasgow's business community. The textile industry was still well represented, by turkey-red dyers and calico printers, cotton brokers and spinners and wool brokers. The Fraser family – 'silk mercers, general drapers, carpet and furnishing warehousemen' of Buchanan Street and Argyle Street – sent two boys to the school. There was every sort of merchant and broker – timber, wine, tea, corn, fish, sugar, flour, provisions.

Growing industrialisation, though, was evident in the coal masters and iron masters, the shipbuilders and ship-owners, the nitrate and sulphate store-keepers, the fireclay manufacturers, the metal and tinplate merchants, the civil engineers, the engineers and boiler-makers. Other fathers had interesting occupations – they included a malt distiller, two shoe manufacturers, a diamond merchant, jeweller and silversmith, a professor of dancing – but the 'philosophical instrument maker' from Edinburgh who bought shares did not have boys at the school. Nor did the 'pyrotechnist', who bought shares and advertised himself in the Post Office Directory as 'firework artiste to the Queen and the Dukes of Argyll and Hamilton, the Marquises of Bute and Lorne etc'.

Robert Scott was appointed as measurer for the new building on 19 September. He agreed to prepare estimates within about ten days of receiving the plans and promised that all would be 'got up in first class style'. Before long, Robert Whyte, a joiner of 345 Gallowgate, had contracted to put the whole building up for some £11000. Provided he was given possession of the completed foundations by the end of November, he undertook to have the work completed by 15 August. If he did so, he would be paid a premium of £500; if he failed to do so, he would pay a penalty of £500. Eventually, he received the premium.

At the end of October the Directors considered four different designs submitted by the Architect and chose the plainest one, without pillars and with cornicing fashioned in wood. Barclay was deeply disappointed and wasted no time in urging the Board to think again. He felt that it was a case of mistaken economy, for he was sure that a building of architectural

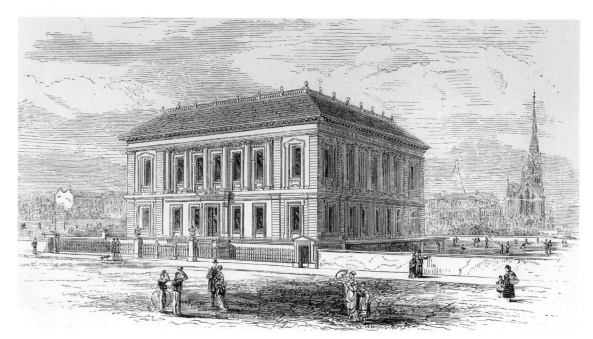

importance would bring in extra pupils. If the Directors adopted his second design, which would cost just £1600 extra, his firm would take up thirty shares, offer certain guarantees about the cost of the building and restrict their fee to what it would have been if the plainest design had been adopted. His arguments won the day.

The masons began their work about the middle of December and by 18 February 1878 the building was ready for roofing. By this time 2252 shares had been taken up and two calls had been made on the shareholders, but expenditure inevitably outpaced income and an overdraft had been arranged with the City of Glasgow Bank.

Staffing arrangements were also made during February. Morrison was appointed Rector, at a salary of £600, and the Head Masters of the various Departments were all invited to continue in the new building, their duties and hours to be similar to those in force at Elmbank Street. Colville, Moir and Macrae would be paid £425 for their responsibilities in the English, Classical and Mathematical Departments, Maclaren would receive £350 as Head Writing Master, and Amours and Schlomka would receive £300 and £160 respectively for teaching French and German. Assistants would be appointed by the Rector and the Head Masters.

The Directors had hoped that Principal Caird of the University would lay a foundation stone but when they discovered in mid February that he was unable to do so they decided that there would be no ceremony of that nature.

There was much discussion with the Hillhead authorities about the type of sanitation to be provided and about the street to the west of the new building. It was agreed to form the street by macadamizing it, with pavements of

from 20/- in First English to 84/- in Fourth, Fifth and Sixth Latin. Where three pupils from one family were enrolled, the third should be charged half fees and when there were four the fourth should be educated free of charge. The school hours would be from 9.30 until 3.30.

The Directors agreed that book prizes should be abolished and replaced by various classes of certificates, a reform which was intended to do away with the prospect of reward and honour as the principal motive for hard work. Explaining the decision in the first prospectus for the new Academy, Morrison argued that it would be better to follow the German model where parents asked at the end of the session not 'How many prizes?' or 'What place in the class?' but 'Have you been promoted?' or 'Have you a good report?' A First Class or Second Class certificate would be given to every boy in First Latin and above who reached a certain percentage of the full value of all the work, in daily marks and written examinations, which had been prescribed for the class. A list of the classes would be published at the end of the session and a quarterly report would be sent home to parents.

ashes, and the Directors thought, when asked by the Town Clerk for their views, that it should be called Academy Street. Their view did not prevail, of course, and the school's address in due course became Colebrooke Street. The Directors were not happy when, some months later, the Commissioners of Hillhead called for the pavement to be formed of Caithness Pavement.

Steady progress was made with all sorts of other matters, including the planting of the slopes running down to the Kelvin and deciding the extent of the playgrounds to the north and south of the building – sixty feet. At the end of March it was agreed that a gymnasium should be constructed on the attic storey. Later decisions which shaped the appearance of the school included the provision of railings and a gateway at the main entrance and along the west front of the school, and construction of the front steps out of cement rather than stone. There was to be fencing round the rest of the site.

As the start of the new session grew nearer, the Directors turned their attention to matters more directly connected with the educational work of the school. Fees were fixed in May. There would be a charge of 25/- per quarter plus a sessional fee which would range

The prospectus included a sketch of the new building together with a plan of the city, showing the various routes to the Academy from the railway stations, including the tramway running along Great Western Road. The Directors had chosen the site carefully, to reflect the continuing move westwards of the sort of families who were likely to send their boys to a school like the Academy – as the success of Park School in Lynedoch Street demonstrated. When the Academy's original building had been opened, Elmbank Street had been more or less at the centre of its catchment area, but things had changed. Academy families had moved into new areas of housing in the Park district, Hillhead, Partick and Dowanhill and at Kelvinbridge the Academy would once again be at the centre of its sphere of influence. The Directors of the new Company were representative of the school community generally, with addresses in Granby Place, Sardinia Terrace and Belgrave Terrace in Hillhead, Eamont Lodge in Dowanhill, Crown Gardens and Prince's Terrace, also in Dowanhill, Belhaven Terrace and Great Western Terrace in Great Western Road, Park Terrace, Park Circus and Lynedoch Place. The Rector lived in Victoria Terrace, Dowanhill.

It was confidently expected that the move westwards, closer to these new residential areas, would lead to a particular increase in the numbers joining the Preparatory Department. Particular trouble would be taken, not only to develop the intelligence of the youngest boys, but also to encourage them to adopt a pure accent both in reading and in speaking. A lady, Miss Campbell, was to be employed to teach the junior section of the First English class.

There would be other developments. The employment of a Gymnastics Master daily from 9 to 4 would allow a systematic course of physical instruction to be offered throughout the school. The teaching of Science would start at an earlier age : in the First and Second Latin classes, Botany would be studied in summer and autumn and Zoology in winter, while Physical Geography and Physiology would be taught to the Third Class, Physics to the Fourth and Chemistry to more senior boys. Singing would be taught up to Second Latin and Drawing up to Third Latin. Instrumental tuition, particularly on the pianoforte, would be available for those who wished it.

Stress was laid on the beneficial influence which would be exercised over the rest of the school by the Sixth Latin, a class which had been instituted three years earlier to cater for those who wished to pursue their studies to a more advanced plane before going on to College. The Rector was now allowed to proceed with the idea which he had put forward on his return from England in 1876, that every boy who completed the Academy's curriculum would receive a Leaving Certificate, an indication of his character and scholarship which could be presented as credentials in any place of business where he might seek employment.

It was planned to inaugurate the new building at the end of July and to invite the Sheriff of the County, the Lord Provost and the Chairman of the School Board, together with the parents of all pupils currently attending the Academy and a number of citizens interested in the cause of education. A certain amount of work still had to be finished, though, before the day of the ceremony : in particular, estimates for the painter work were not obtained until just over two weeks before the inauguration took place.

The Rector obtained decisions on

certain other matters from the Directors when they met in mid July. Some of the teachers had taken exception to the change which was proposed in the hour at which classes would begin and asked that they should be allowed to attend at 10 o'clock rather than 9.30 : the request was declined. Morrison also secured agreement to his proposal that all masters should wear gowns and he was authorised to make arrangements to obtain them.

The ceremony of inauguration and the annual meeting of shareholders were both held in the new buildings on 30 July. Those who visited the school that day could see for themselves what an imposing building it was that had been put up so rapidly. Grecian in style, it was designed to accommodate 800 pupils and occupied only part of the five acre site. Most of the rest had been laid out as playgrounds, with covered verandahs to the south, east and north of the school building which would act as play sheds. The lavatories and urinals stood at the south-east and north-east corners. Senior pupils played to the north and used two entrances to the building on that side; the playground and the entrance for the junior boys were to the south.

The foundation walls which had made it possible to build on the site were eleven feet wide and nine feet high. They enclosed, at ground level, a large central hall, open to the roof of the building some 60 feet above. The hall was to be used for drill and for recreation in wet weather and round the edge of it were arranged numbered places for each boy's cap and coat. It was divided into two sections, 65 feet by 40 and 60 by 26, for the older and the younger boys and at the northern end of it was the Luncheon Bar. On this level, too, was installed the heating and ventilation apparatus which would circulate air

round the whole building through passages between the walls and the plaster work. There were openings from these passages into each classroom. The object was to heat the rooms during cold weather and to increase the natural ventilation during warm weather, so that there would always be a constant supply of fresh air at a proper temperature without any need to open the windows.

The Rector's Room was to be found to the left of the main entrance on the first floor, where there were also seven classrooms, each 18 feet high. Two of the largest, on the east side, had been specially furnished for the younger classes in the Preparatory Department. Of the others, three were used for English, one for French and one for German.

Stairs on the north side of the building led up to the second floor, passing on a half-landing the Masters' Room in which an internal window had been placed so that those inside could see clearly what was going on in the hall and the passages. All the second floor rooms were 19 feet high. The Writing Room, 60 feet by 30, ran along most of the southern side of the building. Including a classroom on the next half-landing, there were four rooms for Classics and four for Mathematics and Arithmetic.

In the attic storey, which was lit only through skylights, was the gymnasium, 90 by 29 feet and 16 feet high. To the west of it were a lecture and examination hall, a laboratory and a room for instrumental music, to the east a kitchen and a dining hall where it was promised

that one of the masters would always preside at table.

The first session in the Academy's new building began on Monday 2 September 1878. Parents who enrolled their children found that, after their time in the junior section of the First English class, the boys moved on to the senior section, where they remained until they had learned to read fluently, had become familiar with numbers and were able to add, to subtract and to write and draw simple figures on a slate. Scottish Geography and History were among the subjects added in the Second Class : Writing, Drawing and Gymnastics were others. After a year in the Third Class and aged about ten, boys then moved on to the Advanced Course.

The study of Latin began in the First Class, where two hours a day were also devoted to Arithmetic. Singing, Zoology and Botany were continued until the end of the Second Class and Drawing until the end of the Third, but Gymnas-

tics and Writing continued throughout the whole course. Algebra and Geometry were begun in the Third Class.

After Third Latin, a boy could continue with the Classical course which was intended for those who wished either to acquire a broad general culture or to proceed to the University or one of the professions. French and Greek were started in Fourth Latin and German in Fifth Latin. The work of the Sixth Class, under the Head Masters, consisted of more difficult Latin and Greek authors, the principles of comparative philology, advanced French and German, Old English, Algebra, Plane Trigonometry, Co-ordinate Geometry and Chemistry. Boys in this class were prepared for the Preliminary Examination, which qualified them to take just a three year course at the University.

An alternative to the Classical course was the Modern Section, from which Greek was excluded. This was designed for those who would be going on to commercial life or public service. There was also the Special English Section, intended to prepare for a business life boys who showed little aptitude for acquiring languages or whose education before they joined the Academy had not equipped them to pursue the study of Latin.

All classes were opened each day with prayer and a scripture reading. In addition, a systematic course of Bible History was undertaken in successive years and selected portions of the New Testament were committed to memory.

On 3 October a meeting was held to discuss the stoppage of the City of Glasgow Bank at which the Academy had had a credit of just under £200. Since the next annual instalment of the cost of the ground was due to be paid at Martinmas, it would be necessary to arrange an advance. The National Bank of Scotland was therefore appointed the Company's Banker and it was agreed to ask for a loan of £6000, with a view to making a permanent arrangement the following year for obtaining a loan over the property of the Company. The Bank was, however, unwilling to lend the money required unless on the personal obligation of the Directors and it was resolved to invite the shareholders to apply for five year debentures bearing interest at 5%, as security for which the Company's property would be conveyed to trustees. The full amount of £5000 was quickly subscribed for The Academy still owed money to the City of Glasgow Bank for the balance of the price of the ground and it was later arranged that £10000 should be borrowed from the City of Glasgow Insurance Company. It is not clear how many Academy families suffered from the collapse of the Bank, which was a disaster for the Glasgow business community : the Rector brought two cases before the Board and was instructed to deal with them in whatever way he though advisable, reporting back to the Vice-Chairman.

The Academical Club took an interest in the playground, where they were given permission to play tennis, and in the facilities offered by the new building : in the autumn of 1878 they held their annual dinner in the Writing Room. The custom is said to have arisen that on the occasion of the Dinner the Club would ask the Rector if the school might be excused classes on the following day – for practical as well as sentimental reasons, since opportunity had to be found to tidy up the room.

Another notable event in the Writing Room was the first concert, given on Friday 9 May 1879 by a choir of some sixty boys which had been formed by John Maclaren and which was augmented for the occasion by twenty men's voices. Accompaniment was provided by a piano and a harmonium and Maclaren conducted with a baton which he had been given by the boys as a token of their gratitude for his labour of love in training them. The proceedings, which were attended by over two hundred parents and friends, began at 8 o'clock with an anthem, *O Lord How Manifold Are Thy Works* and included twelve other pieces, including a cantata, *Sleeping Beauty*, with words by Tennyson, the Poet Laureate. 'Carriages may be ordered at ten.'

So impressed was the Rector with the musical work which Maclaren was doing that it was agreed that he should be appointed Music Master as well as Writing Master for the next session and paid an extra £50. One former pupil recalled that he taught both subjects at once – Music from one end of the Writing Room, Writing from the other.

The examination at the end of the school's first session in its new home was conducted by Professor Geddes of Aberdeen University and Professor Chrystal of St Andrews. Professor Chrystal lamented the shyness of the boys when speaking German : 'there was a tendency (natural enough no doubt) to dispense with the inflexional peculiarities of the foreign tongue'. Even reading aloud in English was 'affected in most cases by the local accent'. He examined the upper division of First Latin, 31 boys, by setting them to spell 'apostrophe' : nine spelt it correctly and there were a dozen different incorrect attempts.

The examination papers for the senior classes that year were re-printed in the prospectus. Boys in the Fifth Class had to turn into

French such sentences as 'Are these men twisting ropes? Would you shear that poodle if you had scissors? Do the Jews go to church? Have you seen the equestrian statue of the Duke of Wellington?' The same boys had studied *Coriolanus* and were asked to mention any 'historical inaccuracies, anachronisms or such like poetical licences' that occur in the play and to write a short account of the rise of the English drama, mentioning in chronological order the principal authors with their characteristic works up to Ben Jonson – this was based on their study of Brooke's *English Literature*.

In History and Geography, the boys were asked to 'Contrast the three great divisions of the United States, viz. the North, South, and West, as to natural features, social, political and commercial peculiarities' and 'Describe the decay of the feudal system in England, France and Germany respectively and trace some of its consequences in these countries'. The questions in Mathematics, Latin and Greek seem just as daunting.

A feature of the school which the examiners may have noticed was the fact that, guided by the Gymnastics Master, the classes moved from one part of the building to another 'with military order and precision', an arrangement which was said to have improved the conduct and bearing of the pupils. As the boys moved from room to room, they passed the museum cases which had been set up on the galleries of the first floor : fifteen of them had been filled with a collection of shells and others soon contained a variety of exhibits.

At the end of the school's first session in its new home, it was possible to reckon up what the new accommodation had cost : £19438/-/5 for the ground, £19192/15/9 for the building and £888/15/- for furnishing and fittings.

The Prize Giving in 1879 was held in the Writing Room, which proved to be too small, so that in 1880 and for some years subsequently the proceedings took place in the Queen's Rooms. By coincidence this building, in La Belle Place at the foot of Woodlands Hill, was another of Charles Wilson's designs, related in character to the building which the Academy had left behind in Elmbank Street.

Among the prizes on offer in June 1880 were one for the best collection of dried specimens of wild flowers and another for the best collection of insects, arranged according to their orders. The system of First and Second Class Certificates did not survive for long without modification, for in 1881 book prizes were given to the boys who obtained First Class Certificates. Writing, Drawing, Music and Gymnastics were excluded from the general totalling of marks though boys who excelled in those or any other subject but did not obtain a Certificate did receive a special Certificate.

In April 1880 Thomas Gilray was appointed to succeed James Colville as Head English Master. Colville had for some time been teaching the highest English classes in the Newton Place School for girls and now he left to take over the running of that school. He would be remembered at the Academy particularly for his love of great poetry and his devotion to the beauty of the English language. Gilray lost no time in setting up a Literary and Debating Society at the Academy. The following year, another of the Head Masters left when James Moir was appointed Rector of Aberdeen Grammar School. William Cooper was appointed to succeed him. As it turned out, neither Gilray nor Cooper remained long at the Academy.

There were other staff changes. In 1880 the Janitor was dismissed without a certificate of character and six hundred applications were received for the post. In June 1881 one of the English Assistants, Gilfillan Letters, was told that his services would not be required for the following session. The reasons were not spelled out to him fully but for at least a year, Morrison had wanted to replace him with a lady who would teach the First English Senior class and who could offer 'greater style and elegance' in reading. Confident that she would endeavour 'to make the children speak gracefully and prettily, with no infusion of provincial tone or accent' the Rector appointed another Miss Campbell to the post.

The Rector believed that much remained to be done to encourage older boys to remain at school longer since there was nothing to stop them from leaving the Academy for the University or for business well before they were really ready to do so. He felt that it would be beneficial to establish in the highest Classes of the Classical and Modern sides a few scholarships or prizes of the value of £10 or £15 each. This would need the help of the Academical Club or other 'friends of education' since there was not yet a fund for bursaries or prizes. His wish was granted and some of the Directors subscribed £5 each so that in 1882 special prizes could be awarded to the two senior boys who passed the best examination in English, Mathematics, Latin and two of the other languages, Greek, French and German.

There were also prizes for excellence in the theory of music, open only to members of the choir, and two for the best description by members of the Fifth and Sixth Modern Sections of works visited during the year, which had included calico printing, paper-making, letter-press printing, engraving, cotton spinning and weaving, shipbuilding and marine engineering. Five boys had submitted 'admirable descriptions' of what they had seen.

In July 1880 Arthur Hart – an accountant in St Vincent Place – had been appointed Secretary and Treasurer, with a special remit to give the Rector what help was needed in collecting the fees. The Writing Assistant was paid ten guineas for preparing the actual accounts. There was, though, some difficulty with arrears and it was agreed that in future no boy should be enrolled for a new quarter until the fees for the preceding one were paid. Morrison corresponded with Hart about the debtors and gave his views frankly : 'Mr Laing's boys are in School. He is perfectly able to pay and only carelessness causes neglect. Mr Stewart is poor, but I should think he will pay in the course of time.'

The financial situation was not, in fact, easy. Income had fallen by over £500 and more pupils had been withdrawn from the higher classes than was usual, perhaps because of the continuing commercial depression in the city. In November 1880 Morrison reported that the number on the roll was 581, 14 fewer than at the same time the previous year, though for only the second time in the Academy's history the First Latin class had been divided into three rather than two. The Directors considered building a house for the new Janitor, since he ought to live as close to the school as possible, but they felt unable to do so and instead paid him a little extra so that he could rent a house in Otago Street.

The Head Classical and English Masters were new to the school and in 1881 the Head Mathematical Master, Finlay Macrae, became ill. He was still unable to resume his duties at the start of the new session in September and the Rector had to write to his doctor, as tactfully as possible : 'The Directors cannot delay longer making a permanent appointment. For Mr Macrae's sake I regret this exceedingly and I have deferred writing you in the hope that through some channel I might hear of his complete recovery.' Macrae did not recover, and the post was therefore offered to James Wood, assistant to Professor Jack in the University, who had been helping temporarily.

Even when that matter had been dealt with and Macrae had been paid three months' salary, there continued to be other staffing difficulties to meet. Gilfillan Letters had not gone quietly and the Rector wrote to him with quite uncharacteristic sharpness : 'I cannot for a moment believe that you mean to deny the fact that I gave you more than a year's notice of the termination of your engagement in the Academy'. He was more sympathetic when he wrote to William Cooper, who in March 1882 was forced by ill health to resign from his post as Head Classical Master. Enclosing his salary, Morrison expressed the hope that 'this rest will strengthen you for some new sphere of labour, which I have no doubt will present itself at some future time'.

The Rector thought carefully about replacing Cooper and came to the conclusion that if certain rearrangements were made it would not be necessary to appoint a new Head Master. By transferring the teaching of Modern History and Geography from the Classical to the English Department, time could be found for William Robertson to take over the work with the highest classes which Cooper had been doing. Robertson had been at the Academy for two years and Morrison felt that it would be difficult to find in Scotland one of the same age who was so well prepared in every way for such work. He had been educated at Ayr Academy and Edinburgh University and had returned to Ayr as Classical Master for a year before joining the Academy where he had become a favourite with boys whom he 'ruled with ease'. Clear and scholarly in his explanations and full of life and energy in his teaching, he was sure to rise to distinction in his profession. Though his salary should be increased, he should not at this stage actually be designated Head Classical Master.

Perhaps this was a cost-cutting exercise. Certainly there were two hours of teaching not accounted for by the proposal, and the Rector undertook to be responsible for these himself, on the grounds that, since fees were now paid

William Robertson as seen by one of his pupils

directly to the bank, his time was not so often interrupted by visits from parents.

Late in 1882, Thomas Gilray was appointed Professor of English Literature in the New University College, Dundee, though he did eventually end up holding a Chair at the University of Otago in New Zealand which had almost claimed him before he came to the Academy. His place as Head English Master was taken by Zachary Ross, who had been headmaster of Campbeltown Academy and Irvine Academy. He continued the Literary and Debating Society, believing that it was useful 'in bringing together boys of all ranks and characters and placing them on their mettle in the fair, open discussion of topics of the day'.

When Ross arrived at the Academy he found that the teacher of the Third English class had not long been at the school. William Melven had arrived in 1881 and had made an immediate impression on one of the school's examiners : 'I am of opinion that the Directors will find that the gentleman just named is an excellent addition to the teaching staff of the Institution'. 29 years old, he had graduated from Aberdeen University and taught at Ayr Academy and the Edinburgh

Collegiate School before coming to Glasgow.

Another addition to the staff was made in February 1882, when Miss Katherine McCallum received notice of her appointment : she was to remain at the Academy for more than forty years.

Despite his insistence that he could spare two hours a day for teaching, Morrison still had innumerable mundane but essential matters to attend to. There were building works close to the school to be coped with, since in May 1881 work had begun on putting up houses on the ground facing the Academy in Colebrooke Street : 'Today the water is turned off in the pipes that supply the Academy. If we had received notice we could easily have provided water for the boys to drink during their lunch hour.'

The Rector also had to keep an eye on the building : 'The rain is falling on the floor of the Gymnasium in at least eight places today. I fear the effect will be injurious to the wood and it might soon penetrate to the plaster of the rooms below.' He even had to order coal as winter approached : 'Please send to the Academy on Saturday before 9 o'clock four loads of Triping and two of Dross, the dross, if possible, to be a little larger than on last occasion.'

There were weightier concerns, too. In March 1882 a Major Sharp approached the Rector with a view to instituting a Cadet Corps in the school. Morrison consulted some of the senior boys and found that at that stage of the session only a very limited number would be willing to join. 'As much depends on a good start in all such things, it occurs to me that it would not be prudent to take action until the commencement of next session.' The Rector felt that membership of a Corps might improve the general bearing of the pupils, but when the question arose again in January 1883, the result was similar. 'I submitted the terms of your letter to the six highest classes in the Academy, containing about 120 boys, and I have given them three days to deliberate on the matter and to consult their parents. I regret to say that the result is altogether unfavourable and as such affords no encouragement to proceed with the matter. Only nine boys have expressed their willingness to join the Corps.'

As Rector, Morrison also had to deal with matters of discipline. Sometimes a gentle warning was all that was needed : 'I am sorry to find that David is not devoting himself to work as earnestly as I should wish. I hope that the mere fact of my complaining of him in this way will induce him to study more diligently.' On other occasions, the matter was more serious, as when he wrote to a mother bringing up her son on her own. 'I am sorry that I did not find you at home when I called at your house soon after 11 o'clock. It is my painful duty to inform you that Frank has been guilty of a very serious offence. For some time books have been mysteriously disappearing from the Academy and information reached me this morning undoubtedly connecting Frank with them. I immediately took him into my own room, when he acknowledged that he had taken and sold all the books that have been amissing except his own. I can scarcely tell how deeply I regret this both for his own sake and specially for yours; and I think it is desirable even in his own interests that he should be removed. From the way in which the information reached me, I believe that his companions will soon know the circumstances of the case; and this, apart from other considerations, would render intercourse with them uncomfortable.' He concluded the letter 'with much sympathy and great regret'.

The number of pupils continued to fall, to 583 in 1880/81 and 535 in 1881/82. Nevertheless, savings had been made and it proved possible both to achieve a surplus for the year and to pay off £1000 of the debentures. Steps clearly had to be taken to attract as many pupils as possible, though, and special attention was drawn in the prospectus for 1882/83 to the opportunities offered in the Sixth Modern class. Modern Languages and Commercial Subjects took the place of Greek and to a great extent Latin. Among their other subjects, boys received a lesson every day in French and German and it was expected that before the end of the session they would be able not only to read but also to converse freely in the languages. The Rector hoped that this would 'obviate the necessity of continued residence on the Continent'.

In July 1883 a further repayment of debentures was made, despite another decline in revenue. Reductions in expenditure had been made but it was clear that further steps would be needed, especially in view of the proposal to erect a Board School in Hillhead. The Directors appointed a committee to take whatever action seemed necessary to protect the interests of the Academy. It became apparent the following spring that, despite joint meetings with the Directors of Kelvinside Academy and strong representations made to the Education Department in London, the Committee had failed to convince the authorities that such a school was unnecessary. The opening of Hillhead High School did nothing to help the Academy's situation : at Christmas 1885 there were 343 boys on the roll; a year previously there had been 405. The position was serious.

The end of an era

Despite its financial difficulties, the Academy had much to be proud of. Morrison believed that few schools could have matched the performance of the Choir which was improving year by year. As early as 1881, the concerts had had to be held in St Andrew's Halls to accommodate all those who wished to attend, and in 1884 a second performance was given in the Queen's Rooms, raising £75 for the funds of the Royal and Western Infirmaries. A magazine – *The Academician* – was founded in 1882 : 'If such a publication can be conducted without materially interfering with the more regular business of school-boy life, it may encourage literary habits and serve as a connecting bond and medium of communication between past and present pupils.' Five issues were brought out before its management was handed over to the Academical Club, who had in fact produced a similar magazine, *The Academical,* in 1870. Under the auspices of the Club *The Academician* became a monthly publication, but it does not seem to have continued beyond June 1884.

Co-operation between school and Club also meant that boys had the advantage of being able to use the large and newly enclosed field at Anniesland which the Club acquired in 1883. Boys were supplied with material for all their games on payment of 2/6 a year and enthusiastic use of the field was expected on Saturdays and during summer holidays. Pre-eminent among the games was football. The first season after Club and school moved to Anniesland began for the Academy XV on 20 October 1883 when the team was beaten by the Academical Third XV. A match against Kelvinside Academy followed, in which Glasgow Academy was victorious. The fixture list also included games against 'Mr J S D Johnstone's Team' (obviously rather a scratch affair, since five of the most prominent Academy players had to turn out for the visitors), George Watson's College, Stanley House, Larchfield, Crieff Academy, College Third XV, West of Scotland Third XV, Blairlodge Second XV, LRV Third XV and the High School, but several of the games were cancelled for one reason or another – including the High School match, later to become such an important part of the Academy calendar. On 9 February 1884 only seven of the High school team turned up. The Academy also fielded a Second XV and a Third XV, each with a limited number of fixtures.

FIFTH CLASS (CLASSICAL).

	Monday.	Tuesday.	Wednesday.	Thursday.	Friday.	Room.
9 – 9·30	..	..	Gymnastics.	Shakespeare,	..	..
9·30 – 10·30	French,*† ..	German, ...	German,*† ..	German, ...	German, ...	{ German. / French.
10·30 – 11·15	Latin, ...	Latin, ...	Latin, ...	Latin, ...	Latin, ...	Classics, 1.
11·15 – 12	Algebra, ...	Arithmetic, ..	Algebra, ...	Arithmetic, ..	Algebra,† ..	Mathe., 1.
12 – 12·45	Latin, ...	Greek, ...	Latin, ...	Greek,*† ..	Latin,†	Classics, 3.
12·45 – 1·15	Lunch, ...	Lunch, ...	Lunch, ...	Lunch, ...	Lunch.	..
1·15 – 2	Geometry,* ..	Geometry,† ..	Geometry,* ..	Geometry, ..	Chemistry, ..	Mathe., 1.
2 – 2·45	Greek, ...	Shakespeare,	Greek, ...	Greek, ...	Greek, ...	{ English, 1. / Classics, 3.
2·45 – 3·30	Eng. Liter.,†	French,......	Eng. Liter.,..	French,......	Gra. & Com.,	{ French. / English, 1.
3·30 – 4	Drill........	..	..	..	..	..

* Written Exercise to be given in.   † Fortnightly Written Examination.

FIFTH CLASS (MODERN).

	Monday.	Tuesday.	Wednesday.	Thursday.	Friday.	Room.
9 – 9·30	..	Science, ...	Gymnastics..	..	..	..
9·30 – 10·30	Eng. Liter.,..	Shakespeare,	Eng. Liter.,..	Shakespeare,	Composition,	English, 1.
10·30 – 11·15	German, ...	German, ...	German,*	German,†	German, ...	German.
11·15 – 12	Algebra,* ..	Arithmetic, ..	Algebra,*	Arithmetic, ..	Algebra,†	Mathe., 1.
12 – 12·30	Lunch, ...	Lunch, ...	Lunch, ...	Lunch, ...	Lunch.	..
12·30 – 1·15	Drawing, ...	Book-keeping,	Drawing, ...	Book-keeping,	French,*	{ Writing. / French.
1·15 – 2	Geometry, ..	Geometry,† ..	Geometry, ..	Geometry, ..	Chemistry, ..	Mathe., 1.
2 – 2·45	{ History, ..} / { Geog.,....}	French,†	{ History,† } / { Geog.,....}	French,*	{ History, ... / Geog., }	French. / English, 1.
2·45 – 3·30	Latin, ...	Latin, ...	Latin, ...	Science, ...	Latin,†	Classics, 3.
3·30 – 4	Drill.........	..	..	..	..	..

* Written Exercise to be given in.   † Fortnightly Written Examination.

SIXTH CLASS (CLASSICAL).

	Monday.	Tuesday.	Wednesday.	Thursday.	Friday.	Room.
9·30 – 10·30	Herodotus, ..	Greek Comp.,	Herodotus, ..	Greek Comp.,	Herodotus, ..	Classics, 3.
10·30 – 11·15	German, ...	German, ...	German, ...	German,†	German,*	German.
11·15 – 12	Latin Comp.	Greek, ...	Latin Comp.,	Greek,†	Latin Comp.,	Classics, 1.
12 – 12·45	Mathematics,	Mathematics,	Mathematics,	Mathematics,	Mathematics,	Mathe., 1.
12·45 – 1·15	Lunch, ...	Lunch, ...	Lunch, ...	Lunch, ...	Lunch.	..
1·15 – 2	Latin, ...	Latin, ...	Latin,†	Latin, ...	Latin, ...	Classics, 3.
2 – 2·45	French,†	Mathematics,	French,*	Mathematics,	French,....	{ Mathe., 1. / French.
2·45 – 3·30	Mathematics,	English, ...	Mathematics,	English,†	Mathe.,†	English, 1.

* Written Exercise to be given in.   † Fortnightly Written Examination.

Timetables in 1884

Within the classroom, the curriculum was under constant review : the Science taught to senior boys on the Modern side was considerably expanded, so that it included Chemistry and such sections of Physics as Mechanics, Hydrostatics, Electricity and Magnetism. Fifth Modern had three science lessons a week and Sixth Modern a lesson every day. It was nevertheless vital for the Rector and the Board to examine in minute detail the working of the school to see what economies could be effected, always provided that no arrangements should be made which would lead to more than 40 boys being taught together.

The Directors had always envisaged that income could be obtained by disposing of a portion of the Academy's ground and in September 1885 they agreed to lease a plot of land for seven years to the Belmont Established Church for the construction of an iron church, the congregation to have the option of purchase at various stages of the term.

In June 1884 it was decided that fees should be reduced for pupils up to and including First Latin but the roll continued to fall and in 1885 the Directors had to report a deficit for the second year running and a bank overdraft of well over £1000. The services of two assistants were dispensed with, a third was asked to accept a reduced salary and more economical arrangements were made for teaching gymnastics.

The Rector found another reason to recommend that boys should stay on until the end of the course. There were forty appointments a year in the Indian Civil Service which were available by competition to young men under the age of 19. The appointments, which carried attractive benefits in terms of salary, furlough and pensions, were 'easily within the reach of a youth of good talent who began early to prepare for such a course'. Two pupils had competed from the Academy and both had been successful.

Another extension to the curriculum followed soon after the departure of Jules Amours to the High School in 1884 and the appointment in his place of Louis Barbé, 'a gentleman of wide culture and considerable

Louis Barbé

literary reputation' who felt that boys in Third Latin could start French, with a view to developing a pure accent. At first Academy boys had started to learn the language in Fourth Latin and the age had been progressively lowered, 'but there is no reason why a boy should not acquire some knowledge of such an easy language as French before beginning Latin'. The instruction would be oral, and there would be no home tasks.

In 1886 the Directors considered proposals from the recently established Scotch

Education Department for the examination of Higher Class Schools and agreed that, despite the facts that the school would have to bear the expense and only advanced classes would be included, the Academy would submit itself for inspection the following year. In the meantime, the masters would conduct their own internal examination, similar to the one which was held annually in the highest class for the Academical Club prize.

In the meantime, though, the financial crisis had to be overcome. Morrison had considered the position of both his school and Kelvinside Academy, reckoning that between them they catered for some 750 boys. This, he thought, was all the pupils that could be attracted from the West End and suburbs such as Pollokshields, Rutherglen, Uddingston and Lenzie. Any increase in the well-to-do portion of the community who would be prepared to pay high fees would be more than counter-balanced by the growing tendency on the part of many less well off parents to take advantage of the cheap education available in the Board Schools. The Rector's proposal, discussed early in 1886, was that the two companies should be amalgamated. If one of the schools were converted into a ladies' school or college, and 300 girls were attracted to it, then the two schools together would have an income sufficient to meet their expenditure. Morrison was confident that all the financial and educa- tional details could be arranged without much difficulty but his scheme did not find favour with the Directors of Kelvinside and nothing more was heard of it.

Another possibility contemplated by the Directors in 1886 was to reduce the fees so that they were the same as those charged in the High School, but they reached the conclusion that this was 'an experiment too hazardous to entertain' and that instead there should be a very thorough examination of the curriculum. The Rector was confident that changes could be made which would attract more pupils, but they would not act quickly enough to resolve the crisis. The only way to meet an anticipated deficit of between £600 and £650 seemed to be to reduce salaries by between one fifth and one sixth, a proposal to which, it seems, the masters expressed 'a very ready acquiescence'. The Rector's own salary was reduced from £600 to £500. No attempt was made to pay William Robertson less : at £250, his salary was still £100 less than the reduced payments made to the Head English and Mathematical Masters. The only other master whose salary was not affected was Louis Barbé, who continued to be paid £300. This was because the services of Clemens Schlomka were dispensed with altogether and Barbé accepted responsibility for teaching German as well as French.

Certain changes were indeed made to the curriculum in 1886/87. More time was to be spent on Science by the Fourth and Fifth Modern classes and parents were reminded that boys who passed through the Modern side could qualify themselves to enter the Bachelor of Science course at the University. More radical was the proposal to permit boys entering First Latin not to do Latin at all but to take Modern Languages and Mercantile Subjects instead. Teaching continued until 4 o'clock : lunch and dinner were available for boys who could not go home during the dinner hour and in addition they were able to devote one half of the hour, under the superintendence of a master, to the preparation of lessons for the following day.

A further deficit was reported in 1886 as the roll continued to fall, to 301 in November compared with 337 a year earlier. There seemed to be a real risk that the Academy would be squeezed out of existence. Urgent measures had to be taken to raise finance, which came in the form of promissory notes granted by the Directors themselves, and a complete re-examination of the courses offered at the school was undertaken, together with a further review of salary arrangements.

For a while, though, it looked as if financial salvation was about to arrive in the form of a proposed underground railway between St Enoch's Square and the Botanic Gardens. At first the Directors registered their dissent to the scheme, but by February 1887 the company involved was proposing to buy a substantial portion of the Academy's land, if their bill passed through Parliament. The following month a provisional sale for £8500 was agreed, but without any penalty if the Bill failed.

At the same time, complex negotiations about salaries took place between the Directors and the staff, culminating in an agreement that the teachers should divide amongst themselves the school fees collected, less £1000 retained by the Board for running expenses. The proportion which each teacher received would be determined by the salaries being paid in May 1886.

It was hoped that these measures would safeguard the position of the school while the new curriculum was proving its worth. Under the new arrangements, the Preparatory course remained unchanged. Instead of choosing between the Classical and Modern sides of the Secondary course, however, boys would now be able to pick one of three possibilities.

The Classical course was intended as preparation for a full university course, for preliminary examinations in Medicine and Law and for the public service of the country. The Scientific course would prepare boys for the Science degree of the University, for the Technical College and for different branches of manufacturing. The Mercantile course, without classics but with extra attention to Modern Languages, was intended for pupils who would enter a counting-house or place of business. They would be able to read and write French and German and to speak those languages fluently. Special attention would be devoted to Geography, Mathematics, Mercantile Arithmetic and Mercantile Correspondence. During the first year of the new curriculum almost the same numbers of boys joined each of the three sections at the outset, signalling success for attempts which had been made to ensure that one course did not seem easier than another.

The new scientific course was taught in rooms properly fitted out for the purpose. In the Lecture Hall on the top floor boys received lectures illustrated by prepared experiments. The Laboratory next door was now fully equipped with all the materials and apparatus necessary to allow individual pupils to take a systematic course of laboratory work, under the guidance of a competent teacher.

The Directors felt that they had introduced into the curriculum at an earlier stage and on a wider scale than was usual various subjects that prepared boys more directly and particularly for a practical business life. The Rector knew that in Germany it was not uncommon for boys to remain at school until they were 19, 20 or 21. He realised that in Scotland, and especially in a busy commercial and manufacturing city like Glasgow, boys could not be expected to remain at school for so long, and that made it all the more desirable that during the comparatively short time for which they were at school boys should not be diverted by attempting all the subjects available in a fully equipped school. Rather, different groups of subjects, each complete in itself and organised from the outset with a definite end in view, should be provided for different classes of pupils.

Preparation at school of lessons for the following day would continue. It had been the intention that this would take place during the extended lunch hour, but since three quarters of the boys had actually gone home to dine, it suited them better to stay on after school for the preparation classes which began at about 4.30 and continued for an hour and a half or two hours. Boys were able in this way to profit from the guidance and assistance of one of the Academy's own masters, rather than their parents involving themselves in the expense of a private tutor.

In June 1887 the Rector reported that the choir continued to sing in aid of some charitable institution, that year the Western Infirmary for which £50 had been raised, enough to support a bed for a year. For many years the Academy had held a prominent place among schools at football, but had not been so distinguished in cricket. Recently the masters, supported by members of the Academical Club, had been using their influence to encourage boys in 'this most healthy and manly game'. On several occasions they had allowed practice for an hour or two in the afternoon, as a change from ordinary school work.

In the summer of 1887 it became apparent that the scheme for an underground railway would not be going ahead. In July 1888 the company responsible for erecting a new bridge over the Kelvin enquired about leasing a plot of ground, but this brought in just £100. The Directors declined the opportunity of earning money from a draper in the New City Road who wanted to erect an advertisement for his own business in the school grounds. They did, though, resolve to advertise the Academy on bills at railway stations and to include in their advertising extracts from the reports on the higher classes which had been received from the Scotch Education Department's examiners.

The reports had made excellent reading. The same tests had been applied to twelve of the leading Scottish schools with a view to fixing a standard for the issue of Leaving Certificates and the Academy had received special notice as one of the two best in Scotland. In 1888 the examination consisted of five consecutive days of written work and a Leaving Certificate would for the first time be issued to mark the end of a completed education in a Higher Class School. Every boy in the appropriate classes at the Academy had been presented, not just the best.

In 1889 boys in the Fifth Class of the Academy had been encouraged to enter for the Lower Grade certificate, with a view to preparing them for the work of the Higher Certificate the following year. There was still a marked tendency in the Science and Mercantile sections to leave school at the end of the Fifth year and in some cases at the end of the Fourth. The Rector felt that this could to some extent be remedied if firms would refuse to employ young men who could not produce a Leaving Certificate.

In October 1888 an Academy pupil had been placed first out of 139 candidates in the University's Bursary Examination and other boys had been first and fifth in the qualifying examination for the Royal Military College. Academic honours of real distinction were also falling to former pupils. In 1887 and 1889 two of them, William Ramsay and William Paton Ker (eldest son of the Academy Company's Vice-President) were appointed to professorships at University College, London, in Chemistry and in English Language and Literature.

The general comments which the inspectors made about the Academy must also have encouraged the masters, the Rector and the Directors. In 1888 one wrote that 'the general tone of the school cannot be spoken of in other than terms of unqualified praise. I have never seen healthier liberty and yet there was no tendency to cross the line where liberty merges into licence. The very walls which no scribbling or scratch has for years disfigured speak volumes'. The following year an inspector commented that 'there is everywhere a healthy spirit of emulation and an entire absence of idle laggards'.

Despite such compliments and the Academy's undoubted academic achievements, financial difficulties continued to weigh heavily. The summer of 1888 had been a particularly critical time. The Directors were faced with legal and other bills totalling over £370. The overdraft stood at £2400, of which £1500 was unsecured and £900 guaranteed by certain of the Directors. No further help could be expected from the bank. The sum of £1000 which had been retained for working expenses had proved inadequate and the Directors regretted having agreed in negotiation to depart from their original stipulation that the figure should be set at £1200.

Morrison was summoned by telegram to a meeting at which it became plain that the Directors were close to giving up the struggle. Eventually it was agreed that the school would be continued for another year. The Directors wished it to be known, however, that they were under no obligation to accept further financial responsibility. They would provide funds to meet the Academy's liabilities through further promissory notes only if the teachers agreed that money would not be made available for their salaries until all other working expenses and interest payments had been met.

Shortly afterwards, Robert Young asked – not for the first time – to be relieved of the Chairmanship and proposed William Ker as his successor. Ker was a leading merchant in the city, his firm Ker, Bolton and Company.

In January 1890 Zachary Ross was given three months' notice that his employment as Head English Master was to cease. He had been absent from school, ostensibly through illness, but had managed to deliver a lecture at Milngavie and attend a Burns Supper. Apparently it was not his first offence. To succeed him Lionel Lyde was chosen, a man who was later to be credited with introducing an entirely new tone to the teaching carried out in the Academy. Lyde had been educated at an English public school and at Queen's College, Oxford, where he was President of the College Debating Society and an Editor of the *Oxford Review*. He had published a volume on the early History of Egypt, Mesopotamia, Greece and Rome, was preparing an edition of Chaucer's *Prologue* and had for three years been Head English Master at Merchiston Castle School, where the Head praised him for his 'power of making a subject interesting by clothing the dry bones of textbooks with fresh thoughts and vivid illustra-tions'.

Lyde's keen interest in games coincided with a new emphasis on physical training and sport within the school. From September 1890, increased attention was given to work in the gymnasium, including musical drill, fencing and dumb bells : this would help to counteract the strain on strength and energy that eight, nine or sometimes even ten hours a day of study produced. In addition, the large playground was made available for the practice of cricket with the help of the masters and of the Academical Club who placed their professional at the school's disposal. The vacant ground next to the playground was used for tennis and golf was played by masters and pupils. Arrangements were also made for the use of the Western Baths and the Arlington Baths at certain times in the afternoon. Prizes were awarded for distinction in these activities, including from 1893 the Masters' Prize, the School Championship for Athletics.

In the summer of 1890 the Rector was at last able to report that numbers in the school, which had fallen to 277 in the previous session, had begun to increase, albeit marginally. The increase continued, indeed accelerated, over the years ahead.

Not only was the enrolment increasing: there had been a threefold increase in the number of boys playing games, thanks in large measure to a committee of masters chaired by James Wood, who also acted as the school's representative in meetings with the Club. The golfers had travelled to the links at Troon and Prestwick. Two tennis courts had been prepared and were kept in excellent order. Four single wicket games of cricket could be played on the playground, which was open from 4 o'clock until dusk.

Morrison was sure that these increased facilities for exercise outdoors, together with excellent sanitary arrangements and the isolation by parents of any cases of infectious disease, had helped to avoid the outbreak in the school of any kind of epidemic during the session which ended in June 1891. It therefore seemed an opportune moment to distribute with the prospectus rules for the prevention of the spread of infectious diseases, a practice which was to continue for over a century. It was nevertheless necessary in February 1894 for Hart and Morrison to send a reassuring circular to parents, following the death from diphtheria of two pupils.

In June 1891 the Directors made representations urging that the Academy should receive a share of the increased government grant which was to be used for the promotion of secondary education in Scotland. For many years the Academy had been 'faithfully discharg-ing the duty of supplying secondary education to a large section of the community'. It was hoped that an appropriate position might be devised for it in the new scheme which would relieve the school from 'pecuniary embarrass-ment'. These hopes went unrealised. The following year it became apparent that 'not only the Academy but the better class of High and Burgh schools would be excluded and the money given almost exclusively to a certain class of Board Schools'.

Other dealings with government officials were more satisfactory. In September 1892 a new Chemistry Master was appointed and successful efforts were made to have the Academy recognised by the Inspector of Science and Art as a school fully organised for the teaching of science.

In June 1893, Samuel Stewart of Dundee was appointed as the new Gymnastics Master. The Rector perceived in him a 'rare faculty of inspiring pupils with something of his own enthusiasm and of preserving perfect order and discipline in all his classes'. Towards the end of his first year in the school, Stewart organised an Exhibition of Physical Exercises, which was much admired. Several other masters had devoted Saturdays to the direction and superintendence of games and moves were afoot to render 'this important adjunct of a public school' still more efficient. The measures, whatever they were, soon paid dividends. In June 1898 the Rector was able to report that the First XV of the Academy had enjoyed an almost unique record, not sustaining a single defeat during the season and so winning the championship of the Glasgow and West of Scotland Schools. They had scored 217 points and conceded none in eleven matches, against the High School (twice), Kelvinside Academy (twice), Speirs School (twice), Greenock Collegiate, Edinburgh Institution, Dollar Institution, Ayr Academy and Glasgow University Second XV. Members of the team, captained by J C Macdougall, were awarded special caps, like the normal trophy cap but edged with a band of silver braid.

In January 1894 John Anderson, who had been Janitor since 1880, resigned on grounds of ill health and emigrated to California. After two men had proved unsatisfactory the job was given to William Smith, Janitor in the Public School at Uddingston. In 1898 he asked for an increased grant to pay for cleaning because the greater number of pupils in attendance meant that more had to be done.

William Smith

The increasing number of pupils on the roll affected the running of the Academy in all sorts of other ways. In June 1893 the Prize Giving was once again held in the Queen's Rooms, after some years when economy dictated that it should take place at the Academy. Additional teaching staff had to be engaged to enable classes to be sub-divided, among them in November 1894 John C Scott, at an annual salary of £90. Scott had been born in Ireland in 1872, but was educated at Carlisle Grammar School before going on to Glasgow University where he achieved First Class Honours in Classics. Appointments in 1895 included those of Duncan Sinclair to teach Mathematics and Science and John Dunlop as Drawing Master. In 1897 George Moffat was taken on as an assistant in the Mathematical Department. In 1898 a separate Science Mastership was created in order to retain the services of Sinclair, who had had offers of appointments elsewhere, and Andrew

Robertson was appointed as a Classical Assistant.

In 1894 salaries were still lower than they had been a quarter of a century earlier and some of the staff supplemented their income by doing additional duties. Melven's basic salary, for example, was £130 but he received £75 for taking preparation classes and another £10 for preparing the accounts. The two lady teachers, Miss McCallum and Miss Wright, took preparation and music classes.

Although the finances of the Academy were now on a much firmer footing, there was still considerable debt outstanding, in the form of both debentures and loans. Unsuccessful attempts were made in 1893 and 1894 to consolidate the debt but in January 1895 hopes were raised that £12000 might be borrowed on favourable terms from the Merchants' House. This would mean that the bonds and some of the debentures could be repaid and both the overdraft and interest payments reduced. In the event, the loan came not from the Merchants' House but through Sir James King, a High School boy who had been Lord Provost of the city and who was responsible for investing funds on behalf of the Trustees of his father, John King of Campsie. The bank overdraft was reduced at once, with further annual reductions planned and the individual financial responsibility of the Directors was cancelled. Salaries were increased in 1897 and the last of the debentures paid off the following November.

In November 1894 the Belmont congregation gave up their site and the iron church was removed. A board was put up, indicating that the Company had ground for sale, but when, just a few months later, the Directors had an enquiry about feuing some ground they decided to do nothing. They had managed for many years not to part with any ground and now the Subway and the Caledonian Railway stations nearby were about to open, perhaps increasing the prosperity of the Academy still further : the new facilities would enable boys coming from a distance, especially from the south side of the city, to travel between home and school much more easily and rapidly. The Directors' confidence in the effectiveness of the developing network of public transport was justified : soon, boys could travel by electric tram along Great Western Road, by cable-driven subway from the centre of the city to Kelvinbridge or by steam train from Central Station to the Caledonian Railway's separate station opposite the school. As a result, although most Academy families continued to live in the West End, greater numbers of boys did come to the school from places such as Bridge of Weir, Kilmacolm, Bearsden, Paisley and Pollokshields.

The Academy celebrated its Jubilee with a Dinner at the Windsor Hotel, St Vincent Street, on 4 December 1895. This was an enlarged version of the customary Academical Club Dinner and each of the Directors tried to be present. Invitations were also issued to serving members of the staff and to certain professors and 'heads of educational institutions'. On 1 May 1896 an entertainment was organised at the Queen's Rooms, intended more for parents and pupils than the Dinner had been. Between two o'clock and four there was a Gymnastics Exhibition and in the evening, between eight and ten, a concert by the Choir. This was marked by the performance of a Jubilee Chorus, with music specially composed by Allan Macbeth, Principal of the Athenæum

through divergence of interest and occupation; old memories now fading through years of absence; old sentiments of affection for school'. To their dinners, which began that December in the Windsor Hotel, the former pupils from time to time invited masters, including William Melven whose first class at the Academy this had been and who 'humorously recalled many reminiscences of the old school and brought back to the memory of those present the worthy masters to whom the class was indebted and graphically reminded them of the scenes in the various classrooms'.

School of Music and father of a boy in the school, and words written by Louis Barbé:

> *Alma mater! fondly, proudly*
> *We, thy sons, our voices raise;*
> *Let the chorus, pealing loudly,*
> *Tell our love, and sing thy praise,*
> *Vivat Academia!*

Reunion dinners for former pupils had by this time become well established. A meeting was held in May 1894 to arrange the first such event for those who had been the youngest pupils in the new Academy, eventually becoming the Latin Class of 1882 - 1888. There was a feeling that a reunion would reawaken 'old ties of friendship in danger of disappearing

Edwin Temple

Donald Morrison

On the morning of Wednesday 29 March 1899, Donald Morrison died, after a short illness. Rector for almost 38 years, he had recently passed his seventy-seventh birthday. The Directors met immediately and entrusted care of the Academy to a committee of the Head Masters, with John Maclaren in the chair as Interim Rector and William Melven as clerk. The late Rector's funeral was held in Kelvinside Free Church at the corner of Great Western Road and Byres Road, where for many years he had been an office-bearer. As the cortege moved from the church to Morrison's place of burial in the Western Necropolis, Byres Road was lined

by Academicals and pupils of the school, shops closed and the blinds of private houses were drawn in respect.

The minister of Kelvinside Free Church, Dr Ross Taylor, had once said of Donald Morrison, 'You'll come across a man like him but once in a lifetime' : he was recalled by another who had known him as 'strict in discipline, just in judgement, generous in approval, apt in instruction and always the gentleman'. When the Directors met again in mid April, formally to record their sense of loss at the Rector's death, their minute laid special emphasis on Morrison's 'administrative power, good judgement and sound common sense' as well as his 'high personal character'. These were the days before pensions but the Directors did offer a gift of £200 to Morrison's widow : in addition, money was raised by subscription to erect a tombstone at his grave. It stands in the Western Necropolis still.

Other memorials to Morrison were placed within the school itself. About a year after his death, a carved oak bookcase was fitted in what had for over twenty years been his study. It was intended to place a reference library in it, for the use of the school. Then in October 1900 J W Arthur unveiled a bronze medallion of Morrison which had been mounted on the wall of the entrance vestibule of the Academy. It was the work of Kellock Brown and its unveiling was witnessed by the Sixth Class and representatives of other classes. When the ceremony was over, the rest of the school marched through to see the likeness of the man who had been their Rector for so long.

The search for a successor to Morrison soon began and the post was quickly advertised. A short leet of four was drawn up at the end of

May, the candidates were interviewed and on Wednesday 7 June 1899, the Directors agreed to invite Edwin Temple to become the third Rector of Glasgow Academy. Temple had been born in 1867, the son of Alexander Temple, an Episcopalian clergyman at Armadale, West Lothian. At the age of 12 he went to Fettes College and from there proceeded as an Open Scholar to Pembroke College, Cambridge. He was Captain of his College XV and graduated with First Class Honours in Classics. Before taking up his career as a teacher, he spent a year in Germany to learn the language, studying for some time at the University of Marburg. Then, in 1890, Temple went as an assistant master to Trinity College, Glenalmond.

Nine years later, the Warden of Glenalmond strongly supported Temple's candidature, staking his credibility on Temple's bringing 'strength and honour' to the Academy. The three decades of service which Edwin Temple gave in Glasgow proved beyond doubt that his aspirations to become Rector fully deserved such a confident endorsement.

In notifying Temple of his appointment, the Directors drew particular attention to the course of Bible instruction which Morrison had conducted himself, class by class – he had apparently favoured the memorising of complete chapters of the New Testament. They hoped that Temple would accept this as part of his duties, too, perhaps wishing to satisfy themselves that the Episcopalian tradition in which the new Rector had grown up would not interfere with this aspect of the school's work. In fact Temple embraced this duty wholeheartedly and changed the Academy's morning routine so that he could do so in his own way.

It had been Morrison's custom to visit the Masters' Room every morning for what passed as a meeting of the masters. In fact he usually did no more than shake each man by the hand before they went off to their classrooms to open the day's proceedings with prayer and a scripture reading. Temple chose to conduct the Prayers himself, with the school assembled as a whole in the gymnasium, rather than leaving it to individual masters with their classes.

'Ted', the boys called him : they must have seen in him a stark contrast with the septuagenarian who was the only Rector they had known. Morrison's silk hat gave way to Temple's bowler, the morning coat to a lounge suit of clerical grey or, at Anniesland, to football shorts or knickerbockers. It was even reported that, after dark, 'Ted' might be seen running along the streets of North Kelvinside in his shorts, for he lived close to the school in Carlton Gardens, Wilton Street. From time to time, he would pronounce on matters which he thought important, sometimes at the end of prayers, sometimes by pinning up a notice, often in red ink, beside the Janitor's shop in the Well. Hugh Douglas remembered one such notice, headed 'All right'. It insisted that 'The words should always be written separate; there is no such form as "alright". E.T.' Underneath in rather unformed handwriting the gloss had been added: 'Alright, Ted.' Douglas, at the Academy between 1919 and 1928, was to become one of Scotland's most distinguished churchmen, a leading light in the Iona Community, Moderator of the General Assembly, Chaplain to the Queen for 22 years and Dean of the Chapel Royal.

The masters were also from time to time recipients of notices penned by the Rector, again in red ink. 'Everyone is aware that when the Certificate examinations are over, it is difficult to keep out slackness in the school. It therefore behoves us masters to guard against it more carefully than ever. Masters are asked to be at school not later than 9.15 am (9.5 am Wednesdays); to be ready to meet their classes when they come down from prayers; to be strict in the matter of intervals, and not to suffer them to lengthen; to be specially careful that no boy is absent in the afternoon – and particularly from the last period – without leave. If a boy is indolent – or if he is likely to get a bad report on the score of industry – I wish to be told of it soon, and not to find it out first from the report.'

Temple, who always looked hard for redeeming features, could be firm and scathing if need be, but more often would reprimand boys gently, almost jokingly : 'Stand up on the form, you miserable fellow'.

Much changed when Temple came to the Academy. Other things did not. One picture which long remained in the minds of those who saw the scene day in, day out, was

James Wood

the meeting between classes of 'Jamie', 'Snubs' and 'Big Bob' – James Wood, Andrew Muir and William Robertson. They leaned on the glass of the museum cases as they conferred outside the Writing Room, invariably at the south-west corner, closer to Wood's classroom, K, and further from Robertson's, M. Occasionally Andrew Robertson, 'Lanky Bob', joined them from Room O.

Before Temple arrived, Lionel Lyde left, to become Headmaster of Bolton Grammar School. He had been an outstanding, almost revolutionary, member of the staff, a deliberately provocative teacher with clearly thought out views on how his subject should be taught. Head English Master he may have been, but for him – and for his pupils – 'English' was a gate which led on to the highways of literature, history, geography and economics. Behind it all was a burning desire to produce good citizens. The Directors decided not to accept William Melven's suggestion that he should directly succeed Lyde as Head of the English Department.

Andrew Muir

Instead, they put the Rector at the head of a single Department including, separately listed, the English staff and the Classical staff, each of which would have a senior master – Melven for English (with a substantial increase in salary) and William Robertson for Classics (with none). It was a cumbersome arrangement, designed to do away with the title 'Head Master' and perhaps some of the associations attached to it.

One of the first fruits of the new Rector's regime was the appearance in November 1899 of the first issue of a new magazine, a *Chronicle* of the doings of the School and of the Academicals. It included the words of the Jubilee Chorus written by Louis Barbé and promised that 'those who toil to raise the reputation of the school, in work or in play, may rest assured that their virtues will not remain unsung' and that the 'very considerable amount of dormant literary talent' that must exist in the school would be cultivated in its pages. There are records of staff changes – the departure of Lionel Lyde and the arrival of Peter Couper – and references to successes at cricket (the Academy had won the Western School Cricket Union's Championship for the first time) and at rugby, with advice to members of the First XV to go for a run twice a week, so as to keep in good training. Boys were now members of all the athletics clubs of the school without extra charge.

The annual concert continued to thrive enough money was raised in 1900 to provide a Glasgow Academy Choir Bed in the National Red Cross Hospital at Cape Town, where there was also to be found a Glasgow Academy bed, provided by the subscriptions of boys, present and past.

Early in 1900 the Directors considered what they might do to extend the course of mercantile or commercial education available at the school : nothing feasible occurred to them, however, and the matter was left in abeyance. A significant development did occur towards the end of May when the Directors agreed to set up a Cadet Corps attached to the First Lanark Rifles Volunteer Regiment, whose headquarters was close to the school, near the Burnbank Coup. One of the Directors, Robert Mackenzie, was not present at the meeting, but when he got wind of the proposal he lobbied vigorously in favour of a connection with the regiment which he himself commanded, the First Volunteer Battalion, Highland Light Infantry. This proved to be a matter of some controversy and was not resolved until October 1901, in favour of the HLI. Parades on Monday and Friday afternoons began on 27 January 1902 and by March, 111 boys had enrolled. The first Commanding Officer was Peter Couper.

A uniform was soon chosen, the tunic of a Cheviot tweed Lovat mixture designed to be worn afterwards as a civilian kilt jacket. At school it was worn with a kilt of Mackenzie tartan, perhaps again as a result of the influence of Robert Mackenzie. Rifles were forwarded so that shooting practice could begin. A Morris Tube Range with two targets was installed in the Gymnasium and inaugurated in October 1902 by Mrs Temple who fired the first shot and was credited with a bull's eye. The Cadet Corps was officially inspected for the first time on 31 October 1902 by Lieutenant-General Sir Archibald Hunter who asked the boys above all to 'keep from the pernicious, mischievous and filthy habit of cigarette-smoking' : he prayed that this country would never be invaded by an enemy, but if ever such a thing came to pass what they were learning in the Cadet Corps

The Corps in 1902. Seated at the front are Peter Couper (left) and Samuel Stewart (right).

would fit them to be of real use in its defence. Hunter had been a pupil at the Academy between 1869 and 1873 and had gone on, at the age of 40, to become the youngest man to reach the rank of Major General since Wellington.

A pipe band was formed, meeting for the first time on 10 April 1902 and making its first public appearance on 12 May 1903 when it marched at the head of the company along the principal streets of the West End. A fearsomely-named Bayonet Squad gave its first public performance at the Gymnastic Display in March 1904.

During the summer of 1901 a board recording the names of all the Duxes of the school was placed on the wall between the Rector's Room and what was then William Melven's classroom, Room A, at the foot of the West Stair. Shields were also placed in the Gymnasium containing the names of the Football XVs for six seasons past. The First XV of 1899/1900 had won the Glasgow and West of Scotland schools championship for the third successive year.

Early in Temple's Rectorship it was agreed to withdraw from sale the ground which had been advertised and to remove the notice board put up in 1894. It was also agreed to enlarge the junior playground and improve its drainage and to relay the four tennis courts. Swimming competitions were inaugurated at the Western Baths : events included the High Dive, the Low Dive, and Graceful Swimming.

On 24 January 1900, a former pupil of the Academy was killed on active service in the Boer War. Hamish Sheriff-MacGregor, 21 years old and a member of Thorneycroft's Mounted Infantry, died at Spion Kop. On hearing of the relief of Ladysmith, the school sent a telegram of congratulation to Sir Archibald Hunter, who replied succinctly : 'Sincere thanks : hope you all become soldiers. Hunter.' Half holidays were given during the spring and summer of 1900 to celebrate the relief of Ladysmith, the relief of Mafeking and the capture of Pretoria.

The reference library had begun by October 1900 and by December a circulating library had also been set up, housed in a recess off one of the Classical classrooms and opened just once a week, at 1.20 on Fridays. The basis

of the collection was a series of 52 volumes of Blackie's School and Home Library, presented by Dr Blackie. On the last school day of December in 1900 there was another innovation, when every boy in the upper school worked a general knowledge paper.

At the beginning of his second year in the school, Temple instituted a Games Committee, which was to have general control of the athletics in the school, with separate sub-committees for the different games, at first football, cricket and tennis, with golf added soon afterwards . The Committee was to consist mainly of boys, but as well as the Rector, who would be President, a master would act as Vice-President and Treasurer. J C Scott took this role and also sat on each of the sub-committees. He was crucial to the Rector's vision of what he

The unbeaten XV of 1900/01. Tennant Sloan is fourth from the left on the back row. Wilfrid, as Captain, holds the ball.

wanted to do with his school, particularly at Anniesland, and when the following year he let it be known that he was interested in a post at Perth Academy he was offered an increase in salary to persuade him to stay, despite the Directors' normal rule that they would review each master's salary only once every three years.

The Academy's footballers and cricketers did well in 1900/01, when both the First XV and the First XI were unbeaten. The Captain of Football was also the Captain of the School, in September 1900 Wilfrid Sloan. The Sloans were a remarkable Academy family : Norman had been Captain of the School in 1886, Tom in 1888, Alec in 1891 and now Wilfrid in 1900. William, the fourth son, had died in 1887 and Tennant, the sixth and youngest, reached the top of the school at the same time as Wilfrid, who was preferred perhaps by virtue of his age. The Sloans' remarkable record of four Captains has never been beaten.

Wilfrid Sloan was also the first President of the Academy's revived Debating Society, which held its inaugural meeting on 16 November 1900. Boys of 14 years and upwards were invited. Meetings were to be held every alternate Friday and for the first year at least no masters were to be allowed to attend the meetings. The first debate was held a fortnight later, and the motion was 'Would a Channel Tunnel be an advantage to Great Britain?' Ten voted for the affirmative, 52 for the negative. In mid December a Hat Night was held, with topics such as 'Should teetotallers be tolerated? What is love? Has the Liberal Party any hopes for the future? Could the rules of Rugby be improved? Should the electric poles in Great Western Road be removed?' Further motions included 'Should athletics in a day school be compulsory?' (yes)

and 'Should compulsory Army service be introduced into this country?' (no). The Society's affairs were not always conducted in a very dignified manner – in October 1902 the Chairman protested that he 'did not propose to come down every second Friday night to take the chair if better order was not kept' – but serious topics were debated. In January 1903, members decided by a narrow majority that capital punishment should be abolished though just over a year later they rejected the proposal of a Mr Reith that corporal punishment in schools should be abolished. Mr Reith would go on to become Lord Reith, a man renowned for his strong moral stance and identified through and through with 'The Establishment' – so it is interesting that at the age of 14 and in his last year at the Academy he should so publicly question received wisdom about the education of the young. Reith attained high honour and renown, not just for his work at the BBC but as Rector of Glasgow University, a Knight of the Thistle, and Lord High Commissioner to the General Assembly of the Church of Scotland.

Early in 1901 the Rector reported that the school was to all intents and purposes full. Healthy numbers of pupils were reflected in a healthy financial position and in July that year the Directors recommended for the first time the payment of a dividend to shareholders and of a 5% bonus to the teaching staff.

With the death of Andrew Muir in December 1901, the Academy lost a master of 28 years' standing. A small man with a bald head and a beard, 'Snubs' may have been a little unpolished in his rough tweed morning coat and bowler hat and the boys may sometimes have made fun of his broad accent, but he was a splendid teacher whose invariable rule was to encourage his pupils to find illustrations from real life of the particular arithmetical problem of the day. He was also a devoted and passionate golfer. A tablet in his memory was soon placed in the Academy.

The football season of 1901/02 was not quite the success that the previous year had been. Most significantly, on 30 November 1901 the Academy was beaten by the High School, one try to nil. According to legend, the players approached the Rector the following Monday morning and asked if football could not be played on Wednesday afternoons. Temple is supposed to have announced the very next morning that alterations had been made in the arrangements for Wednesdays and indeed it is true that at about that time the Wednesday timetable was altered. School began at 9.10, the dinner interval was shortened by fifteen minutes, afternoon school ended at 2.30, and Games could then be played by Third Latin and above. First and Second Latin played Games on Tuesdays and Thursdays respectively. Another measure which helped to make Games practice more effective was the use of the First LRV Football Club's pitch, opposite the Academy's field, whenever it was available. The change in timetable was thought to have paid off, since in the return fixture in mid January the Academy succeeded in beating the High School.

Conscious efforts were made in 1902 to encourage boys in the school to develop further their sense of continuing allegiance to it. The first portraits in what was to become a collection of distinguished Academicals was hung on the first floor, Sir William Hunter and Sir Archibald Hunter being chosen for the first two photographs. In April the annual meeting of the

Academical Club was held in the school Dining Hall. Members of the First and Second XVs and of the Fifth and Sixth Classes were invited for the first time and care was taken to make it an enjoyable introduction to the Club : tea and coffee were served after the meeting and a concert was then held in the Gymnasium. Forty boys accepted the Club's invitation

It became important, too, to offer a further mark of distinction to those who represented the school at the highest level in rugby and in cricket. Tasselled velvet honours caps had been awarded for some years but in 1902 and 1903 the Games Committee discussed the design of a special blazer of blue and white stripes to be worn only by members of the First XV and First XI and a cap for day to day use, to and from school, in place of the plain blue cap with white school badge which every boy wore.

Perhaps of more practical use was the decision to buy fifteen jerseys of a design different from the school jersey for use during football practices, to help avoid stupid mistakes. Football, of course, meant rugby football, though its supremacy seemed sometimes to be in doubt, at least amongst the boys themselves. A letter in the *Chronicle* of October 1903 warned about the effect of the increasing popularity of Association football – a splendid game, but detrimental to the best interests of school football. 'I have enough faith in the present generation of Academy boys to believe that, once having realised the harm that Association is doing, they will do their best to stamp it out.'

That same year, Temple told the Royal Commission on Physical Training that 'games are not compulsory but the boys are advised as strongly as possible to go in for them. I should like to have them compulsory , but I don't see my way to have it'. The Directors shared his enthusiasm. Indeed they attached such importance to 'the outdoor life of the boys' that in November 1903 they gave J C Scott another considerable increase in salary.

A year earlier, the suggestion had been made that the school and the Academical Club should between them purchase playing fields, rather than rent them. An area of some ten acres was identified, about 200 yards to the west of the existing field at Anniesland, to the south of what was then the line of Great Western Road but is now Anniesland Road. There would be space for three football pitches, a cricket pitch, a curling pond and a pavilion, and the Academy Company would contribute £3000, about one third of the cost.

The new ground, which has always been known as New Anniesland, took some time to prepare and lay out and it was not formally opened until 9 May 1908, when the Annual Games were held in delightful weather. Sir William Bilsland, the Lord Provost, declared the ground open and the President of the Academical Club, John Knox, was presented by Arthur Hart, in the name of the Academy and the Club, with a piece of antique silver plate to commemorate his work in promoting such an important development. Sir William Bilsland's son was a pupil at the Academy when his father was invited to open the new ground : as so often, Steven Bilsland followed his father's example of public service and brought distinction both to himself and to the school of which, as Lord Bilsland of Kinrara, he eventually became an Honorary Governor.

Later in 1908, the Company agreed to pay the Club £50 each year towards the cost of maintaining New Anniesland, rather less than it had been paying for the use of its predecessor. In 1910 a new pitch was obtained for junior games, in the field to the north west of the new ground. This was the area known as the Alps because of its curious ridge-like formation.

Another far-reaching project on which the Directors embarked in 1902 and with which they were actually able to make more rapid progress was the provision of increased laboratory accommodation. The original laboratory permitted twelve boys at a time to do practical work. It was complemented by a large and bright lecture room for demonstration purposes, but the emphasis had shifted and training in science was now chiefly of a practical nature. A demonstration was given only occasionally, to cement the practical work as Duncan Sinclair, the Science Master, put it and the lecture room had become 'sometimes more ornamental than useful'. Furthermore the Leaving Certificate in Science required that two scientific subjects should be professed and studied for three sessions. What was needed, then, was a Physics laboratory for 20 or 30 boys, with a dark room adjacent, and a lecture room, and above them a Chemistry laboratory of about the same size, together with a lecture room, balance room and store room.

The building was lit by electricity and heated by hot water pipes and radiators. The laboratories were fitted with seats and desks for up to 30 boys, clear of the working space and in front of a demonstration table and blackboard, so that no lecture room was required. The opportunity was taken to provide an art room on the first floor, well lighted from the top and from the north and having windows provided with shading blinds so that the light was under complete control. The seats were arranged in concentric arcs so that every boy was able to get the best view possible of the object under study. The building cost just over £4000, of which the electric lighting accounted for more than £1000.

Armed with a clear view of the accommodation which Sinclair needed, the Directors commissioned Hugh Barclay to recommend a site and submit both a sketch of his proposed building and an estimate of its cost. In November 1902 it was decided to put up an oblong building to the north of the school, between the main building and the tennis court. Delays were experienced through the use of faulty material, but by the end of 1903 the building was ready and in use. Lord Kelvin agreed to conduct a formal opening ceremony on 22 December, but poor health prevented him from attending. There were hopes that he might come in the spring, but he did not in fact do so.

The old lecture hall, Room S in the main building, became the library. In 1909 a partition was removed, making it a more spacious and convenient area, and it came to be used as a reading room for the Sixth Class.

It was important to make the best possible provision for senior pupils. Temple believed, as Morrison had done before him, that the highest class should be larger than it was and that more boys should go on to complete the full curriculum. 'Any superiority which

Germany may possess – if it is true that this superiority exists – is probably due to the fact that school education lasts longer in that country.' He had a useful ally in the Inspector who reported in June 1902 on the school's Mathematics and on the habit of taking boys away before the end of the course : 'it seems to me most deplorable that this practice is so prevalent in Glasgow, and that the two highest classes of such a school as the Academy are so much smaller in numbers than those just below them'.

Her Majesty's Inspectors had other comments to make. The written work of the Upper School should receive more attention. There should not necessarily be more of it, but it should always be written in ink and 'where exercises are corrected by the boys themselves, the supervision by the master should be most vigilant'. In the Prep School 'great pains had been taken with the handwriting, but we should be glad to see slates altogether discarded'. The manner of the Prep School boys 'was frank and attractive, their expression lively, and their pronunciation very seldom marred by local peculiarities of speech'.

Sometimes, as in 1905, there was quite trenchant criticism. 'Even the smallest of pupils should not be allowed, I think, to point with their fingers or their pencils to the actual words as they read them. The staff seems to me to be far too small for the numbers which have to be dealt with. Classes of 30 and 40 and even more are far too large for efficient secondary work. I am strongly of opinion that there should be at least one member on the staff who has undergone the best possible University training in such important and advancing subjects as History and Geography. If there is a lantern in the school it should be used.' There was, in fact, a lime-light lantern available which the Club and the School had purchased in 1904. Occasional Geography lessons were given with its aid and by December the First Latin class had already had views of India and of Canada – 'an agreeable change from the ordinary lesson'.

Inspectors also commented on the use of the Direct Method in French. 'Not a word of English was used either by master or boys during the lessons which I heard. The weakest point is certainly the pronunciation.' The Directors had been worried about the work in Modern Languages, where in 1902 and 1903 the Leaving Certificate results had been below the national average instead of above it, as they were in Mathematics, English, Latin and Greek. The Rector's view was that until quite recently the teaching of elementary German had not really been tackled seriously but left 'to a chance man, who was not always a good teacher'. Furthermore, Barbé had 'hitherto been too much of the Professor and too little of the Schoolmaster'. By 1904, things had been put right.

Extra-curricular activities flourished. A Chess Club was started, meeting at lunch time and on alternate Friday evenings. A Photographic Club was also formed and before long had a dark room of its own, off Room Q on the top floor. In December 1904, the Club organised the first 'At Home' to be held in the Academy. It was attended by some 450 people who were treated to tea in the dining hall, where about 300 photographs were on display. Boys played the piano and members of the band the pipes. There was also a programme of vocal and instrumental music and reading, and lantern slides made by members were shown in the Gymnasium. The Photographic Club had an interesting outing in June 1906, travelling on the Forth and Clyde Canal steamer *May Queen* to Cadder, where they were shown the spots most suitable for photographic pictures and then entertained at the Manse by the Watt family, whose boys were pupils at the Academy.

Temple believed that 'the ideal which a school like ours should strive to attain is that all boys above a certain age either join in regular games or be a member of the cadet corps'. Games certainly had a strong appeal : an Academy poet addressed a sonnet to a trophy cap:

> *O blue and silver emblem of the fight*
> *That intermittent thro' the year has raged;*
> *A symbol thou of battle bravely waged;*
> *A meet reward for whom such prize is right:*
> *How fair thou seemest to the envious eyes*
> *Of those who have thee not; oh, fairer far*
> *Than wisdom and her calf-bound volumes are*
> *Which once a year she scatters to the wise.*
> *How does the proud possessor toss and flick*
> *Thy tassel, faring forth with jaunty air;*
> *With dignity restrains the step too quick,*
> *And deems himself admired of all the fair:*
> *But soon that pride-inspiring cap so gay*
> *By time and air becomes a soft-toned grey.*

Not everyone felt quite the same way. When one of Andrew Robertson's pupils won his Second XV cap he was reckoned by his master to have joined the ranks of 'those flannelled fools with their tasselled velvet bonnets'.

All boys, of course, had to wear a cap and, from 1903, either a dark blue tie without pattern of any kind or a tie of dark blue and white stripes, the Academy colours. Before long, the Games Committee returned to the subject of blazers, deciding that the blue and white striped version should be abolished and that there should in future be two blazers. One, for the general use of the school, was to be dark blue, bound with white cord; the second, for the exclusive use of members of the First XV and First XI was to be of dark blue serge or flannel without bounding but with brass buttons. On the pocket were to be the school arms and the letters GAFC or GACC as appropriate.

Steps were taken to improve the games. In 1909 an experimental system of going for runs was devised, part of a scheme for better football training, especially on wet Wednesdays. But J C Scott was disappointed, especially with the football after a season of 17 matches in which 11 were won and 6 lost. 'We might as well stop playing the "Public Schools" altogether and deprive ourselves of our most interesting and educative matches, unless there is going to be a greater degree of keenness in the whole School. Far, far more boys should be playing and the attendance at School matches should be multiplied tenfold.' But things did not improve and the following winter boys who should have turned out to practise for the Third and Fourth XVs preferred instead to go skating.

In June 1910, therefore, an experiment was started which it was hoped would promote a competitive interest in football. The number of inter-school fixtures had been increased by inaugurating a Fifth and a Sixth XV, and there had been occasional under 14 and under 15 matches, but now it was decided to introduce a House system. Residence in one part of Glasgow or another would qualify each boy for membership of a House, which would be in the charge of a master and a committee and which would take part in football matches, generally

J C Scott's North House of 1915/16 — "footer", cricket and tug-of-war champions

on a Wednesday afternoon. Monosyllabic names were chosen 'to lend themselves to easy and full-lunged shouting by boys whose houses are playing their matches' : Hill, West, North and South. The first House Matches were fought with great keenness and Hill House emerged as winners of the Challenge Cup.

In the meantime, the War Office had informed the school in 1908 that the Cadet Corps was to be transferred to the Junior Division of the Officers' Training Corps, thus severing its official connection with the First Volunteer Battalion HLI, then the 5th HLI.

Members of the Corps were soon issued with brass shoulder badges with the designation 'Glasgow Academy OTC'. It was not long before the *Chronicle* wrote approvingly about the Corps and particularly about the benefits of attending Camp : 'the training a boy receives in orderliness, method, and self-reliance as well as consideration for others instils in him a sense of manliness he did not before possess'.

A clear sense of what the Academy felt it had achieved for its pupils also found expression at the time of the school's Diamond Jubilee. It had 'given their early training to those who have shown capacity for diligence in affairs, for leadership and for administrative power. It has turned out pupils who have learnt to think and reason for themselves and who are thus enabled to take in after life a thoughtful and intelligent view of those public affairs, imperial or municipal, that come before them.' The *Chronicle* also asserted that the Academy had been responsible for an important advance when under Donald Morrison it had been the first educational body in Scotland to recognise and remedy the evil which had made individual attention to boys' needs impossible, the practice of limiting the size of a class only by the number of pupils who had reached the same stage and were more or less fit to go on together. Now, the Directors urged the Rector always to take immediate steps to divide any class which had begun to grow too large and the new building made that easier to do, as there was plenty of accommodation.

Another problem which had vexed Morrison continued to tax Temple, though boys were increasingly staying at school until the end of the course, prompted by a growing feeling that seventeen was really the youngest age at which it was advisable to enter the University. Increasingly, too, boys who hoped to win Bursaries and to take a degree with Honours stayed for two years in the Sixth Class and if there were enough of them arrangements were made to teach them in what amounted to a Seventh Class.

Other changes affected these senior boys. In the summer of 1908 the prefectorial system was introduced to the school and five prefects were appointed to help the Captain, A D Laird, 'to expand and diffuse his authority'. The following year the Rector let it be known that in future the Captain of Football, who was also Captain of the School, would be chosen by him and not elected by the Games Committee : his first choice was C W Andrew.

In March 1907 the Directors heard of J C Scott's intention to start a Boarding House and of his wish to have their agreement and support. This came in the tangible form of an addition to his salary and the Boarding House was soon established in 23 Lansdowne Crescent.

Another important development in the management of the school affected only the teaching staff. In 1907 the Directors implemented a pension scheme in association with the Commercial Union Assurance Company. The normal retiring age of the staff would in future be 65, though the Directors reserved the right to retain the services of a master after that age, and membership of the scheme would be compulsory.

The boys would have known nothing of this, but they would have noticed other changes – the decoration of some of the classrooms and the Dining Hall with reproductions of good paintings; the installation of eight fire extinguishers throughout the buildings; a weekly lesson in English composition for the junior classes, so that they would learn to write their own language 'with correctness and ease'; an essay prize to encourage senior boys to apply themselves to the art of good composition and the study of good literature; collections each December for various charities; the appointment in 1907 of a new lady, Mrs Grace Sinclair, to manage the dining hall and luncheon bar.

They would have noticed the departure of long-serving teachers, too. At Christmas 1907 Miss Elizabeth Wright retired after 21 years with First English (Senior). She and Miss McCallum, her colleague in First English

(Junior), were extraordinarily painstaking ladies, determined to instil in the boys a sense of manners, manliness, teamwork and honour. One pupil recalled in later years that Miss Wright had only one arm, another that she was the daughter of a butcher in Main Street, Gorbals, rather a grim lady in an Inverness cape. Andrew Robertson, by contrast, recollected her invariable cheerfulness.

A year later, John Maclaren retired after 47 years as Writing Master, only to die the following April. Always immaculate, with a flower in the buttonhole of his dark grey frock coat and his silvery white hair parted in the middle, 'Bulldog' Maclaren's main contribution to the life of the school was not his teaching of penmanship but his work with the choir. Over the years he had organised 22 concerts, raising in the process a considerable sum for charity and building up for himself and for his wife a considerable fund of affection. In 1889, when he had been ill and no concert had been possible, some two hundred former pupils had presented him with a purse of over 200 sovereigns and a diamond bracelet for Mrs Maclaren. The concert on 29 March 1904 had been Maclaren's last, and the principal work had as usual been a new cantata, in this case *Ruth*, by Alfred R Gaul.

A year after his death, the Academicals in India let it be known that with the money which they had raised for a retirement present to Maclaren they had placed a memorial in the Writing Room and instituted a prize, to be awarded to the boy who seemed best to combine work with play, who was diligent and successful at his studies and 'helped the general outdoor life of the School by his skill in games and by the general example of keenness that he set'.

The first recipient of the Indian Trophy was Charlie Andrew, who had been in the First XV for three years and the First XI for four, three of them as Captain. He had also been notably successful in the Athletics Sports and in 1910 had established a record for throwing the cricket ball – 100 yards 1 foot – which stood until 1953.

Not every activity was as satisfactory as John Maclaren's choir had been. In October 1908 the Rector called a meeting of the Fifth and Sixth Classes to discuss the future of the Debating Society. It could not go on as it had, since the previous year many had joined with no intention of speaking and sometimes with the intention of having a 'rag'. This year it was to be a society for real debating, as it had been in the past : there would be monthly rather than fortnightly debates, with a master in the chair, and members were to take part. The following session the practice of having occasional lectures was instituted, with a talk in December about Icelandic sagas and another the following February on experiences in the Boer War. In 1910 the fortnightly meetings were restored and about this time an annual debate or lecture held jointly with the High School was introduced.

In 1910 it came to the notice of the recently established School Committee of Directors that Edwin Temple had received no increase in salary for eight years. It was suggested, therefore, that £100 should be added, making his salary £800. For comparison, Andrew Robertson's payment was increased in the same year to £210 and J C Scott's to £300. The following year it was decided to change the basis on which increases were awarded : they would no longer be based on length of service alone but on other considerations, including promotion to posts of greater responsibility.

In 1911, too, the Company's borrowings of £13000 fell to be repaid. £2000 had been paid off early in Temple's time but a further £3000 had soon been borrowed to finance the purchase of the Company's share of the new field. It was now agreed to approach the Scottish Widows Fund Life Assurance with a view to borrowing £12000 on the security of the property.

An increasing variety of activities away from the classroom now characterised the life of the school. Masters played boys at golf. The Gymnastic Display went on annually, with 250 boys taking part in 1912, doing best at the Indian Clubs, the Bar-bells and the Maze. Unofficial magazines appeared from time to time. In 1912 First Latin brought out one called *The Mag*, full of rather bad poetry, some stories, competitions and so on. In February 1914 an Academy branch of the Public Schools' Scripture Union was started. Perhaps instrumental music did not fare as well as some of these other activities : when the Directors were approached by a lady who wished to teach violin at the school, they had to decline, on the grounds that the present teacher had no pupils.

The dominant figure in the sphere of games continued to be J C Scott. On 21 October 1911 he was so keen to let the Rector know how one football match had turned out that he sent a telegram from Perth : 'Academy five points College nothing hooray Scott' – in other words the Academy had beaten Temple's previous school, Glenalmond. He was pleased with the way in which school football was developing, with as many as 130 boys from the four senior classes turning up for rugby on a Wednesday afternoon, to say nothing of the

40 or so from Second Latin on Thursdays and not many fewer from First Latin on Tuesdays. 'Cricket has been a small plant but an extremely healthy growth'; golf was spasmodic; tennis had given exercise to very many without startling feature; the annual swimming competitions had been interesting, sometimes almost exciting; the sports had revealed ever improving standards. 'Better that a hundred boys should each be striving to do his best, at work or play than that from time to time an intellectual or physical prodigy should be produced to dwarf all the others by his prowess and be a thing for others to gape at.' House matches in football, cricket, the tug-of-war and the relay race were giving a zest to games for boys who never had much to look forward to before. A correspondent in the *Chronicle* who wanted swimming to be added was told that 'Competitions cannot be multiplied indefinitely'. One sport which Scott did not mention was shooting, but during the summer of 1911 representatives of the Academy had been at Bisley for the first time – not an VIII but two cadets who secured sixth place in the Junior OTC Challenge Trophy.

In October 1912 Scott suggested to the Directors that they should themselves acquire a house to accommodate boarders. The Board agreed to commit up to £1000 and came to a financial arrangement with Scott, who paid all annual outlays but received a capitation grant. The house at 12 Belmont Crescent, conveniently situated, was soon obtained for £800.

In July 1912 the Directors had learned of the death of William Ker, who had been their Chairman since 1890. He was succeeded by John William Arthur. Arthur, a former pupil, had been a distinguished friend of the Academy and a distinguished figure in other circles, too.

John W Arthur

He had been instrumental in organising the first rugby match between Scotland and England in 1871, playing in that game and the return match of the following year. In 1873 he had been part of the group which had met at the Academy in Elmbank Street to form the Scottish Football Union – later the Scottish Rugby Union. Arthur's abiding interest, though, was in church work and he was well known in Glasgow for the religious meetings which over a period of many years he organised for young people. Married to a member of another notable Academy family, the Sloans, he was the first in a line of Arthurs which was to be connected with the school through four generations.

On 1 December 1912 Edwin Temple heard of the sudden death that morning of James Wood. Wood, sixty years old, had been Head Mathematical Master since 1882. A native of Banffshire, he had won First Class honours in Mathematics at Aberdeen University and then proceeded to Queens' College, Cambridge, graduating there as the tenth Wrangler. He soon became assistant to the Professor of Mathematics at Glasgow and while there had been recruited to the Academy during Finlay Macrae's illness.

He might have returned to Aberdeen as Professor of Mathematics had he not been seen on the Sabbath rowing a small boat in Aberdeen Harbour : as it was he remained at the Academy, a short and stocky man with a smart little curly moustache, his ginger hair parted in the middle, always well turned out in short jacket and top hat and perhaps rather scornful of those who were not such accomplished mathematicians as he was : ''Tseasy' was his favourite expression. His interest in philosophy and especially literature continued and expanded, he possessed a fine library, he enjoyed travel, and he walked : indeed, on the day before he died he had walked sixteen miles. George Moffat was appointed Senior Mathematical Master in his place.

The Cricket XI of 1913 was regarded as the best all-round side that had represented the Academy for very many years. In its turn, the First XV of the following year gained the reputation of being the best-balanced and soundest side for some time : they played 20 matches, winning 11, drawing 2 and losing 7. South deposed Hill from the first place it had enjoyed since the inauguration of the House system, and North came second.

As well as football and cricket, the Corps and what it stood for achieved great importance in the Academy of those pre-war years. In 1912 the Directors expressed their thanks to Frank Adam, who had presented prizes to promote among the boys a sense of patriotism, esprit de corps and high tone in conduct. Then, on the afternoon of 3 October 1913 a flag staff was inaugurated on the grass opposite the south east corner of the school, a gift to the Academy from J W Arthur, President of the Directors.

In February 1914 the first Corps

Concert was held, in the Dining Hall. Tea was served to the hundred or so cadets and others who attended and then there was a programme of vocal and instrumental music, much enjoyed by the audience. It was noticed, though, that of the 300 boys eligible to enrol in the Corps, only 135 boys were 'patriotic' enough to belong. A commentator in the *Chronicle* remarked, prophetically, that 'the youths of this nation are those to whom in the future we shall look to defend our shores'.

PRESENTATION OF UNION JACK TO GLASGOW ACADEMY 3/10/13.

War

Edwin Temple was on holiday in Somerset when war was declared on 4 August 1914. The next day, Arthur Hart wrote to tell him that the Academy and playground had that afternoon been requisitioned by the Government for billeting the Glasgow Group of the Royal Engineers (Territorials). They took possession of the school, sleeping in the classrooms and keeping their horses and equipment in the playground. In particular, the tennis courts were used as wagon lines and horse standings and a ramp was constructed from the courts into Colebrooke Street. The occupation was not expected to last for longer than a week, though in fact it went on for about a fortnight, and the Janitor was on the spot, so there was no need for the Rector to break his holiday : but the annual redecoration had had to be interrupted. 'What an appalling time!' wrote Hart. Neither he nor Temple could possibly know what a profound effect the war was to have on the Academy.

On 13 August Peter Couper sent a circular marked 'Confidential' to members of the Corps, instructing all those who were in Glasgow or nearby to report at once to the Academy. They were not to wear uniform. A more serious mobilisation began about a fortnight later when the War Office sent a telegram requesting the services of Colour Sergeant Instructor Stewart : 'Could you spare your gymnastic instructor until 10 January 1915. Urgently required for training New Army'. He left for Aldershot on 7 September and was not to return for some three years. At the end of the month, Frank Reid, who had joined the Classical staff in 1910, left to join the 2nd Glasgow Battalion of the Highland Light Infantry at Gailes Camp.

And of course Academicals went to war. On 4 September Temple wrote to the *Glasgow Herald* drawing attention to an advertisement in the paper that day which called on all old Academy boys willing to join an Academy Company to be attached to one or other of the Glasgow Battalions in Lord Kitchener's Army to send their names at once to the Secretary of the Academical Club or to Major Couper at the Academy. The football section of the Academical Club decided not to play football that season, but rather to support the effort to raise an Academical Company. Former pupils of the Academy and of other Glasgow schools at first made up No 2 Company of the 3rd Glasgow Battalion, HLI.

The boys who were too young to fight had their part to play. The *Chronicle* had words for them in the early months of the war, warning them that it was 'A Long Way to Go'. 'To subdue a brave, though arrogant and misguided people, fighting on their own soil, will be no speedy business. What can I do to help? Occasional definite opportunities to be of service – for example be kind and helpful to the Belgian refugees in our midst. Do your school work and home lessons as well as you can – harder work means fewer chance of friction between you and your masters, between you and your parents – less friction means easier running, easier running gives grown men more time for national tasks. Join the Academy OTC. Give up something of your pocket money for the weekly collection. Knit. Even ten minutes a day should produce a goodly crop of articles for men at the front.' The author of this sound and prophetic advice was Walter Barradell-Smith, editor of the *Chronicle* and English master at the Academy since 1907.

Early on, before the truth really dawned, a Glasgow Highlander wrote from the front : 'On Wednesday night we went into the front line of trenches. Our section's part of the trench was only 25 yards from the Germans. I have everything I want now except a clean shirt. We are having a sort of holiday and are in great form. I knock about with four very decent men, two golfers and two rugger men, and we share all our grub parcels.'

On 31 October 1914 Stuart Bulloch-Graham of the 2nd Battalion, Gordon Highlanders, was killed. His was the first name in a list which grew and grew as the months passed, until of the 1375 members of the school who saw active service, 327 were dead.

Every sphere of Academy life was touched. There were the Academicals who gave up their football and decided to fight instead. The Academical First XV of 1913/14 had been an outstanding one, winning twenty two of their twenty five matches, scoring 500 points and conceding only 76. Their season had ended on 28 March 1914 with a match against West of Scotland at Partick which the Academicals won by 27 points to 3. Six members of the team scored that day.

George Warren scored four tries that afternoon. By Christmas he had joined the 9th Battalion of the Highland Light Infantry, the Glasgow Highlanders. He survived the War. Thomas Burton scored a try. He, too, joined the Glasgow Highlanders. He was wounded in July 1916 and again the following month and in January 1917 was sent home, an invalid. He was mentioned in despatches and awarded the Military Cross. Arthur Russell scored a try. Another Glasgow Highlander, he died on 16 July 1916 of wounds received in battle, 23 years old. William Barras scored the seventh try. By Christmas he had joined the Argyll and Sutherland

Highlanders and for his bravery he was awarded the Military Medal : but on 21 March 1918, aged 23, he died of wounds.

Charles Andrew dropped a goal. He joined the Glasgow Highlanders before Christmas but transferred later to the Royal Field Artillery. Wounded at the Battle of the Somme, at the Battle of Arras, and at the Battle of Ypres, he was mentioned in despatches three times and awarded both the Military Cross and a bar to the Military Cross. Arthur Laird converted one of the tries. Captain of the Academical side that season, he had been Captain of the School and Captain of Cricket and had won the Masters' Prize as the outstanding games player of his year. One of the first to join the Highland Light Infantry, within weeks of the war starting, he was killed at the Battle of the Somme on 1 July 1916 at the age of 26.

Two internationalists were in the team that afternoon. John Warren played against Ireland in 1914. He fought during the War with the Royal Engineers in France, was wounded three times, mentioned in despatches and awarded the Military Cross. Eric Young played against England that season. He joined the Cameronians and fought at Gallipoli where on 28 June 1915 at the age of 23 he was killed.

Eight more Academicals make up the official list of the team. John Smith also fought at Gallipoli with the HLI and was wounded in March 1917. John Sandeman joined the Argyll and Sutherland Highlanders and fought also with the HLI. Twice he was sent home as an invalid, from France and from Palestine. Frank Sandeman joined the Glasgow Highlanders early in the war and fought in France and in Mesopotamia. He was invalided in June 1918.

8th Battalion The Cameronians (Scottish Rifles)
WAR STATION. DECEMBER 1914.
OLD GLASGOW ACADEMY BOYS.

Lieut. H. M'Cowan.   Lieut. W. N. Sloan.   2nd Lieut. W. Maclay.   2nd Lieut. T. Stout.   Lieut. E. Maclay.   Capt. Chas. J. C. Mowat.
Lieut. A. D. Templeton.   Capt. W. C. Church.   Capt. A. B. Sloan, R.A.M.C.   Capt. J. W. H. Pattison.   Capt. E. T. Young.

Eight of these Academicals died on a single day, 28 June 1915, at Gallipoli. A ninth was killed elsewhere.

Robert Arthur of the Queen's Own Royal Glasgow Yeomanry was mentioned in despatches six times and awarded both the Military Cross and the Belgian War Cross. George Speirs fought with the 6th Battalion of the HLI in Egypt and in France. He was awarded the French War Cross, wounded in 1916 and on 1 October 1918, aged 25, killed. George Macewan also joined the 6th Battalion of the HLI. 22 years old, he died on 12 July 1915 of wounds received at Gallipoli. Archibald Templeton was a Cameronian. Fighting at Gallipoli, he was wounded and reported missing on 28 June 1915, and his body was never found: he was 26 years old.

Thomas Stout was another Cameronian, a lieutenant in the Scottish Rifles. He, too, was killed at Gallipoli on 28 June 1915, trying to save another officer. He lived in Belmont Crescent, just across the road from the school. He started at the Academy when he was six, stayed until he was nearly fifteen and died when he was 23. A writer in the *Chronicle* remembered him as a keen sportsman and a loveable lad : 'No more shall we see Tommy Stout scoring a try for the Accies, with that wonderful swerve of his and with his hair flying in the wind.'

Only two members of the Academical team of 1913/14 went through the war unscathed. Six received wounds. Eight were killed.

There were families like the Galbraiths, who had lived just opposite the school in 3 Colebrooke Terrace until they moved to Dowanhill. There were seven of them and they all served except the youngest, Alexander, who was only ten when war broke out.

Walter Galbraith was the oldest. He had come to the Academy in 1895, when he was six. Eventually he took up the study of medicine at Glasgow University and served with the Royal Army Medical Corps in France and Italy. He maintained his connection with the Academy, proud of the fact that he was born within sight of it, and in time became a Governor of the War Memorial Trust.

Tom, the next, had joined the Royal Navy by December 1914, serving aboard HMS *Audacious*. He saw action in the Dardanelles and remained in the Navy after the War : eventually he entered politics, sitting as the Member of Parliament for Pollok between 1940 and 1955 and serving as Minister of State at the Scottish Office. As Lord Strathclyde, he later became an Honorary Governor of the Academy, so helping to perpetuate the memory of men like his brothers.

Brodie was the third boy, remembered by his friends as 'frank, transparent and always cheerful'. He served in the 7th Battalion HLI but died of wounds at Gallipoli in 1915.

David, 'graceful and fleet of foot', had also joined the 7th Battalion by Christmas 1914. He was wounded on 12 July 1915 and killed in action just over a month later, on 20 August, at the Dardanelles.

Norman joined up as a trooper in the Queen's Own Royal Glasgow Yeomanry but soon joined his brothers in the HLI. He fought at Gallipoli, in Egypt and in France, where he was killed on 22 August 1918.

By June 1917 Robert, the sixth son, was a cadet in the Officer Cadet Battalion. He became a Lieutenant in the Royal Garrison Artillery and fought in France until he was gassed in September 1918 and invalided out.

Six of the Galbraith boys of Colebrooke Terrace were old enough to fight. Three of them died.

There were men like Wilfrid Sloan, Captain of the School in 1900 but a married man in his thirties, with children, by the time duty called. On 14 April 1917 he led his Company straight at the enemy after his Captain had been killed until he too fell, shot through both legs, unable to move. He lay all day in a shell hole and at dark was brought in and taken to a Base Hospital. Fourteen days later, at Camieres, he died. 'No matter what it was – a run over Kelvinside roads on a murky night in November, to get more wind to better stay the full football time, a day's fishing on a hill loch, a sunset in the Western Highlands, a mountain climb, the delights or discomforts of camp life, anything, everything, came to this man as a fresh zest to life. His breeziness and good fellowship marked his entire life.'

59 Academicals were mentioned in despatches during the war and 78 were awarded the Military Cross. 11 were decorated with the Distinguished Service Order and of the thirteen men from Glasgow who received the Victoria Cross, two had been pupils at the Academy and

were killed during the actions for which they were decorated : Lieutenant Donald Mackintosh, Seaforth Highlanders, on 11 April 1917 and Lieutenant-Colonel William Herbert Anderson, Highland Light Infantry, on 25 March 1918.

By June 1915 a third member of the staff, J A MacGregor, had joined Sam Stewart and 'Freddie' Reid on active service. The following spring John Macbeth was commissioned into the HLI and John Sutherland into the Royal Scots. Their work at the school was taken over by three retired headmasters.

By October 1916 Walter Barradell-Smith had joined the Artists' Rifle Corps. 'Freddie' Reid had been wounded when 'the great push' began. John Macbeth was about to leave for Egypt : it turned out to be an ill-fated voyage, for his ship was torpedoed and he lost his kit. Then, in 1917, he was killed in Palestine. He had joined the staff in 1905.

John Sutherland was killed in action on 23 April 1917 He had been on the staff since 1904 and had had charge of the library. After the war and at the instigation of J C Scott, John Dunlop designed and executed a tablet to the memory of John Macbeth and John Sutherland. It was unveiled by Edwin Temple in the Masters' Room on 18 May 1922.

Academicals made their mark during the war in a remarkable variety of ways. Two winners of the Dux Medal made special contributions. Carl Browning, Dux in 1897 and the first incumbent of the Gardiner Chair of Bacteriology at Glasgow, discovered the antiseptic properties of acridine dyes such as flavine and so helped to save many lives in the latter part of the First War – and in the early days of the Second. Arthur Turnbull was Dux in 1901 and

a pioneer in radiology : in 1915 he was in France with the Royal Army Medical Corps and felt so strongly that British troops should be equipped with steel helmets that on his return home in 1916 he visited the Strangers' Gallery of the House of Commons, left his seat, hung by his hands from the balcony and dropped twenty feet to the floor of the House. As he was led away, he shouted, 'I ask you to protect the heads of British soldiers against shrapnel fire'.

Early in the war, Barradell-Smith had urged the boys to knit. In October 1914 Katherine McCallum began work on the Fearnought Gloves Scheme, which became the principal focus of war effort for those with Academy connections. The object was to provide strong thick gloves, gauntlets a foot or more long, for the crews of destroyers who without them would in severe weather lose all feeling in their hands and arms in a very short time.

On 15 and 16 December 1916 a 'Café Chantant' was held in aid of the Gloves Fund. A Sing-Song in the Writing Room on the first day was managed by the Largie Timber Campers : rarely had there been a more enthusiastic concert in the Academy. Admission was sixpence – 'a small sum considering the enormous expense involved and the talent' – and the whole school was exhorted to attend. 'It's your duty and you'll enjoy it.'

The following day, the classrooms downstairs were devoted to games of various kinds; in the Masters' Room and the room above it, cakes were sold; the Dining Hall played host to a collection of war relics and curios ; the Writing Room was the scene of a Photographic Exhibition, various competitions, the tea-room, a palmist and a series of concerts each timed to last half an hour.

By June 1915 over 1500 pairs of gloves had been supplied. Production then accelerated and in some years as many as five thousand pairs were made. By the time the final meeting of the Work Party took place in June 1919 the tally was reckoned to be over 15000 pairs. Over £1800 had been collected and a balance of almost £500 remained, which was eventually divided among four charities.

The 'Timber Campers' who had performed at the Café Chantant were among those who contributed in other ways to the war effort. During the first week of July 1916 an unofficial Corps Camp had been held on the Corporation Estate at Ardgoil and on the way there the Cadets had been addressed about a timber cutting camp which it was planned to hold at Largie, between Tarbert and Campbeltown, towards the end of the month. Several Academy cadets spent five weeks providing pit props and other timber for the Board of Agriculture. Seven thousand lengths of larch and spruce were felled and prepared, a total surpassed during the following year's camp at Banchory, when some nine thousand trees were dealt with. The master in charge was E P Kaye, who had been on the staff since 1913 and had succeeded Duncan Sinclair as Science Master in 1916. Sinclair had gone to America, where in time he became editor-in-chief of the *Christian Science Monitor*.

Fund-raising activities continued at the school. There were weekly collections and in May 1915 the profits from the Sports were handed over to Red Cross funds. The Sports continued during the war, shorn of all their gala trappings – no band, no tea-tent, no formal presentation of prizes at the close – and without the comic events, such as the wheelbarrow race

Sports Day in 1915

and 'Academical pick-a-back' of earlier years. In March 1916 a Seven a Side Schools Tournament was held at Myreside, which also raised money for the Red Cross. Other help of a practical nature was provided : First Latin A and First Latin B each took under their charge the care of a prisoner of war, keeping them supplied once a fortnight with parcels of food and occasional articles of clothing. There were five Belgian refugees in the school during 1915 and 1916, recalling for some the time in 1907 when André Hervieu, a French boy, had been a pupil. He had joined the French Army in November 1913 but was killed in 1915, a Sergeant Major of the 168th Infantry Regiment.

Temple started a Ramblers' Club in March 1915, to give boys something to do on Saturday afternoons when there were no Academical matches to watch. Anyone in the Fourth Class or above who felt capable of walking not less than ten miles was invited to join. On the first Saturday of March a party of nearly thirty met at Killermont Car Terminus and went by farm roads to the Roman Road at Bearsden Cemetery and on to Baldernock Church and up the hill to the Auld Wife's Lift. The keeper on the moor was 'unexpectedly kind' and did not turn them back when he met them. On the return journey the party went by Baldernock Linn and from Bardowie Station walked along the railway till they reached the Cars again about 6.30, tired and hungry. The walk in October that year was from Milngavie, Craigallion Loch, Strathblane and Mugdock back to Milngavie, while the following month, with the ground covered in snow, they went again from Killermont to Baldernock Linn.

There were other diversions. On 24 February 1916 the Writing Room was the scene of an elaborate Mock Trial, complete with costumes and make up, with parts played by boys and masters. Cassius was on trial for the murder of Caesar, who had stolen Cleopatra's needle when he saw that it was used for 'furiously fashioning Fearnought gloves for gladiators' which he feared might be used against Rome's fleet. The proceedings were interrupted from time to time by the appearance of Caesar's ghost and by Nero, who gave selections on his fiddle, and Horace, who did the same on his 'lyre' – but the eventual verdict of the court was that Cassius was guilty. Caesar's ghost was played by Guy McCrone, who went on to make his name in rather more conventional theatrical circles as the first manager of the Citizens' Theatre. He is also remembered as the author of the *Wax Fruit* trilogy, novels which evoked most vividly the spirit of Glasgow at the time when the Academy was establishing itself at Kelvinbridge.

Games continued to be taken seriously. In 1915 a new privilege was announced for members of the First XI : they were to be allowed to wear a straw hat with a white band and the school arms and date or dates worked in dark blue silk on the front.

13 February 1915: Academy, 10 points; High School, nil

That was headgear for the select few. A change which affected everyone occurred towards the end of October 1917 when a new school cap appeared in the shops. The existing one was very neat, but not easy to distinguish from those of many other schools, and now the Lyon King of Arms had asked for a large sum of money for the privilege of wearing the city arms, so a change was to be made. The new cap was to be in dark blue and navy blue and the monogram GAC in a third shade of blue would take the place of the crest. There was still no school motto, though the phrase 'Vivat Academia' was used on the cover of the *Chronicle*.

The change in the school cap meant that there had to be changes in honours colours, too, though as far as possible dark blue and white were retained as the school's athletic colours. Ritual and tradition were stabilising forces and bolstered patriotism still further at a time when some boys were leaving the Academy for active service as soon as they reached the minimum age for enlisting. Each year in May the ceremony of Saluting the Flag was held. The OTC paraded, with the rest of the school ranged around the flagpole, cadets presented arms and a verse of the National Anthem was sung.

Steps were taken, too, to commemorate some of those who had died, and families endowed prizes to be competed for on the sports field, in the OTC and in the classroom. An imaginative proposal was made in December 1916 by Nicol Paton Brown, a Director, who arranged with the office-bearers of Kelvinside United Free Church, at the corner of Great Western Road and Byres Road, that he would install in the tower a peal of bells in memory of the boys of the congregation and of the Glasgow and Kelvinside Academies who had fallen or might yet fall in the war.

The most far-reaching suggestion of all, though, came in response to a note in the *Chronicle* of April 1917 which mentioned that 'the subject of a suitable memorial to those many Academicals who have fallen in the war will soon come up for decision. We invite suggestions and we shall be glad to publish briefly such suggestions as are sent.' It was in response to this invitation that Peter Rintoul wrote the letter published in June 1917 in which he first mooted the idea which evolved into the formation of the Glasgow Academicals' War Memorial Trust. Rintoul had spent five years at the Academy from 1882 and had then come to prominence in Academical circles, serving as Secretary and Treasurer of the Club, as Vice-President and then, just before war broke out, as President.

In the meantime the Academy continued to be governed by a Board of Directors, many of whose concerns were financial. In 1916 it was agreed to reduce the Company's indebtedness to the Scottish Widows Fund by £2000 over four years. The financial position of the school was strong and the fees collected for the year were a record, over £9500. In December 1916 it was agreed to pay the staff a special bonus 'with the compliments and good wishes of the Directors'. In the same month Arthur Hart resigned as Secretary, after a connection with the Company of some 35 years : he had gone to live in London. In his place the Directors appointed their former auditor, D Norman Sloan, who had been Captain of the School in 1886/87 and for sixteen years Secretary of the Academical Club.

Fees were increased in May 1917 and it was also agreed to change the concession allowing abatement of fees if boys were absent from ill health for over four weeks. The Academy's practice was exceptional and had actually been quoted against Kelvinside Academy and the Glasgow Girls' School Company, which had never had any such concession.

A general increase in salaries was implemented in September 1917. Reflecting the general economic situation, the Authorities had awarded their teachers around 15% and increases for the permanent staff at the Academy ranged from 10% to 25%, so that Temple was paid £900 and the Heads of Department £330. The Chairman felt that the Rector was doing too much and had asked him what he felt about

engaging a 'capable lady typist' to act as his Secretary. Typically, Temple preferred to engage another teacher. He was instructed that when engaging new junior masters he must endeavour to get the best men possible, from both a social and a teaching standpoint, and that with this in view, such masters should be started at a salary of not less than £200.

The Rector, the School Committee and the Board of Directors as appropriate dealt with staff matters. In October 1916 William Melven was unwell and absent from school, replaced temporarily by a man who had left the army in May 1915 and was the author of *Echoes from*

The Sixth and Seventh Classes of 1917-1918.
Edwin Temple is flanked, from left to right, by Messrs Barrie, William Robertson, Moffat and Kaye.

Flanders – sketches giving 'a remarkably vivid insight into the innermost conditions of camp life at the front, our soldier's daily talk, his constant danger, his buoyant comradeship'.

Melven was able to return briefly after Christmas but in February was told by his doctor to seek leave of absence for the remainder of the session. In view of his 36 years' service, it was agreed that he should be paid his salary in full and allowed to attend to the fee accounts as usual. His health did not improve and he offered his resignation from the end of the session. In a further bitter blow, his wife died at about the same time.

William Melven therefore retired alone to Gullane, where he died on 26 April 1919. Temple missed him : 'I continually find since his departure how much the Rector has owed to him since he entered on his office. He was a careful, thorough, methodical teacher, with a great knowledge of boys, a fine sense of discipline and a power of organisation to which we owe much'.

'Bill' Melven was undoubtedly a remarkable man. It was said later that 'the memory of him could unite two utter strangers in a remote corner of the globe in a flood of delighted mimicry and reminiscence'. He walked each day from his home, first in Gibson Street and later in Jedburgh Gardens, left his hat and coat in the Masters' Room and then stayed in Room A throughout the day, even for luncheon. With his magnificent full brown beard he was striking in appearance, and he insisted on absolute orderliness and discipline, on method in everything. There was a rule of thumb for every contingency, too rigidly applied to suit everyone: 'to begin a sentence – let alone a paragraph – with a conjunction was probably

William Melven

the deadliest of the seven deadly sins'. There were those who said that 'he had a voice that congealed the marrow' and there were those who could see that with the strictness went a sense of humour. There were those who gathered each day in the 'horse boxes' – the cap and coat partitions of the Well – to laugh over the 'Melven Diaries' which showed their hero going through various degrading and absurd activities and there were those – only a few, no doubt – who knew that with his wife he shared an enthusiasm for fine old china and toby jugs. There were those who delighted in a fantasy that as a sideline he ran an old clothes shop and there were those who recognised his interest in his pupils as individuals and who knew that no boy taught by him ever faded from his memory. There were those who recalled the staccato cough and violent expulsion of breath which marked the delivery of a sarcastic witticism and there were those who recognised that he was a man who loved literature and much else. 'I never saw him idle for a moment; even his relaxations were a change of work. A walk with him was in itself an education. He knew all the flowers, the geological structures, the lore of the countryside, its historical and architectural points of interest. He showed Marischal and King's Colleges in Aberdeen with pride. He was the last of his race.'

In William Melven's place, Peter Couper became the Senior English Master. J C Scott undertook the fee account work which Melven had formerly done for payment of £20 or so. The Directors felt that this was far too low and that £40 should be paid. The Rector suggested that this should actually be divided, so that there was £20 for the fees and £20 for the supervision of athletics. Scott had undertaken this work without payment for many years, but the Rector wished to have some hold on the master responsible – hence the suggestion.

Louis Barbé was the next to retire, in 1918 after 34 years at the Academy. A Channel Islander by birth, who always rode a tricycle, he was a distinguished and learned man who in 1911 had conferred upon him by the French government the distinction of Officier de l'Academie, equivalent to the honorary degree of Doctor of Laws : but he was said to lack real interest in any except the brighter boys. Perhaps daunted by what one former pupil called 'the heartbreaking task of imposing a correct French accent upon our native Glasgow accent' he told his classes to study long passages of French on their own while he wrote reviews or articles for the newspapers which reflected his special interest in little known areas of Scottish history.

Louis Barbé left the Academy afflicted by great sadness, for his second son, Adrien, had been drowned earlier in the year while returning on board a troop transport from Egypt. It was a tragedy which nearly broke his father's heart.

The Directors knew that the principal work in the Modern Languages Department had for some years been under the care of George Barrie and they were happy to appoint him as Head of the Department.

During the summer of 1918 'Free Nights' were granted to commemorate General Allenby's victories in Palestine, the defection of Bulgaria and the capture of Ostend and Lille. The war was at last drawing to a close. Peace finally came at eleven o'clock on the morning of 11 November 1918 and less then a month later, during the afternoon of 6 December, the whole Corps, including all boys down to Third Latin, marched to Kelvinside U F Church to take part in a solemn Memorial Service at which the peal of bells given by Nicol Paton Brown was dedicated to the memory of the fallen.

The War Memorial Trust

Peter Rintoul

On 10 January 1919 a meeting was held in the Merchants' House, at which Peter Rintoul spoke of the wish among former pupils and their fathers and friends to see a Memorial established to the old boys of the school who had served in the Great War and in particular to those who had fallen. He had in mind words of Sir Archibald Hunter, the distinguished Academical soldier, whose belief was that 'a memorial to the dead should take the form of something useful to the living'. Rintoul recalled that in June 1917 he had explained in a letter to the *Chronicle* that he felt that the best memorial would be to place the Academy on a more

permanent foundation and to enable it to devote all its energies to the education of the boys of the future, untrammelled by any consideration as to possible benefit or otherwise to its shareholders. He felt that action should be taken now while the bulk of the shareholders were people with fairly close Academy connections. His proposal was that a Trust should be established, to which would pass, by purchase or donation, the shares of the Academy Company. Administration of the Trust would be vested in a Board of Governors, some of whom would be elected by members of the Trust, others nominated by bodies with Academical connections. It might prove to be possible to confine membership of the Board to former pupils of the school, which would, as he put it, 'preserve the esprit de corps in the highest degree'. Since the Trust would have no dividends to pay, it would be possible to pay good salaries and so attract good masters who would raise the standard of the education in the school. It would also be possible to spend money from time to time on improving the school accommodation. The current position was that 226 shareholders between them held 2379 shares, the true value of which was probably £6 each. There was also a bond over the school of £10500, which was being reduced to £10000. To purchase the shares would cost £15000, though there was reason to believe that some would be gifted.

The meeting greeted these proposals with approval and suggested that, in addition to the Trust, a visible War Memorial should also be established, perhaps on the Great Western Road frontage immediately to the west of the Kelvin. A committee was appointed to look into these matters and to communicate with the Directors of the Academy Company.

The Directors, acknowledging that the scheme was a desirable one and that the price of £6 per share was fair and reasonable, determined to write to the shareholders, recommending that they should sell at that price. By March a sum of about £2000 had been promised, in cash or in shares, and 1839 shares had been offered for sale, just a little less than 80% of the share capital. The next step was to hold a public meeting at which a subscription list would be launched.

The meeting was held on 13 May 1919. The proposals were outlined again, and some further details added. There would be an annual Founders' Day which would ensure that successive generations would realise the circumstances under which the Trust had been created. A Founders' Book would be kept, in which would be recorded all subscriptions, given as a Memorial to any Academy boys who had fallen in the War or as a thank-offering for those who had been spared to come through the ordeal.

By September over £10000 had been promised or paid and it was decided that subscription cards should be issued at school so that the present generation of pupils could make a contribution. In October the name The Glasgow Academy Trust was suggested, later amended at the request of the Board of Trade to The Glasgow Academicals' War Memorial Trust, and proposals were made about the constitution of the Board : it was suggested that there should be 15 Governors, 8 elected and the remainder nominated by a number of bodies in the city of Glasgow : the University Court, the Senate of the University, the Royal Faculty of Physicians and Surgeons, the Merchants' House, the Chamber of Commerce, the Faculty of Procurators and the Institute of Accountants and Actuaries.

In the meantime the Directors of the Academy Company were still responsible for running a school which was gradually returning to normality after the war. In February 1919 Barradell-Smith, Reid and MacGregor returned from war service, allowing the three former headmasters to return to retirement. The Directors knew that there was a danger that Reid would be attracted to a post at George Watson's College, where he had been a pupil. They particularly wished to retain him at the Academy as they hoped that he would share the supervision of athletics with J C Scott, who wished to give it up. Accordingly Reid returned to find that he was to be paid £25 a year as well as his salary of £300.

Scott also wished to give up the Boarding House and efforts to interest another master in taking it over proved fruitless. Consideration was given, fleetingly, to giving charge of the House to Mrs Sinclair, Superintendent of the Dining Room, but in the end the Rector was asked to advertise for a suitable master.

J C Scott in fact left the Academy altogether at the end of that year to become Rector of Hutchesons' Grammar School, where he remained until 1932. He was awarded the degree of Doctor of Laws by the University of Glasgow in 1929 and later served the city as Councillor and as Bailie, a figure who had earned high respect in the community and in the two schools which he had served. He had arrived at the Academy in 1894 a young man, clever but inexperienced. One of his pupils later recalled seeing him on his very first day. During a break between lessons he came out of his room holding his head in his hands and crashed both elbows down on and through the glass top of one of the museum cases. His despair, if that is what it was, did not last long, for the school was won over by his seemingly limitless enthusiasm, both for the Latin and Greek which he taught in the classroom and for the games at Anniesland over which his influence was immeasurable.

He became an almost legendary figure, 'pugnacious, witty and debonair, bustling about in knickerbockers every Wednesday afternoon and Saturday morning, wet or fine, cheerfully organising games for a hundred and fifty or two hundred noisy shouting boys by sheer enthusiasm mixed with a great deal of shrewdness and knowledge of Rugby football'. When he came to the school, football and cricket and games generally were in the doldrums and things needed wakening up. J C Scott woke them up and achieved a transformation.

There was an extraordinary muddle over Scott's final salary payment. He was paid on 19 December 1919 and the Secretary later had to admit that he had overlooked the fact that salaries were paid in advance. Scott had been paid for the whole quarter, which ended two months after he left the Academy's employment, and had written to thank the Directors very cordially for their generosity. The Directors took a pragmatic view : in view of Scott's long service to the school they would in all probability have paid the full quarter's salary anyway – so Scott kept the money.

His successor in the Boarding House was Paul Mallam, a master at Cargilfield, who took up duties in the autumn of 1919 as a member of the Mathematics Department. The Directors agreed to lend him the capital sum he needed to acquire the Boarding House furniture from Scott and to furnish his own quarters. He had served in the Coldstream Guards, had been awarded the MC, and was very soon immersed in school activities. By mid October he was in the chair of the Debating Society and during the Christmas holidays of 1920 he was instrumental in laying on a series of entertainments in aid of the Red Cross – a sing-song, a concert, a whist drive and a dance.

Mallam, clearly, was a man of what the Chairman of the Directors called 'the proper stamp' and so, too, was Frank Batchelor, who arrived in 1919 from St Andrews, Balliol and war service to teach Classics in Room P. The Rector was having difficulty, though, in recruiting suitable masters and in the meantime three of the lady teachers who had helped out during the war were re-engaged. The ranks of the temporary teachers had included Temple's own sister, who had braved the dangers of an Atlantic crossing in wartime to come to her brother's assistance.

Questions of salary and pension engaged a great deal of the Directors' attention in a changing post-war world. The new scales which the Glasgow School Board adopted during 1919 entailed considerable increases in salary which the Directors eventually implemented, at least for senior members of the staff. Fees were raised by £2 per annum to help pay for the increases, which meant that Temple was paid £1000 and the Heads of Department between £400 and £450. The immediate reaction of the staff was to write letters of appreciation and thanks.

Matters were complicated, though, when the School Board awarded its staff a further increase. Temple calculated that if all the staff were paid the maximum on the new scales the salary list would amount to £12000 instead of £8300. Even though the whole staff would never all be on the maximum salary, it would nevertheless cost some £3000 to implement the new scale in the Academy. The Directors decided to find out what was being done about the matter at other schools and discovered that Edinburgh Academy, the Girls' School Company and Kelvinside Academy all proposed fee increases to enable them to pay the Authority scales. This, of course, was what the staff at Glasgow Academy wanted, too. A deputation of masters met the Directors at the beginning of 1920 with a number of points to make about salaries, pensions, the recruitment of younger men and the effects on the school of setting up the War Memorial Trust.

The Directors were broadly sympathetic. Under the War Memorial Trust the school would in general be administered by the same men as before. The staff would benefit from the provisions of the Government's superannuation scheme, though progress was slow and it was some five years before the first contributions to the Government scheme were made. The Board had been surprised by the new salary scales, which had appeared in the middle of a session and could not immediately be reflected in increased fees, but they would adopt the new rates with effect from June that year, inserting an intermediate step between the scale for ordinary teachers and that for Heads of Department. Fees would need to be increased by rather more than one third to meet the increased expenditure.

The salary of one member of staff, however, continued to prove contentious. Under the Authority scale, the Gymnastics Master was to be paid £410, which the Directors regarded as exorbitant. Instead, they offered Samuel Stewart £300, which itself was an increase of £110. Stewart protested, and was asked to submit his certificates so that the Directors could have them examined by the Clerk to the Glasgow Education Authority who would then be able to say what salary the Authority would pay him. The answer was £410, which the Directors were very unwilling to pay. They therefore gave Stewart the option of being paid £410 until he reached the age of 60, when he would be required to retire, or £300 without conditions. He chose £410.

Not all the Directors' concerns were so weighty. They had to find a new place in which to hold the Prize Giving in 1919, as the Queen's Rooms were no longer available. They chose the Berkeley Hall. Another ceremony took place in the Academy itself later in the year when on 11 December Lady Ramsay unveiled a memorial to her late husband, Sir William, which was mounted on the east wall of the first floor, opposite the Rector's Room. The plaque remains in the school but is now displayed in the Chemistry building. Ramsay had come to the Academy in Elmbank Street at about the same time as Donald Morrison's term as Rector began and had become a chemist of remarkable distinction, honoured by no fewer than sixteen universities. When the *Chronicle* noted the presentation to him in December 1904 of the Nobel Prize for Chemistry it remarked that 'its value is £7825, so the members of the modern side should be encouraged by the thought of the possibilities they can achieve'.

Consideration was given in 1919 to dividing the Writing Room with a sliding partition and the decision was taken to employ a man to help the Janitor, specifically during the six winter months when the boilers had to be stoked. A man was found who was able to work between 5.30 and 8.30 before going off to his other job, which was looking after the Pleasure Ground in Athole Gardens.

As far as the Academy's own grounds at Anniesland were concerned, the Directors were told in October 1919 that there was a need to find more pitches, as the additional ground which had been rented before the war was being encroached upon by building operations. The Secretary was asked to look out for additional ground to lease.

Sloan soon reported that the only piece of ground close to Anniesland which would be suitable for playing fields lay to the north west of the present ground and was bordered by the avenue to Jordanhill House and Great Western Road. The Rector and J C Scott thought that it would make quite a satisfactory field and the Directors decided to buy it at a cost of £650 per acre, with possession on 1 April, though the farmer in possession would be allowed to take the summer's hay crop off it before it was put to any use. It was also agreed to rent from the farmer the part of the field which the school had not bought. This would cost £4 per acre and some payment for 'unexhausted manures and foggage', perhaps £12 to £14 in all.

In May 1923 it was decided to pay £600 per acre for just under four acres to the west of the new ground, on which three football pitches would be laid out. The Bank was asked to lend the purchase price. The Board also bought the Lodge at Anniesland for use by the second groundsman, though it was in fact first used as a pavilion. The cost of laying out the new ground turned out to be well over £4000, considerably more than had been anticipated, and the Bank was approached again, eventually agreeing to a loan of £10000, repayable at £1000 a year. This would help to meet other costs which it was anticipated would arise. Members of the Board consoled themselves by reflecting on the fact that when all the work was done they would have a field with excellent drainage – over four thousand cart loads of ashes, giving a covering of a foot, with eight inches of soil over it.

The Directors had embarked on another important project in October 1919 when they heard that of the 770 boys in the school 200 were dining there daily and that it had been necessary to use the end of the Gymnasium as additional Dining Room accommodation. It was therefore suggested that a new and 'semi-temporary' Dining Room be put up in the school grounds. What was envisaged was a building about 100 feet by 30 feet which would cost about £1600 if the existing cooking apparatus could be transferred. To this would have to be added the cost of partitioning the original Dining Room to allow it to be used as additional classrooms, so the total would be something over £2000, compared with a projected surplus that year, after paying a 5% dividend, of £1600.

The matter was an urgent one and before the month was out, a site had been chosen, north of the Science Building and fronting Colebrooke Street, with the kitchen wing further to the north. It was decided to put up an expanded metal building which it was optimistically envisaged would take five weeks to complete. In the event, the new Dining Hall was first used on Tuesday 30 March when a sing-song took place there, part of a Grand Fete intended to swell the school's contribution to the War Memorial Fund. On the previous Friday evening a whist drive had been held in the

Gymnasium and the old Dining Hall, but the chief day was Wednesday 31 March, when at three o'clock the school was transformed into a sort of fair. The Writing Room became a store, with concerts in the afternoon and evening, a cinema performance in the intervals and an auction sale. Elsewhere various scientific devices attracted attention and contributions, visitors could have their characters read, and a talking parrot was on display. The whole enterprise raised the remarkable total of £525.

The War Memorial scheme was progressing well. At the AGM of the Company in September 1919 it had been reported that £10500 had been subscribed, which Peter Rintoul considered 'distinctly satisfactory'. The purchase of shares went ahead and by the end of April 1920 only 275 had not changed hands.

GLASGOW ACADEMY
MENU
20TH DECEMBER 1921

SOUP
KIDNEY
FISH
BAKED SOLE

TURKEY AND SAUSAGE

ENTRÉE

SWEETBREAD AND MUSHROOMS

SWEETS
TRIFLE   MERINGUES
MINCE PIES   JELLIES
SUNDAE
FRUIT   FRUIT
COFFEE

The Trust was officially incorporated on 25 June 1920 and in August Sir Robert Mackenzie was elected Chairman and G H R Laird Secretary and Treasurer.

Sir Robert Mackenzie had divided his school days between the Academy and Uppingham, but had returned to the city where he was born – in Blythswood Square – for his University studies and to pursue his career as a chartered accountant. He was a member of the Glasgow Stock Exchange and served as President of the Institute of Accountants and Actuaries in Glasgow. He was also elected President of the Scottish Rugby Union, having been capped four times for Scotland, and held the Glasgow University record for the quarter-mile. Mackenzie was best known in Glasgow, though, for the leading part which he took in the Volunteer and Territorial Forces, an interest reflected in the Academy's association with the Glasgow Highlanders.

Laird, too, was active in the Territorial Army and he, too, had moved on from the Academy to complete his education elsewhere before returning to the city, in his case to practise as a lawyer. But he was devoted to the Academy, supporting all school occasions and serving as Secretary of the Committee whose deliberations had resulted in the establishment of the War Memorial Trust. A lover of books and literature, a writer and a poet, he was a Deputy-Lieutenant of the County of the City of Glasgow and – in the words of the *Chronicle* at his death – 'a great Academical'.

In the meantime the day to day life of the school went on. On 25 February 1920 Major Couper handed over command of the OTC to Captain Reid who was assisted in his work by a large number of masters. The old uniform jacket had been abandoned in favour of tunics of officers' pattern. A whole day of field manoeuvres was organised in the neighbourhood of Mugdock Castle, Milngavie, early in June that year.

In October 1919 a Scientific Society was started which during the session organised ten meetings and two excursions, to an oil and varnish works and to Glasgow Observatory, where members were favoured with a perfect night and saw Orion's nebula, Jupiter and its moons and Saturn's rings. A Literary and Debating Society Sing-Song was held on the last Friday before Christmas in 1919, with the hope expressed that, now that it had come into being, it would remain as a school institution. In September 1920 the Photographic Society resumed after a lapse of five years.

The Academy was full. Indeed the Rector reported in March 1920 that there were 770 boys on the roll, 90 more than could properly be accommodated. In planning the level of fees which would be needed to meet the increases in salaries which the Directors had awarded to the staff, they should therefore base their calculations on a roll of 680 boys, 40 in each of the First English classes, 35 in each of the Second English classes and 30 in each of the other classes. There would be three classes in each year from Third English up to and including Fourth Latin, two classes in Fifth Latin and some thirty boys in Sixth Latin. The fees which were proposed ranged from £12 annually for the youngest boys to £33 for the oldest.

If, briefly, we imagine ourselves visitors to the Academy in 1920, we approach by walking up the broad steps to the main entrance. Opening the front door with its engraved glass panel, we pass into the entrance hall, perhaps taking a seat on the carved oak bench which remains there still and noticing the bronze medallion of Donald Morrison, the brass shield memorial to Andrew Muir – and the head of an ibex, mounted on an oak shield. Having rung the bell to summon the Janitor, we might be shown through the door to the left leading into the Rector's Room or perhaps into the main part of the school, taking in the engraved gas globes for lighting in the winter months, the Dux board, the memorial to Nigel Watt – a former pupil accidentally drowned at Corps Camp, the panel commemorating Sir William Ramsay and a selection of framed photographs. Looking down into the open area of the Well we see the large clock, two busts on wooden pedestals, a variety of plants, notice boards and cleaning equipment. The luncheon bar is there, equipped with a cooking stove and tiled fire-place, a sink and a service counter.

If we are invited into the Rector's Room, we notice the marble fireplace, the roller blinds at the windows, the Axminster carpet, and the dozen mahogany vase-back chairs with buttoned leather seats. Edwin Temple works at a large mahogany table with a leather top and a movable writing slope. On the walls are an array of photographs, including one of William Melven. There are seven classrooms on this floor and we absorb just some of the details : in Room B, across the entrance hall from the Rector, a battery of maps – of England, Scotland, the British Empire, Europe, Ireland, Australia – and pictures on the walls of scenes in India, Australia and Africa; the Children's Encyclopaedia at home in Room E; Room F, furnished with ten long desks and forms for the infants – and with a piano.

As we go up the stairs on the north side of the building, we look briefly into the Masters'

Room on the entresol floor. There is a marble fireplace here, too, and a carpet, eleven chairs and an octagonal table. There are all sorts of books about and on the walls two dozen or so framed photographs of school teams.

On the second floor there are eight classrooms, two of them with small box rooms leading off. Most striking is Room L, the Writing Room, furnished quite differently from the other rooms with their desks and masters' tables. The master here has an imposing pitch pine rostrum fitted with cupboards and a desk, atop a two step platform, and seating for the pupils is on backless forms at nine desks, each 21 feet long. The Thurmer grand piano and the tablet commemorating John Maclaren remind us of musical activity.

The gallery on the upper floor is enclosed to the ceiling, with 'bound work' in the lower part and glass sashes above, the upper parts formed into arched tops. Photographs of teams decorate the walls of the passages. On the west side there are three classrooms. Room Q must have been the old music room, for there is a piano. Next door, in Room R, we find the library, 1200 volumes or so housed in pine bookcases. The heating needs to be supple-mented by coal stoves in some of the rooms up here. The gymnasium is full of equipment – the rack holding rifles, the bar bells, the Indian clubs, the vaulting horse, the Avery weighing machine which Samuel Stewart uses at the beginning of each session to weigh every boy. He records their height and tests their eyesight, too. Returning along the passage on the east side of the building, we notice that Room U, the large room which used to be the Dining Room, has only its heating stove and a small number of desks. The old kitchen next door is now the armoury.

A striking and moving addition to the main building was being planned during 1920. The Governors of the War Memorial Trust agreed in April to accept the design for the Memorial Panel which had been submitted by T Andrew Millar and a year later preparations were in hand for its unveiling. The Directors of the Academy Company decided to play their part by having the woodwork around the cupola of the school repainted and the hall, landing and corridors thoroughly cleaned up, so that the Academy would be in good order for the unveiling ceremony. The work of installing the panel took place when the school was quiet during the holiday and the painstaking work of gilding the names then followed, a four or five week task in itself. It had been hoped that General Sir Archibald Hunter would be available to perform the unveiling but in fact the ceremony was carried out on Wednesday 22 June 1921 by General Sir Ian Hamilton, another most distinguished soldier. There remained still the erection of an outside memorial to be considered.

At Easter 1920, the Academy lost the services of one of its most distinctive and memorable masters, William Robertson. He did not return to work after the holidays and in May asked the Directors if he might be allowed to retire. It was agreed to grant him leave of absence on full salary. In an act of real generosity, the Directors decided in August to retain him on the staff until the superannuation position was finally decided : they hoped to ensure that he eventually received a pension under the new scheme based on his full salary, even though he was unable to work. In fact, Robertson died suddenly on 24 January 1921. He had no surviving relatives and his estate therefore fell to the Crown : rather grudgingly, the Directors paid the balance of his salary to the King's Remembrancer.

'Big Bob' had taught at the Academy for forty years. He was a tall, burly man with a red-brown wig, not particularly smart in appearance with his vast morning coat, baggy trousers and, occasionally, brown golfing boots. He was a shy man, who talked little in the Masters' Room and who was embarrassed into stammering and blushing if any of his former pupils ever returned to visit him.

Although at first he lived close to the school, at the turn of the century he moved back to Ayr, travelling from there by train and subway each day. Hence the picture of him which lived on in the minds of many, 'rolling over the bridge from the subway with his umbrella hooked into his handkerchief pocket to save him the trouble of holding it' and then leaping up the front steps several at a time. Hence too, or so it appeared, his reluctance to keep boys in after school : 'Observe! Take up your books. Back seat. Four o'clock for an hour. I'll be there ... so will you. Toch! I've got to catch the four ten. Besides, it's no prison when it's raining. I'll have to forgive you.'

There was more to it than that, though, for Robertson was a kindly and sensitive man of almost childlike simplicity, with the gift of humour and an extreme desire to be fair and just to every boy. His classroom was not an orderly place and indeed was at times the scene of incredible buffoonery, but when occasionally he erupted into anger the outburst would be followed at once by a display of remorse. Punishment was abhorrent to him.

He loved Latin and Greek and he loved teaching them to those who wanted to share his knowledge. He encouraged them but never spoon fed them, and there were those who did not realise or accept the responsibility which his methods of teaching laid upon them. But if they did want to learn, as one of them later recalled, 'we felt at once that all his scholarship and all his kindness were at our disposal to help us'.

Among William Robertson's favourite lines were two from the fourteenth Ode of Horace:

Eheu fugaces, Postume, Postume,
Labuntur anni.

They are lines of great poignancy, which Robertson liked to render in his own way: 'The years that roll on are lost to me, lost to me'.

In 1921, when the Directors expressed some concern about the size of the seven classes in the Preparatory School, Temple had to concede that although he tried to limit the two First English classes to 40 boys between six and seven years of age – 'by no means too large a number for a class at that stage, when little written work is done' – they had in fact become somewhat larger. First English Senior, though, was in the hands of Miss McCallum and even at 48 pupils was not too big, as she had 'marvellous disciplinary powers'. It was not possible to add to the number of teachers in the Junior School because there was not room, but when Miss McCallum retired it might be a good idea to put a master or mistress in overall charge under the Rector.

Temple's son David had been one of Miss McCallum's pupils and concurred in his father's judgement of her, recalling the 'ring in her voice that kept generation after generation of restless, primitive little boys in the most perfect discipline imaginable, the order that comes not from fear but from instinctive, immediate respect for the born teacher'.

When J C Scott left, the Rector tried but failed to get a master to undertake the task of supervising all the games. George Brotherston, a Watsonian who had been appointed in 1920, helped Reid, who was also relieved of teaching for an hour a day so that he could devote time to his work as Commandant of the OTC, but the Directors expressed the view in September 1920 that this was not really a suitable combination of responsibilities. Brotherston's help was in any event cut short by his death in August 1922. So began what turned out to be a protracted debate about the priority which should be given to games when making appointments to the staff. The Directors recalled that Arthur Campbell, a former Captain

of the School and Dux, had been temporarily employed when he was invalided out of the army at the end of the war and they were strongly in favour of making another such appointment if a suitable man could be found. Perhaps a University student could be specially employed to help with the games?

The Directors continued to press the matter. In March the following year the Rector agreed to give special consideration to the possibility of appointing a man to look after the whole physical training of the boys, including gymnastics and sports, and then in June found himself confronted by a report from Peter Rintoul that he had had an offer from a man who was not a teacher but who would be prepared to come to the Academy as Sports Master. Temple was fortunately able to deflect this suggestion by referring to the possibility that a vacancy on the teaching staff would arise during the summer.

Although in September there turned out to have been no vacancy, the Rector did consider the possibility of engaging an additional master who would be able to relieve him and take the place of absent teachers as well as undertaking the duties of Sports Master. It was a question of finding the right man and with that in mind three names were obtained from the Appointments Boards of Oxford and Cambridge Universities. Perhaps conscious of the considerable pressure they were exerting on Temple over the matter, the Board did acknowledge that any appointment would naturally require the candidate to be suitable for the educational scheme of the school as well as supervising sports, and that selection must lie with the Rector.

In the end, nothing came of these moves, and the following summer Norman Sloan wrote at length to the Rector, intimating that it was unlikely that there would be help from Academicals at Anniesland during the forthcoming session. He knew that Temple was looking out for one or two new members of staff and anxious to say how convinced he was that the school should gradually get together five or six members of the staff who would take a real interest in the sports and give assistance in organising them 'as masters do in other schools'. In that connection it was important that masters should live near the school. 'I think there should be one man in charge who would have little or no teaching to do after the luncheon interval – on three days each week at least.' At the moment, the younger boys were often left quite uncontrolled at Anniesland and games lost much of their value as an aid to character building if they were not carried on under discipline. If it could be achieved, though, efficiency in athletics would bring prestige to School and Club.

As it was, 'considerable anxiety' was felt by leading members of the Academical Club and there was a growing feeling as to the real urgency of the matter. The Board would grudge no reasonable expense which had to be incurred to improve the position. 'I think we are only now realising how great a loss J C Scott was to the School in its Athletic side at least.'

In 1922 additional changing accommodation for the boys was provided at Anniesland by installing an Army hut. In the main building of the school, an oak cabinet was fitted into a disused doorway into Peter Couper's room, Room D, to house cups and trophies which had been donated to the school over the past ten or twelve years. Trophy winners had in the past been allowed to keep them at home and the Rector insisted on consulting the boys before implementing any change to the practice, but it was eventually agreed that trophies would in future be kept at home for part of the year only, after which they were to be returned for display. Boys were given small replica trophies as a permanent memento of their achievements.

The Directors made a conscious effort during 1921 to acquaint themselves further with the management of the school and made some quite pointed enquiries of the Rector. Temple offered them his assurance that the text books in use were entirely satisfactory : 'no book would be clung to if a better offered itself'. He was also happy with the system of dividing the classes into parallel divisions for all subjects. Setting for individual subjects would lead to timetabling difficulties and he did not believe that boys were good in one subject and weak in another, except perhaps in Mathematics.

The provision made for the most senior boys could, on the other hand, be improved. Ideally, the Seventh Class should be taught quite separately, though it was not clear how many would stay on if an entirely separate Seventh Class were provided, or where they would be accommodated. Anything which would encourage pupils to stay on for another year was to be welcomed, though, since boys at the Academy were younger than their counterparts at the top of other schools, such as the High School and Allan Glen's, because they were not bound by the strict regulations about the age at which various stages of the Leaving Certificate might be taken.

There was a feeling that although numbers were being reduced – from 771 in

1920 to 753 the following year – the school was still too full and the Rector was asked to aim for a total in 1922/23 of 725. The financial position remained healthy and the Company elected to resume half yearly repayments to the Scottish Widows Fund rather than pay a higher rate of interest. Contributions to the Academical Club for the upkeep of Anniesland were gradually raised and a contribution was made towards the cost of additional stand accommodation. The Trust made its contribution to the financial well-being of the school by returning, as a loan, £600 which it had received by way of dividend from the Company in 1920. In September 1922, as the Trust began to assume control of the school, the Governors learned that the salaries being paid in the Academy were still the same as those which had been paid by the Glasgow Education Authority before their scale was reduced by 7.5% in the early summer. They decided that in the Academy the original scale would be maintained, subject to the deduction of 5% as a contribution to pensions.

In February 1922 the roof of the Boarding House required renewal and Paul Mallam took the opportunity of letting the School Committee know that in his view the house was too small to generate a large enough surplus to make a worthwhile contribution to the Company. The Committee tended to agree with him but could not contemplate a change at that moment.

Mallam was fully involved in the life of the school. Together with Walter Barradell-Smith he had taken a leading part in the performance of the sketch *Cox and Box* which had formed the second part of a most successful Concert and Entertainment held in the Dining Hall in December 1921. He had also made the scenery and stage properties.

On 15 March 1921 J W Arthur, a Director since 1878 and President since 1912, died in France, just as the final moves began which would lead the following year to the planned change in the Academy's status. The Directors of the Company and the Governors of the Trust all felt that the time had come for control of the school to pass into the hands of the Trust. The only obstacle took the form of a number of shareholders who would not part with their shares and, since legal opinion ruled out such options as the Company leasing the school to the Trust, the way forward was to make another effort to get the shares transferred. The number outstanding continued to be reduced little by little until eventually all shares in the Company were transferred to the Trust, including those which had been deemed derelict and those whose owners had been prepared to sell only at prices exceeding £6. Additional subscriptions had been obtained to meet the cost of acquiring them and a promise that the whole amount needed would be forthcoming had been made by Gilchrist Macbeth, a pupil at the school between 1894 and 1897.

In the meantime, the Board of the Company decided that by making some of its number Honorary Directors it would be possible to create vacancies which would then be filled by Governors of the Trust. In this way all the Governors of the Trust had by October 1921 become Directors of the Company, and all the Directors of the Company were members of the Trust, with the exception only of Professor James Moffat and Norman Sloan who, although a Governor of the Trust, could not become a Director by virtue of being Secretary to the

Company. Control of the school had effectively passed to the Trust.

On 5 June 1922 Norman Sloan was appointed as liquidator of the Glasgow Academy Company which held its final meeting on 31 July. On 18 September Sloan informed the Governors that he was prepared to transfer to the Trust the whole assets of the Company on consideration of a payment of £150. Once the Company was liquidated, G H R Laird resigned as Secretary and Treasurer of the Trust and was succeeded by Sloan.

On Friday 16 June 1922 every boy in the school from Second Latin upwards attended the first Commemoration Service, which was held in the Dining Hall. An address was given by the Revd Dr George Morrison, the congregation sang *Oh God of Bethel*, *For all the Saints* and *Fight the Good Fight* and the passage from the Epistle to the Ephesians was read in which Paul urges his brothers to 'Put on the whole armour of God, that ye may be able to stand against the wiles of the devil'.

The following day was observed as Commemoration Day. Temple had given advice about this, based on his experience at Fettes and Glenalmond, and had pointed out that Anniesland offered better accommodation than the School. There were two cricket matches – an Academical XI against the First XI and an Academical Veterans XI against the Second XI. There was tea, and the band of the Royal Scots Fusiliers played, but it was a cold day.

That month, too, Edwin Temple himself was honoured. The University of Glasgow conferred upon him the degree of Doctor of Laws : one observer remarked that 'no graduand received a warmer welcome and he felt certain that much of the deep-throated cheering came from old boys who first found their lungs at Anniesland and within the Academy grounds'. The degree was conferred for reasons in which all who knew the Academy heartily concurred, to mark the Senate's 'sense of the solid achievement of the Rector of the Glasgow Academy in the past and its confidence that under the new constitution the Academy will, thanks to his guidance, advance to still greater heights of prosperity'.

1922-1932

A decade of peace

As far as the boys in the school were concerned, the appearance of electric light during the summer of 1922 probably seemed far more significant than the passing of control to the Trust. The contractor responsible for installing the new lighting was an Academical, and when the work was done he presented the school with a wireless set. E P Kaye applied for the necessary licence and at a ceremony in the Physical Laboratory on 28 November the apparatus was formally handed over. Earlier in the evening broadcasting from Manchester had been received in the form of news and song, but results were somewhat disappointing during the ceremony itself. Small groups of boys subsequently 'listened in' to Manchester, Birmingham, Marconi House and Chelmsford. The growing interest in wireless was reflected in the contents of a new magazine, *Science*, published in 1922 by the Scientific Society and including in its twelve foolscap pages, printed on the hectograph or some similar jelly machine, articles on how to make a wireless receiver, broadcasting, and 'the science of today'. The Scientific Society continued to offer its members a variety of opportunities, including the chance to visit works and factories – in 1924, for example, the Richmond Park Laundry at Cambuslang and the Bryant and May Match Factory at Maryhill – so continuing a tradition that had started in Donald Morrison's time. Cricket in the playground had also been encouraged under Morrison and in 1922 another new amenity which the boys were able to enjoy was a concrete pitch, or more strictly a granolithic pitch, which was placed between the Dining Hall and the bank of the Kelvin, on ground which had been used since the war as a kitchen garden.

Another successful OTC concert took place in December 1922, perhaps most notable for the fact that the first item on the programme was the performance of John Ireland's *Ragamuffin*, a pianoforte solo given by a master newly arrived at the school, Frank Roydon Richards. Two other masters had arrived at the same time, Alexander Todd and Cyril Engledow. All three were helping with the football and were taking a great interest in the boys, both in and out of school hours. To assist with the recruitment of staff the Rector proposed in 1924 that a special travelling allowance of £10 should be paid to masters whose homes were in England and the proposal was adopted. The practice continued until the end of 1946, when there was only one man on the staff who qualified for the payment – and he did not know about it.

Temple fought shy of a suggestion made in 1922 that the Governors should hold a dinner for the staff in the school Dining Hall, since he did not think it would achieve the intended purpose of bringing the Governors into touch with the masters. He preferred to suggest that Governors should pay occasional visits to the school, either for lunch or while lessons were in progress.

Two of the mistresses in the Junior School, Miss Katherine McCallum and Miss Olga Gentles, were absent from their classes for the whole of the spring term in 1923. Temple felt that he should plan for the following session on the basis that Miss McCallum, who was suffering from the after effects of influenza, would never return. He would discontinue Third English C, a class which had begun during the War and which he maintained he had always regarded as 'more or less temporary', and he would transfer its teacher, Miss Margaret

Walker, to Miss McCallum's class, First English Senior. This would allow him to appoint an extra master and so provide staffing for an extra division of Sixth Latin, where he expected there to be 70 boys rather than the usual 50 : clearly his wish that boys would stay on longer was being fulfilled.

The Rector was correct : on 29 May Miss McCallum wrote to him from her home in Belmont Street. 'My doctor has finally advised me that it would not be judicious for me to resume work in the Academy in September.' She computed her service at over 41 years when she sent in her resignation to the Governors. She received a testimonial cheque for £500 and a wealth of good wishes from those who were grateful for her work in First English Junior and then First English Senior, classes in which she had exercised her determination that the boys should be guided to become not only well educated scholars, as Temple put it, but good citizens. Temple had told her that 'many mothers looked back with pleasure to the time when their boys were with her and some may even wish it could return'. She was touched, and replied that 'to have been in touch with youth at its freshest is a great privilege and to have had the trust and loving companionship of hundreds of small boys a joy for ever'.

Like her aunt Miss McCallum, Miss Gentles never returned to teach at the Academy, where she had had charge of First English Junior for thirteen years, for she died on 17 September 1923. Miss McCallum, whose retiring allowance the Governors made up to half her salary, died in April 1936.

In February 1924 the Governors discovered that the previous August Samuel Stewart had reached the age of 60, at which he was supposed to retire. They agreed to do nothing in the meantime, as they were on the lookout for a suitable man from the Royal Navy to replace him. In any case the Rector was confident that he knew he would have to retire, and at the end of the session he did so, succeeded by Jack Coleman Smith. Stewart was later remembered as 'an able and honoured exponent of older fashions and more spectacular exercises involving horizontal and parallel bars and other apparatus upon which the pundits of Board and Department had begun to frown severely by the end of the War'. His great joy was the Gymnastics Display which was held annually for twenty years until the war put a stop to it, the war in which he lost two sons. He had been a professional soldier, a Dundonian who joined the 2nd HLI in 1881 and fought with them in Egypt and in India. He eventually returned to Dundee to teach at Morgan Academy, but in 1893 he moved to Glasgow and the Academy. When the Corps began, he became its Colour Sergeant Instructor and when he was released from his war service, he returned to the school and devised a war effort of his own, the kitchen garden which at first produced vegetables for the Dining Hall and then, in times of peace, flowers.

The old Dining Hall was at last divided into two during 1923, so providing an additional classroom, and a new heating system was installed, with individual radiators in each classroom in the main building, a move prompted by the complete failure of one of the boilers the previous winter.

The Miniature Rifle Range was inspected late in 1923 and found to be not altogether safe, but its shortcomings had clearly not impeded the progress of shooting in the school, which Frank Batchelor had greatly assisted. In July 1923 for the first time an Academy VIII shot at Bisley and the following year a shooting blazer was devised, basically the same as the one for the First XV except that on the pocket there was an emblem of two crossed rifles with the Roman numerals VIII beneath them.

In the autumn of 1923 the Governors discussed with the Rector the Academy's showing in the Leaving Certificate and Bursary examinations. Temple believed that it was partly because in certain subjects Academy boys sat a year earlier than was normally the case that the Leaving Certificate results were not as good as the Governors might have wished. Turning to the Bursary Competition, he explained that it referred to the Arts Course, which was not now usually taken by Academy boys 'as the Arts degree is not of so much account in these days as it used to be, except in the teaching profession'. There was also the point that few Academy boys felt the need of the financial assistance of a bursary : they were satisfied with results that allowed them to enter the University.

Temple would nevertheless be glad of anything which would induce the boys to stay a year longer at school and suggested an Academy Bursary. The following spring, therefore, the Governors instituted the War Memorial Scholarship, to be awarded to a boy in the highest class who had entered in the Third Latin or earlier and had spent at least five years in the school. It was to be worth £50 a year and tenable for four years.

The Upper School was at this stage still divided into three sections from the Third Class onwards, Classical, Intermediate and Modern. All boys took Arithmetic, Mathematics, English,

History, Geography and French. Those in the Classical section added Latin and Greek, in the Intermediate Latin, Science and Drawing, in the Modern German (from the Fifth Class), Science and Drawing. Intermediate and Modern boys could also take Book-keeping and Commercial Subjects. Changes in the Leaving Certificate arrangements in 1924 included abolition of the Intermediate Certificate. To qualify for a Group award, boys had to pass two Lowers and two Highers, which they could take only in the Sixth or Seventh Classes of the Academy.

At the inauguration of the War Memorial Edwin Temple, George Laird and Sir Robert Mackenzie

The Prize Giving in June 1924 was held in the Methodist Central Hall, Maryhill Road. On Armistice Day that year the outside War Memorial was unveiled by Sir Robert Mackenzie. It had been decided that the most suitable location was the corner of Colebrooke Street and Great Western Road and A N Paterson, an Academical, had been responsible for its design, which incorporated the statement that the Academy was a 'living and enduring memorial to the former members of the school who served in the war of 1914-1918 ... in the confident hope that the memory of their sacrifices will be an inspiration to all who come after'. In order to give the Memorial a fitting setting, the existing fence was replaced by a wall, and trees were planted.

Conversely, trees were being removed at Anniesland, where the work of laying out the new ground involved removal of a line of fine specimens which had marked the avenue to Jordanhill House. The contour of the hillside had also been altered. The ashes and the top dressing of soil would be laid by direct labour under the supervision of Joe Ward, the grounds-man, but it would not be possible to sow the grass before the onset of winter and by January 1925 it had become apparent that the extra pitches would not be ready that autumn. In the meantime two small pitches had been made available on ground immediately to the south-west of the Club Ground. Joe Ward had come to Anniesland from the Watsonian ground at Myreside in 1902 : he was shortly to be joined in his work for the Club and the school by his son, so that 'Old Joe' and 'Young Joe' would be working together.

'Old Joe' Ward

The Governors were perhaps more conscious than usual of the work of non-teaching staff at this time, since they heard in January 1925 that two important figures had died. William Smith had come to the Academy as Janitor in 1895 and had won high esteem for his over-riding sense of duty. Mrs Grace Sinclair had been Superintendent of the Dining Hall since 1907 : she had said then that she had had no experience of such work but that she would try and she had remained for 18 years, taking a deep interest in the boys and the life of the school.

In 1924 Norman Sloan and his sister had entertained the Governors and staff to a Reception in the Dining Hall. The precedent having been set, the Governors themselves organised a similar evening on 13 March 1925 and made it the occasion of a presentation to Edwin Temple, marking with the gift of a silver tea service and tray his completion of twenty five years as Rector of the Academy.

Temple had for some years had the vision of an additional block of buildings at the Academy containing some classrooms, a library and a school hall, perhaps the gift of a generous benefactor. There was no benefactor in 1925 and there was no new building, but the Academy did secure for itself new accommodation by looking across the road. In October 1924, the first house in Colebrooke Terrace came on the market and, imaginatively, the Trust expressed an interest. The price was too high, but the Governors waited and in February their offer of £1500 was accepted.

By the following autumn the new Janitor, Thomas Winderam, was living on the top flat and plans were in hand for the rest of the house. There would be rooms for the lady teachers and for the masters, the dining room would make a useful classroom and the drawing room was already in use as the school library. An appeal was launched for donations towards the cost of furnishing the new room. Book-cases, chairs and tables would be needed, of a high quality. Pictures were given by his brothers in memory of Wilfrid Sloan and a book-case in memory of William Melven.

Another Senior English Master was remembered through a similar gift : in March 1926 his colleagues made a presentation to the library in memory of Peter Couper, who had died in June 1925 at the age of only 59, another victim of influenza. A native of Rothesay, he had graduated from the University of Glasgow in 1895 and taught at the Albany Academy and the High School before joining the Academy in 1899. When the Cadet Corps was founded he volunteered to take command and indeed was long remembered for his staccato military voice booming across both playground and classroom: 'When I am forgotten, comma, as I shall be, comma, and sleep in dull cold marble, semicolon, say that I taught thee, period'.

The rigours of his class were the stuff of many stories, for he was what one pupil described as 'a fiery chap' and 'suffered no slackness of any sort', determined as he was that his pupils should be trained as much in habits of industry and order as in the intricacies of English grammar. Temple had for some years regarded Couper as his right hand man.

The Rector felt that Barradell-Smith could be appointed in Couper's place as Head of the English Department but because he knew that some Governors had reservations about him he suggested appointing another master to the staff without making a definite appointment of

Senior English Master – though Barradell-Smith's salary would be increased. Ben Aston was appointed to teach English and after a year Walter Barradell-Smith was confirmed as Head English Master.

It is difficult to see why there was a feeling that Barradell-Smith needed to prove himself. He had been at the school for 18 years and had played his part outside the classroom as well as in it. Perhaps there was disapproval of the fact that, under the nom de plume of Richard Bird, he wrote and published school stories for boys, such as *The Gay Adventure* which he brought out shortly before the war.

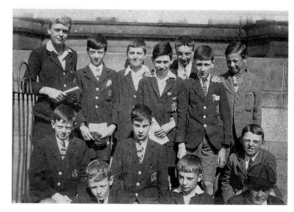

Prize-winners in First Latin, 1925

Perhaps it was because there were those who remembered that, like so many others, he had been exhausted when he came home from the war and, if schoolboy stories were to be believed, perhaps not always as attentive to his classes as he might have been. It was said that he used to set the class a subject for an essay, put his feet on his desk, cover his face with the *Glasgow Herald* and fall fast asleep. One day the subject was 'On a piece of string'. In the middle of the hour the door opened and there was the Rector, who surveyed the quiet scene for a minute or two, put his finger on his lips and went out, closing the door quietly.

The Barradell-Smith of those days that Ben Aston later recalled would have enjoyed that story. He was 'a jolly man of early middle-age, solid, four-square, inclining perhaps to the portliness that Rugger forwards later allow themselves; rubicund of face; his eyes twinkling behind his glasses, as likely as not at a joke against himself'. The two men worked together for almost twenty years and were a powerful influence over many Academy boys.

After Coleman Smith had been at the school for a year, he was anxious for change. The gymnasium, at the very top of the school, was badly ventilated, but he believed that matters could be improved by installing equipment supplied by a company called Thermotank. When the Governors discovered that the cost would be up to £700, they decided to do nothing, and it was to be ten years before the problem was tackled. All that could be offered in the meantime was altering the roof light windows so that more could be made to open.

When it came to installing new apparatus, the Governors were more receptive and changes were made. These involved moving the honours boards : the First XV boards were mounted on the east wall, the First XI boards went into Room Q and the names of boys who had won the OTC and athletic prizes were to be found on large boards in the east passage leading past Room U to the gymnasium.

Changes were made, too, to the arrangements for Sports Day, which was still a mixture of serious events and novelty competitions such as the Cockie Leekie race, in which competitors had to eat buns, drink lemonade and thread needles. There had been a feeling that the Commemoration Day had not been the success that had been hoped for, and it was proposed in 1925 to amalgamate it with the Sports, abandoning the cricket matches and incidentally the first Saturday in May which had for years been the traditional timing for Sports Day. In 1927 a challenge cup was presented by the London Branch of the Academical Club for the House which did best at the Athletic Sports. The Houses wore distinctive colours for the Sports – South was Red, North was Blue, Hill was Yellow and West was Green.

Less athletic pursuits also took new directions. During 1925 the school was visited on several occasions by members of the British Association whose mission was to raise the taste in music of pupils in schools like the Academy by giving short and good concerts. Then in December 1925 a new club was founded, The Circle : it met chiefly to read plays, mainly those of modern authors, and it was expected that membership would be limited to about fifteen from the Sixth and Seventh Classes – 'a good sociable sit-by-the-fireside size'. Two years later a junior equivalent, The Orb, was started for boys in the Fifth Class.

During November 1926 senior classes attended a Shakespearean recital given in the Writing Room by an actor called Hubert Carter, who was appearing with Sybil Thorndike's Company in *Henry VIII*. He gave extracts from *Othello*, *Hamlet* and *Macbeth* and caused quite a stir by doing part of the ghost scene from *Hamlet* in American. The following month the Scientific Society revived its magazine, *Science* : this time the articles included one on Aircraft in

Naval Warfare, another on Flashlight Photography and an imaginative story entitled *The Last Man Left*. Early in 1927 the boys in the Sixth Class met and decided that it would be an excellent thing if every boy on leaving gave one book to the Library. On two evenings in March 1928 a dramatic performance was given in aid of Library funds 'by half a dozen boys performing a few scenes from *Much Ado* in semi-darkness'. They also performed *The Tiger's Ghost* by Richard Bird (alias Walter Barradell-Smith).

During the General Strike in the spring of 1926, members of the Sixth and Seventh Classes offered their services, some on the railways, some on the cars, at least one on the docks. Some of the staff drove tramway cars in their spare hours, some acted as conductors and others were special constables.

Numbers in the school remained about the same – 741 in October 1925 compared with 742 a year previously. By 1927 enrolments had risen slightly, to 746. In every case where application had been made before the lists closed, sons of old Academy boys received a preference. The Rector did not know how many boys had been refused admission as he had not kept records of this kind.

Despite the healthy enrolment, the Secretary reported in January 1926 that if he paid all the outstanding accounts, the overdraft facility at the Bank of £10000 would be exceeded by some hundreds of pounds. Was an increase in fees necessary? The Academy's fees were significantly lower than those of Kelvinside Academy and Edinburgh Academy. At their next meeting, the Governors decided that they would make an increase in the fees to cover the next four years. They decided not to ask for payment termly instead of four times a year,

although they did acknowledge that if fees were paid just three times a year, John Dunlop would be saved a good deal of work in filling up forms. Dunlop had taken over the task of assisting with the school administration in this way, following in the footsteps of Peter Couper and William Melven.

The Boarding House was contributing very little to the Academy, financially. Indeed the surplus for 1924 was just £50 and since at the beginning of 1925 there were only ten boys in residence it seemed likely that there would be no surplus at all that year. Matters did not improve : a year later there were still only ten boys.

Although the Governors did not hold Paul Mallam to blame for the situation, he let it be known in June 1926 that he wished to give up the Boarding House at the end of the session. There was a feeling among Governors that enough was enough and that 12 Belmont Crescent should be sold, but the Rector intervened with the suggestion that the house might be useful in the future as a residence for the Rector. The Governors agreed to wait and in the meantime to let it for a year to Solbé who would also be given a loan to take over the furniture from Mallam. The reprieve lasted much longer than a year and Solbé himself remained until 1930, suggesting to the Governors in 1928 that they should install electric light. When he gave it up, Mr and Mrs Coleman Smith took over the Boarding House.

In 1927 pressure was again exerted on the Rector in connection with school games. This time, the particular anxiety amongst members of the Academical Club concerned cricket and in January Temple agreed, perhaps rather wearily, that he would take the needs of the game into account when next making an appointment to the staff. Then, six months later and in the absence of the Rector, one Governor raised the matter again and said that he had spoken to Reid, who wished to be relieved of the supervision of cricket. The Governors went on to record their wish to see on the Academy staff a man who was then at Kelvinside Academy, and the Secretary was instructed to communicate this wish to the Rector. It seems likely that the man in question was Sandy Forrester, a Glasgow Academical who had represented Glasgow University at rugby, golf and tennis and had been the University's Captain of Cricket for three years. He taught at Kelvinside Academy – where in time he was to serve as Acting Rector –

but maintained close links with his old school and particularly with the Glasgow Academical Club, for whom he played cricket for a quarter of a century.

The Rector, though, had his own suggestions to make. It would help the cricket, he believed, if Sports Day was moved from June to the end of March : nothing came of this suggestion until his successor revived it in 1934. Temple also thought that it would be a good idea to engage a cricket professional and it was later noted that the Clydesdale professional had been coming to the Academy twice a week to give coaching to members of the First XI. The Governors were not satisfied and minuted again in June that 'the only real solution was to get a

The Staff, 1926-1927
Back Row: Messrs Kaye, Aston, Batchelor, McVey, Clark, Wilson, Bolton, Jones, Engledow and Winderam (Janitor)
Centre Row: Messrs Runcieman, Reid, Rees, Campbell, Mallam, Barradell-Smith, Solbé, Parry and Carr
Front Row: Mr Moffatt, Miss Reid, Miss McEwan, Miss Wilson, Dr Temple (Rector), Miss Walker, Miss Alexander,
Mr Dunlop, Mr Robertson and Mr Barrie. Absent: Mr Coleman Smith

master who would really take a keen interest in school cricket matters'. In May 1929 a meeting of the Board was held especially to consider the whole question of games, as a result of which a small number of Governors met the Rector to discuss the matter further. Roydon Richards was to affirm more than twenty years later that these manoeuvres caused Temple much anxiety.

The Rector greatly valued the contributions which members of his staff made outside the classroom. During a discussion of salaries in January 1927 he made it plain that, rather than having the maximum salaries higher in the Academy than those which were paid by the local authority, he would 'like to be able to grant special payments from time to time to those masters who voluntarily made themselves specially useful in the general life of the school outside school hours'. That summer the Board decided to raise the Rector's own salary to £1250, as they had discovered that Edinburgh Academy had had to offer £1500 'to get the sort of man they wanted'.

Some of the matters with which the Rector occupied his time were taxing, others perhaps less so. In February 1927 the Games Committee exercised itself over exactly when it was expected that school caps and ties should be worn. Temple's ruling was that they should be worn during term time from Monday morning to Saturday night, 'with licence allowed on Sundays and during holidays'. The rugby trophy cap was to be worn only when a boy was changed for rugby : a year later, this was extended and boys were permitted to wear the trophy cap with ordinary clothes when going to and from certain rugby matches – but not under any circumstances after 7 pm.

The Governors and the Rector let it be known during the summer of 1927 that they would welcome 'any benefaction which those who have the interest of the school at heart might see fit to trust to their care'. They had a clear idea of the uses to which they would put such a gift. What was needed most urgently was a School Hall worthy of the Academy, the lack of which was a very serious hindrance to the corporate life of the school. They would like, too, to be able to build an entirely new gymnasium and workshops for engineering and woodworking. Some day the Dining Hall, which was not a permanent building, would need to be replaced. Increased attendance at the school brought with it the prospect that all debt would soon be eliminated, but not until that was done would any new scheme involving considerable expenditure be embarked upon.

Minor improvements were carried out, including provision of facilities for the OTC in the cellars on the east side of the school. First, in 1926, came the installation of a sand table, twenty feet by ten, in the basement under Room D. Its purpose was to give members of

Off to Gailes! The OTC at St Enoch Station in 1927

the Contingent greater familiarity with the use of ground and with the working out of tactical schemes. Then, two years later, the armoury was moved to the basement from the old kitchen on the top floor. At the beginning of 1928, command of the Corps changed hands, on the retirement from the post of Major Reid. He was succeeded in command by Paul Mallam.

The Corps Entertainment, 1927

Although the Board felt that they could not embark on any major projects, they did redecorate the main hall right up to cupola level in 1931 : a light buff took the place of the previous dull maroon. More signficantly, they took the chance when offered it of buying 2 Colebrooke Terrace. The house came into the school's hands in January 1930 and, because the Governors had no immediate use for it, it was let. Three months later 4 Colebrooke Terrace was also acquired. It, too, was let.

The Academy bought 2 Colebrooke Terrace from one of its former pupils, William Beckett, who had been at the school between 1891 and 1900, ending up as Captain of the Second XV and a prize-winning swimmer. His mother had continued to live in the family home until her death in September 1929.

Academy boys of the late twenties undoubtedly had more opportunities than those of the eighteen-eighties and nineties. Some would simply have enjoyed inter-class sports in the playground. Others, in the First Latin class of summer 1929, would have enjoyed their trip to Edinburgh, which they explored from the Castle to the Zoo. Others still would have relished the opportunities offered by the Hill Climbing Club which was started the same year : the first target, in May, was the Cobbler, with some members of the party going on to Ben Ime.

During the Easter holidays of 1929 a still more adventurous excursion took place. For the first time in the school's history, a party of boys and staff travelled abroad. Under the

The Academy party visiting Heidelberg Castle in April 1931

leadership of Cyril Engledow 62 boys and four of his colleagues went first to Bruges and then to Paris. In 1930 a party visited the Loire and at Easter 1931 Mainz.

Another important development began with a meeting in Room D on 21 January 1930 called by Ben Aston to discuss the setting up of a Shakespearean Society. Seventeen boys attended and discussed first the society's name. The first proposal was 'The Mermaid Tavern Club', but 'The Globe Players' was preferred. Six days later the Players met again and Aston read Hamlet's instructions to the players which members of the society were urged to follow. Then members of the Fifth Class gave a reading of the ghost scene from *Macbeth* followed by the sleep-walking scene : and so the play-reading activities of the Players began. At the end of the following meeting it was agreed that a whole play should be read, and *Twelfth Night* was selected. The first four acts were read at the end of February and on 11 March the decision was taken to produce the play during the Summer Term.

Two performances of *Twelfth Night* were given, on 23 and 24 June 1930, with a cast of seventeen and an orchestra of two violins, a cello and a piano. Aston remembered rather ruefully having cast as Feste a boy whose voice was breaking. Paul Mallam put together an enlarged stage, Mrs Aston made a 'splendid background of curtains' and Herbert Sowrey, a new science master, arranged the lighting effects. The later recollections of one participant suggested that the whole effect was actually rather makeshift : he remembered that the Players 'commandeered the dining hall tables and arranged them with as few undulations as possible into a stage; they caused seven naked electric bulbs to be set above their heads and seven more at their feet, draped the cheapest of curtains from the roof beams, borrowed a valuable chair and table from unsuspecting friends, struggled into hired costumes and were ready'.

The choice of play in 1931 was the First Part of *Henry IV*, followed in 1932 by

Macbeth which would 'long be remembered for its thrills and horrors'. Dick Smith, who played the Third Witch, had vivid memories of one moment of excitement on the first night. The cast changed into their costumes in one of the Laboratories and then made their way along the semi-permanent corridor which had recently been put up between the Science Building and the west door of the Dining Hall. There, dressed in their long heavy black gowns, with pointed witches' hats and pointed black shoes, they waited to go on. The School Captain, Jimmy Risk, had been cast as the First Witch. All went well until the Cauldron Scene in Act IV : to give flashes of real fire matching the chanting of the witches some chemicals had been put in the brazier beneath the cauldron. 'Unfortunately the fire blazed up higher than we had expected and caught the trailing draperies of Jimmy Risk's gown. In a matter of seconds he fell on the stage, smothering and extinguishing the flames. Mr Aston came on stage from the Prompt Box, called in a loud voice, "My God! James!" and left the stage again. My own father leapt on to the stage, ready to rescue me, and returned to his place in the audience. We witches resumed our interrupted dance and the play continued without a line being left unspoken. We did not again have real fire beneath the cauldron.'

In 1933 the Globe Players put on *A Midsummer Night's Dream* and Miss Wilson was offered special thanks for training the fairies – 'such raw material' – to dance. Miss Wilson had also helped in December 1931 when Paul Mallam had produced *H M S Pinafore* which that year, with ladies in the cast, replaced the usual OTC entertainment.

These events took place in the Dining Hall. So, too, did the Supper and Reunion to which each December the Rector invited boys leaving from the Seventh Class, winners of Leaving Certificates, the First XV, the First XI and the shooting VIII. 'You are particularly requested to bring your music, if you sing or play.'

The OTC had a Field Day each summer. The boys came to school in full uniform : Glengarry bonnet, high-necked brass-buttoned tunic, belt and webbing, Mackenzie tartan kilt with sporran, green hose-tops with red flashes, and spats.

'Thus equipped, we paraded in the playground after Prayers and headed by the pipes and drums of the band marched off down Colebrooke Street, across Great Western Road, into Otago Street and passing behind Caledonian Mansions we filed down the steps on to the city-bound platform of Kelvinbridge station. Soon there burst out of the tunnel-mouth a long train of the most ancient and filthy carriages headed by an even more ancient and filthy tank engine. This was our "military special" and in it we travelled to Cambuslang station. There we formed up again and commenced our long journey to Dechmont ranges.

'The march was uphill all the way, and the distance was between two and three miles. At first the Pipe Band played us along valiantly, but presently we were reduced to the tap-tap-tap of a single kettledrum.

'When we reached our destination there was a delay to allow the defenders time to "dig themselves in", but then the mock battle began. Ours was the attacking force and we had to make a frontal attack, uphill, to capture a hilltop position held by B Company. All was noise, smoke and confusion, and hard running, partly in a crouching position, alternated with lying prone or worming one's way forward on one's stomach, then taking aim and firing uphill at the defenders.

'Some must have been named by the umpires as casualties, but the section of which I was a member was eventually pronounced to have reached its objective. The battle was declared to be over and we drank from our flasks and sat on the ground in the shelter of a clump of trees to eat whatever provisions we had brought with us in our haversacks. Very soon afterwards the homeward march was begun and our grubby train transported us back to Kelvinbridge. There we formed up once again, and marched the short distance to the school, where we were dismissed.'

In April 1930 the *Daily Record* carried an article on the Academy in a series on 'Famous Scottish Schools'. The Rector preserved the cutting, but it is difficult to know what he or the Governors would really have thought of the piece. In the writer's time 'if two small boys were found fighting by a Prefect he would take them up to the gymnasium and give each of them a pair of boxing gloves and with him as referee let them settle their quarrel. The aim of the education here is to turn out sportsmen in every sense of the word. The Academy places more importance on character formation than acquiring book knowledge, and it is for this reason that so much importance is attached to sport, which helps the pupils for all time "to play the game"'.

Whether or not the Academy placed more importance on character formation than acquiring book knowledge, the Governors were pleased to learn in April 1930 that the school had been bequeathed £3000 by Ronald Wallace Mowat to institute a scholarship associated with the names of his sons, Ronald Douglas Carlton

Mowat and Charles James Carlton Mowat, who had predeceased him. The Mowat Scholarship as then established was an award of £50 a year for three years. The following November the proposal was mooted that holders of the Mowat Scholarship should, if they proceeded to Oxford or Cambridge with a college award, be eligible for an additional £70 a year to be known as a Temple Scholarship in recognition of Edwin Temple's great services to the Academy.

When Her Majesty's Inspectors visited the Academy they, too, were ready to pay tribute to Temple's leadership. In 1929 it was recorded that he presided over the school's 'manifold activities with unabated vigour, enthusiasm and success'. To meet criticism of the way in which science was taught at the school – there were not enough science teachers and class sizes in science, ranging between 22 and 36, were excessive – a new science master was appointed.

In October 1928 rumours had circulated that Edwin Temple was about to resign. The Rector told the Governors that he felt it might be best if he did in fact retire, not because as he put it he wished 'to be laid upon the shelf' but from a desire for the welfare of the school. He was pressed to remain and replied that he would be glad to continue until he reached the age prescribed under the Super-annuation Scheme. On 15 November 1929, however, the Board met to consider a letter of resignation which they had received from the Rector. The Governors hoped that he would change his mind and remain at the Academy until August 1932, a month before his sixty-fifth birthday. Temple agreed to do so.

In April 1931 a committee was set up to take steps to appoint the next Rector of Glasgow Academy. By October 35 applications had been received and on 30 November in the Central Hotel four candidates were interviewed. The Committee's choice was Frank Roydon Richards, whose appointment was ratified by the Governors on 10 December 1931.

Richards, who was 32, was of course known to the Academy. He had left Christ's Hospital, Horsham, in 1917, joined the Royal Garrison Artillery Cadet School and then served in France, where he was injured. On demobilisation he entered Queen's College, Oxford, where he took a First in Honour Moderations and a Second in Greats, graduating also as Bachelor of Music in 1925. He played for the College XV and XI. He joined the Academy in September 1922 but left at Easter 1924 to become Sixth Form Classics tutor at Christ's Hospital. There he remained until in July 1928 he became Headmaster of Bridlington School. It was now arranged that he would return to the Academy as the school's fourth Rector on 1 April 1932.

A committee decided that Temple's retirement should be marked by asking him to sit for his portrait. Any money left over would be used to obtain personal gifts for him and for Mrs Temple and subscriptions of up to one guinea were invited. The Governors intended to bid farewell to Dr and Mrs Temple at a luncheon on 23 March : but they were unable to do so.

Edwin Temple suffered a heart attack on Wednesday 16 March 1932 and died at midday two days later. Every boy in the school except the young ones of the First and Second English attended his funeral in St Mary's Cathedral on Monday 21 March. The school's own commemoration of their Rector was held in the Dining Hall the following Wednesday.

Edwin Temple did much else, quietly and modestly. In January 1931 one of those whom he had helped sent from Helmsdale in Sutherland a letter of earnest thanks : 'When I first met you, I was in need of a helping hand and you (under Providence) held out yours generously and continuously till I achieved the great ambition of my life – to give all my family a University education'.

After his death an impartial observer – one of Her Majesty's Inspectors – paid public tribute to the fact that 'for thirty three years he had filled the Rector's chair with distinction and his rich humanity had won honour and affection from all who knew him. To die in harness would have seemed no bad thing to one who spared others but never spared himself'.

During his last month at the Academy, Temple gave to each pupil in the school a copy of *A Boy's Prayer* :

Oh God!
Give me clean hands, clean words, and
clean thoughts;
Help me to stand for the hard right against
the easy wrong;
Save me from habits that harm;
Teach me to work as hard and play as fair
in Thy sight alone as if all the world saw;
Forgive me when I am unkind, and help me to
forgive those who are unkind to me;
Keep me ready to help others at some cost to myself;
Send me chances to do a little good every day,
and so grow more like Christ.

The last words that Edwin Temple was heard to speak were 'A little rest'. His grave at Comrie describes him simply and accurately as 'A workman that needeth not to be ashamed'.

Edwin Temple was greatly loved. He was missed by his colleagues and he was missed by his pupils. He was the kindly man to whom in February 1930 over thirty boys had written a letter which he had kept : 'Dear Sir, Would you be good enough to permit our having a skating half-holiday'.

Edwin Temple knew that Academy families were privileged and set amongst those who were not privileged. For several years he sent a circular each autumn to the mothers of Academy boys, appealing for their sons' cast-off clothes and boots, which he then passed on to the headmasters of local schools. He relied upon, and obtained, a generous response.

1932-1939

Roydon Richards

The portrait of Edwin Temple was painted by James B Anderson ARSA and unveiled on 18 June 1932. The following spring the Governors decided that it should be hung on the second floor, facing the War Memorial Panels.

Soon after he returned to Glasgow, Temple's successor made it clear that his Rectorship would bring changes. 'What work is done, what games are played, are matters of tradition, and change in them is not to be sought, for it might mean forgetfulness of the ideals to which they are means. But *how* the work is done, *how* the games are arranged, those are questions of organisation, in which experiments *are* helpful from time to time as every school develops. Yet, ironically enough, such changes in petty detail sometimes attract more criticism than the most revolutionary changes in fundamentals.'

The changes began even before Richards had been introduced to the school on 12 April 1932 and had asked 'for a friendly judgement on any changes I might think it desirable to make' : in January he had told the Governors that he would wish to appoint new masters. New masters would require rooms to teach in, and the tenants of 2 and 4 Colebrooke Terrace were therefore given notice that they would have to leave the houses.

As soon as Richards arrived he appointed Miss Hilda Sloan as his Secretary and bought for her use a typewriter, a table and a duplicator. At first her office was in what had been the Ladies' Room in 1 Colebrooke Terrace but by the following autumn she was installed in Room B, formerly the home of Second English B and opposite the Rector's own room. In 1939 an assistant secretary began to work in the afternoons.

Richards had many other plans. No time was lost in changing Morning Prayers by

Frank Roydon Richards with a group of prefects

moving them to the Well and introducing a hymn : 'the general singing was hearty'. The Captain of the School signalled for silence by blowing a whistle and the lesson was read by one of the prefects, taking it in turn week by week. In 1936 copies of the *Public School Hymn Book* were obtained for the use of the Choir, which soon began to lead the singing at the assembly : 'we look forward to the day when the whole school may be singing in four-part harmony'. On Armistice Day the two minutes' silence was observed in a more formal fashion : the School assembled in the Well for an address from the Rector, a hymn, the sounding of the Last Post and the Rouse, and the rolling of drums. In 1933 Armistice Day fell on a Saturday, but the pause and silence were observed on the fields at Anniesland 'where once the heroic dead were wont to play'.

The Prize Giving, too, was altered : the Rector had written, in Latin, a School Song which in 1932 was 'rendered by the school and some of the audience'. In 1933 the ceremony took place for the first time in St Andrew's Hall and as well as Richards' *Carmen* the Battle Hymn of the Republic was sung. In 1933, too, on 16 June, the Commemoration Service was held for the first time in the Cathedral. The OTC paraded in Cathedral Square and marched into the Cathedral, and the staff entered in procession. The service was conducted by the Rector and the sermon was preached by the Very Revd Charles Warr, Minister of St Giles', Edinburgh, Dean of the Thistle and Dean of the Chapel Royal. Warr, who had been at the Academy between 1904 and 1910, became an Honorary Governor of his old school the following year.

From an etching by Wilfred C Appleby

The four original Houses were abolished and replaced by six new ones, temporarily named A, B, C, D, E and F. All boys above Second Latin were included in the Houses, each of which had the use of a classroom equipped with periodicals and even gramophones and ping-pong tables. By June 1933 proper names had been chosen : Morrison, Arthur, Temple, Clyde, Kelvin and Albany. Two honoured past Rectors, a third commemorated the distinguished Academical family of Arthurs, a fourth recognised the close links there had been with the Albany Academy and the remaining two

recognised Glasgow's rivers, one of which flowed past the school. The following winter at least one House, Temple, organised a 'House Night', with competitions, a cinema show and a treasure hunt, altogether 'a jolly evening' organised by the House Monitors.

Games also changed. The Games Committee was reconstituted so as to include more representation from masters, to 'eliminate the element of extreme youth', to secure house representation and to dissociate if necessary the office of School Captain and Captain of Football. Rugby was reorganised so that fewer school teams were fielded and more boys took part in House Matches. A School Sixty was selected – four XVs – which were divided into two 'practices'. Each House then selected two XVs from the remaining boys to take part in a league competition. When that was over, the School Sixty could be included in the house teams for a knock-out competition. After two seasons House matches were reduced somewhat and rugby was practised in 'Clubs', each under a master assisted by a member of the First XV.

And, inevitably, the academic life of the school changed too. Richards had set out some of his beliefs during his first Prize Giving address. He deplored the attitude of those who urged that what a commercial community needed was a vocational and utilitarian educa-tion : he believed strongly in the value of a high standard of scholarship, for brilliance at the top tended to raise the level of ambition in a school, not only of the clever boy but of the moderate boy.

Certain changes were made for the Session 1932/33, mainly in preparation for a more extensive overhaul the following year. Principally, First Latin no longer started Latin and French but followed a curriculum similar to the Preparatory School's. Each Block, as Richards called the year groups, consisted of about 90 boys and a system of setting was introduced so that in each of the more important subjects there were three or four divisions, the grading being carried out separately, subject by subject. In Block Three, choices were made. A boy could either continue with Latin or take Geography and Commercial Subjects. He could also opt for Greek or German or Science with Art. This combination of options was intended to supply the right kind of training for the various types of mind – classical, modern linguistic, scientific and 'the type which needs to combine elementary commercial work with the other subjects'. The Seventh Class was intended for the special training of boys for University Bursary and Scholarship Examinations.

By the beginning of the following session 1 and 2 Colebrooke Terrace had been reconstructed and provided enough classrooms to house the existing Preparatory Department together with a new class of five year olds. The old system of naming the classes was swept away. The new class became Prep 1, what had been First English Junior became Prep 2 and so on. The class which had been known as First Latin in the Senior School became the senior class of the Preparatory School but stayed in the main building : it was called not Prep 6 but Transitus 'as befits their station in the school'. Second Latin became the First Form in the Senior School – and this meant that what had been the Seventh Class now became the Sixth Form, a genuine post-Certificate class 'in the accepted sense of the word Sixth Form'.

The overdraft finally having been cleared, it was agreed in October 1932 that the Trust would purchase 3 Colebrooke Terrace. The Governors declined, however, to take over No 13, presumably on the grounds that it was too far from the houses which the school already owned. More than sixty years later their successors rather rue the day when the house was allowed to slip from the Academy's grasp : it and No 14 next to it are the only two houses in the Terrace which have yet to come into the ownership of the Trust.

Houses 3 and 4 were to accommodate the library, some classrooms, a music room and common rooms for the masters, mistresses and prefects. The Rector had set aside the first floor front room of No 4 for the library. In the past, he maintained, the Academy library had aimed only to help a few boys at the top of the school, whose reputation for scholarship was already well established. What he wanted to see was 'a room to attract everyone and to be a cultural centre radiating a definite influence', a library adequate to house 4000 books.

When the Preparatory School moved into its new home, Miss Wilson, who had joined the Academy in 1918, was formally appointed Head Mistress. New appointments to her staff included Miss Kate Gentles, sister of Miss Olga Gentles, niece of Miss McCallum – and sister of three Academicals.

There were changes on the staff of the Senior School, too, and the Rector signified his belief in the value of music as a subject in the curriculum by appointing Eric Coningsby to teach it. A Musical Society was formed, with an orchestra and a choir, and £20 was allocated for the purchase of a gramophone, a stand and a stock of records. The first School Concert was given on two evenings in May 1933; the second, a year later, ended 'with some jolly sea-shanties in which the audience joined'.

The gramophone made it possible for records to be used in the teaching of French, too : a course of recordings had been presented in March 1933. New equipment was also beginning to be used elsewhere : the 'cinematograph projector' which had been acquired in 1931 had been used the following summer to show two films in the Science Building and 'had illustrated a new departure in the science teaching' In 1936 the London Branch of the Academical Club presented two epidiascopes to the School, one for use in the Senior School, the other for the Prep School.

Several links with the nineteenth century were broken by retirement or death in the mid thirties.

In June 1933 John Dunlop intimated his retiral after 38 years without a single day off for illness. A shy and retiring man, who had trained in the Glasgow School of Art, he had led the Photographic Club and during the War had held a commission in the OTC. Within four years he had died, to be remembered as 'a craftsman, a golfer, a bowler, a motorist' and a dedicated church worker.

George Moffat died at Helensburgh on the last Sunday of the Easter holidays in 1934. Educated at George Watson's College and Edinburgh University, he had taught briefly at Dumfries Academy before coming to the Academy in 1897, where he succeeded James Wood in December 1912 as Head Mathematical Master.

'Geordie' Moffat was remembered for fluent, sound, rapid teaching, for the fact that he made little use of textbooks and for the fact that he set no homework. He was remembered too for his dryly humorous voice and 'a certain acidity of humour' : he was reckoned to be both 'wonderfully patient' and 'deadly sarcastic'. He read widely, particularly in history, theology and philosophy, and had readily given assistance with the new arrangements for the school library. His colleagues remembered that there was never a story that he could not cap : but they reflected, too, that for the second time in little more than twenty years their senior mathematical colleague had been taken from them by the 'sudden visitation of death'.

Nathaniel Clapton, Mathematical Master in Watford Grammar School, was appointed in Moffat's place.

Andrew Robertson retired as Head Classical Master at the end of the session in 1934. He had joined in 1898, having followed his time at Kilmarnock Academy and Glasgow University with four years' teaching at Ayr Academy, and had succeeded William Robertson as Head of the Department in 1921. He used to remark that he had inherited Donald Morrison's classroom and tawse and had 'stuck to both of them for 36 years'. Robertson was a tall man – 'Lanky Bob' to distinguish him from 'Big Bob' – and his face was 'such as one might have expected to see stamped on a coin of ancient Rome'. He was an austere man and a man of rigid routine.

Andrew Robertson

Each boy in turn would be called to the desk in front of Robertson's chair. Sitting there, the pupil would first read the Latin and then offer a translation which Robertson, who was deaf, would receive through a battery microphone held out to the speaker and connected by a cord to a disc which he held to his ear. If a mistake was made, Robertson would invariably say 'Repeat without alteration' and on hearing the repetition would send the guilty boy's book flying away to the wall. When eventually the correct answer was supplied by one of the boys described by Robertson as 'a worker', his face would shine with approval, he would say 'Of course, yes' and he would throw one more shaft of searing scorn at the culprit, reinforced with the words 'Go home and work'. Those who were not in favour were dubbed 'the granite section'.

Just as boys remembered William Robertson's approach to school in the mornings,

others remembered Andrew Robertson 'leaving school each day in his raincoat and velour hat, carrying his battered attaché case on his way to the Pollokshields tram'. They thought of him as a lonely man, even though he had an Academical son, a doctor, and even though he could occasionally be persuaded to talk about golf, an abiding passion.

One Academy tradition which Robertson had maintained was the conference with a colleague outside the classroom between periods. Years before, he had from time to time joined in the talk outside James Wood's room. Latterly the meeting had moved to the opposite corner of the building where Robertson from Room O met 'Foxy' Clark from Room M, a Classical colleague who in 1932 had gone as Rector to Kelvinside Academy.

Robertson was succeeded by Frank Reid, his colleague since 1908, who in turn was succeeded as master in charge of Athletics by George Preston.

George Barrie did not belong to the Academy of the nineteenth century, in which his cousin Alexander Ogilvie Barrie had taught, but he had nevertheless worked at the school for over thirty years before he retired in 1936. Proud of his kinship with the author of *Peter Pan*, he had been born in Kirriemuir and had attended both the Grammar School and the University in Aberdeen before, like George Moffat, beginning his teaching career at Dumfries Academy. He moved for just a few months in 1903 to Ardrossan Academy before joining Glasgow Academy where he succeeded Louis Barbé as Head of the Department in 1918. For many years he had spent practically every holiday attending courses for foreigners at French or German universities or in travel with a view to developing and perfecting his languages, though at least one of his pupils remarked that 'he spoke French slowly and with a broad Angus accent so that when one heard a Frenchman use his native tongue the sounds were, so to speak, double Dutch'. Christopher Varley was appointed as Head of the Modern Languages Department in place of Barrie, who died after only two years' retirement.

Miss Marion Brown was as well known to Academy boys as any member of the teaching staff when she retired from the Tuck Shop in October 1935. She would miss 'the daily inrush of the famished at the end of morning school, the time-honoured salute to a breakage, the more subdued 10 o'clock queue of Form 1, and the occasional casualties whom she kept warm by the fireside before they were sent home'. Within a year, her domain had been transformed as part of considerable work undertaken during the summer of 1936. A new classroom was constructed between Room C and Room D by roofing over part of the cloak room area in the Well and moving the staircase to one side. At the northern end of the Well a new office was provided for the Janitor and a platform from which Prayers could be conducted. The Luncheon Bar (as it was officially known) was

moved to the south east corner, where 'Chocolate Addicts, Doughnut Dabblers, Soup-Absorbers and Bibbers of Bourn-Vita could conduct their devotions aloof from curious eyes'.

The more formal provision of food continued in the Dining Hall, the patrons of which were from time to time consulted about their preferences. Lentil soup and Scotch Broth were favourite soups, sausage and chips consistently the most popular main course. The puddings that were especially enjoyed included chocolate boats, fruit salad, banana custard and vanilla cream. Haricot of mutton and tapioca found few enthusiasts.

There can have been scarcely a single area of school life into which change was not introduced during Roydon Richards' first year or two as Rector of the Academy. He started a system of detention for boys whose work or conduct was unsatisfactory and paid Paul Mallam £15 to supervise it. He devised schemes for keeping boys' property safe, adding lids and fasteners to lockers and locks to the new desks with lids and storage space which he was also gradually introducing. He started a school register, since there was no record of boys attending the school. He designed forms – for ascertaining from staff their qualifications and experience, for admission to the Academy and for application for fee rebates.

Up to £1000 was being allowed each year in fee reductions, largely 50% rebates granted to the sons of ministers or teachers, apparently without any reference to the parents' financial circumstances. The Governors wished to establish a series of principles to govern the future allocation of rebates, which they hoped to see restricted to something over £800. Certain financial guidelines were drawn up and categories were established of boys to whom a rebate would be awarded if certain financial conditions were also satisfied : the father might be an old Academy boy or unable to pay the full fee 'owing to active service with H M Forces, self dedication to one of the less remunerative professions or causes beyond his personal control'; the boy might have a brother in the school; the applicant might be a widow or the Rector might for some other reason especially wish the boy to be enrolled. Masters in the school had from the earliest days had their sons educated free of charge and this continued.

The appearance of the *Chronicle* also changed, for in 1933 it was given a new cover design based on the front door of the school but seen very much as an interim measure. There were high hopes that before long the design would be heraldic, for a committee had been appointed soon after Richards became Rector, to look into the possibility that the Trust might be granted the right to bear arms.

On 26 May 1937 there were delivered at the Academy Letters Patent bearing the seal of the Lord Lyon King of Arms, granting that right. The design adopted had been put forward by Wallace Orr, an Academical who in 1935 had joined the staff as Art Master. On a quartered shield the City of Glasgow was represented by the symbols of St Mungo and Scotland by her Lion. The Torch of Learning was included as an appropriate symbol for a school and the Crosses of Sacrifice were chosen to recall what was then described as 'the perpetual mainspring of the school, the spirit of sacrifice and service' and in particular the fields of Flanders and France. The familiar school colours were heraldically represented as Azure and Argent, but for the first time a definite school motto was adopted.

'Keep Faith' was chosen, the suggestion of Ben Aston, but turned into Latin as 'Serva Fidem' with the verb deliberately cast in the singular to appeal more forcefully to members of the Academy as individuals.

Perhaps unfortunately, for both would have been appropriate, neither arms nor motto was available when in 1933 the Roll of Honour was published in its final form, recording details of service undertaken and casualties sustained by Academy boys during the war. The first edition, which had owed so much to the work of Peter Couper, had been published in October 1918 and had necessarily been incomplete. Now it was possible to make a permanent record of the part which Academy boys had played.

The establishment of the War Memorial Trust had of course been the principal step taken to honour the Academical dead. Its inception had been the idea of Peter Rintoul, who died in 1933, just as the Board took stock of what the Trust had achieved since he brought it into being. The Governors had always endeavoured to let the Rector feel that they were solidly behind him in every step which he saw fit to take for raising the educational status of the school. Since the war they had reduced debt by £5000, provided £1800 for scholarships and spent over £27000 on projects such as the Jordanhill Ground, the external War Memorial, the new Dining Hall, installation of electric lighting and new heating and purchasing and altering the four houses in Colebrooke Terrace.

Much remained to be done. Their vision of the future still included a new building at Kelvinbridge – a school hall, a new dining hall and kitchen, a gymnasium and workshops – and a pavilion at New Anniesland. Conscious that the War Memorial Scholarship and the Temple Scholarship were funded from the revenue of the Trust, they hoped to establish a capital fund for scholarships, as there was for the Mowat Scholarship. The Governors hoped that friends might be able to help and enable the School to develop and more than maintain the traditions it had already established.

Among those traditions was a strong OTC, where change was also in the air. The Governors had heard in 1931 that a grant would no longer be made for boys under 15 and that rifles and other equipment used by them would also be withdrawn. A Cadet Corps for boys aged 13 to 15 was therefore formed : its affiliation to the 5th Battalion Highland Light Infantry renewed a link which had been broken in 1908. Paul Mallam, who had been awarded the OBE in the King's Birthday Honours of 1933, retired as Officer Commanding the OTC early the following year and took responsibility for the new Cadet Corps. He was succeeded in command of the OTC by Frank Batchelor, under whom the Shooting VIII had been doing well at Bisley, securing fourth place in the Ashburton in 1931 and winning the Brock Shield in 1931 and the Strathcona Shield in 1933. Batchelor found the financial responsibilities of running the OTC particularly onerous, resigned his command after some two years and was succeeded by Engledow.

The Academy's team at Bisley in 1931, Paul Mallam to the left and Frank Batchelor to the right

Mallam was assisted with the Cadet Corps by A S Kelly, whom the Rector had recently appointed to teach Classics. He 'needed to do some teaching for three years before becoming an Inspector', was currently a Professor's Assistant at the University, having a Double First at Oxford and was to be paid a specially enhanced salary. Another new appointment was that of R H Kelley who took a special interest in the teaching of Geography, an area of the curriculum identified by the Rector as in need of improvement. He was allowed to spend £25 on a globe, a new stock of wall maps, storage for Ordnance Survey maps and a set of meteorological instruments and the Rector was also authorised to hire 'conveyances' to take Geography candidates into the country two or three times a year for practical work in connection with the Leaving Certificate examination. To accommodate Kelley, what had been the Writing Master's 'beautiful broad domain' was divided in 1932 by a movable partition, the two resulting rooms being known as L and LL. As well as Geography, special attention was paid to the improvement of facilities for German and Higher Science, including the equipment of a room in Colebrooke Terrace for instruction in mechanics. For the first time candidates were presented in the Leaving Certificate in Geography and Music.

Richards had made clear from the outset his intention to achieve the highest academic standards and success was soon achieved. In 1933 Douglas Bailey became the first Academy boy for many years to come top in the Glasgow Bursary Competition. Small divisions of the Sixth Form were established, specialising in scholarship work for Oxford and Cambridge, at first in Classics and History and later in Mathematics. This policy first bore fruit in 1934 when J M Hunter won an Open Exhibition at Christ's College, Cambridge, and between 1934 and 1938 eleven open scholarships or exhibitions with an annual value of £790 were awarded at Oxford or Cambridge to Academy boys, in Classics, Mathematics and History.

In December 1938 it was decided that the Academical Club Prize should be replaced by six prizes, in English, Latin, Greek, Modern Languages, Mathematics and Science and that there should no longer be a Dux of the Academy. Roydon Richards prepared a Latin inscription to be added to the Dux Boards explaining that the award had ceased. Deciding who should be Dux had been straightforward when all the boys who stayed at school for a year after gaining their Leaving Certificates had done the same work but now that boys were staying on as a matter of course for two or even three years and each studying different subjects it was impossible to achieve a common measure of their ability.

The Governors discussed the arrangements for the Academy's scholarships during 1934 and expressed the conviction that only the Mowat Scholarship should be tenable at a Scottish University. The War Memorial and Temple Scholarships should be awarded only to boys whose intention was to proceed to Oxford or Cambridge.

By the autumn of 1934 Richards had arranged that the Academy should be included in the list of schools eligible for representation on the Headmasters' Conference and regarded as a Public School for the purpose of, for example, inclusion in the Public Schools' Year Book. By the end of 1935 he had been elected to membership of the Headmasters' Conference.

Excellent provision was clearly being made at the Academy for the best scholars, but a warning note was sounded by HMI in 1937 : 'perhaps in certain directions more might be done in the interests of the less able boy'.

The emphasis under the new régime was not, of course, exclusively on the work of the classroom. Societies continued to flourish : in October 1933, for example, the Scientific Society visited Blochairn Ironworks and the Photographic Society was revived. The Globe Players tackled *Hamlet* in 1935. A Sixth Form literary and philosophical society, the Humanists, was founded in the autumn of that year. Its members met once a week in the Masters' Room ('out of hours of course') to hear lectures on, for example, art, archaeology and geology, and to discuss what they had heard. 'To speculate even idly on one's own place in the whole universe is a chastening experience.'

A group of boys and masters
at the summit of The Cobbler, May 1935

Games, too, maintained their important place in the scheme of things. In June 1933 the Academy's annual grant to the Club was further increased, in recognition of the fact that having the new ground involved the Club in paying wages to an additional groundsman and to an extra man during the summer. A new cricket pitch had been laid at Anniesland that spring. Another move made in the hope that it would improve the cricket was to hold the Sports on 29 March 1934, immediately after school had finished for Easter. The weather did not favour such an arrangement and the experiment lasted only two years.

There were successes in rugby. Captained by J R Henderson, the First XV of 1935/36, like that of 1900/01, was undefeated by a school side. Nevertheless, it was felt desirable to revise the arrangements for afternoon games at Anniesland. Junior games had largely taken place after school, with Wednesday a 'semi half holiday' to cater for senior games, but from September 1935 matters were rearranged to allow senior pupils between the Third and the Sixth Forms to play on Tuesday afternoons, when the Second Form would also play if ground was available. Boys between Prep Three and the First Form would play on Thursdays. The intention was that junior games would be able to continue throughout the winter and not stop in November as they had done in the past.

These and many other changes must have struck home particularly to R C Wylie, an Academical, who in 1934 was appointed to teach Classics in place of the Revd John Hutcheson Bolton who had died on 3 September. Bolton had arranged chamber concerts for the Debating Society, conducted the first Gilbert and Sullivan production in the Academy and looked after the library. An article in the *Chronicle* soon after Wylie's appointment contrasted the Academy in which he was a master with the Academy which he had known as a boy a quarter of a century earlier. Then there had been 22 staff; in June 1935 there were 33 and in September there would be 36, of whom 7 would be ladies. (Sixty years later, there were 80 members of the teaching staff, 36 men and 44 women.) The three extra staff in 1935 were to strengthen the Mathematics Department, to teach in Transitus and to make possible the establishment of a second Prep 1 class, though in the event that was not needed for some while. The Rector noted that the main centre of recruitment to the Academy had shifted to the lowest classes of the Preparatory School. In March 1937 he was given permission to admit to Prep 1 boys who would reach the age of five by the end of the year in which they entered.

The school continued to attract large numbers of pupils, though careful arrangement of the classes meant that in 1934 the average number in each was just over 27 and the highest number in any was 35 in IIIA. In October 1934 there were 793 on the roll; by the end of the session in 1937 the total had risen to 810. Strength in numbers made judicious improvements possible, from time to time. A fence still divided the south playground in two : it was repaired in 1933. The state of the playground itself gave cause to complaints that it was dusty in dry weather and muddy in damp and consideration was given to laying tarmacadam. There must also have been complaints about the lack of facilities for washing hands, for in 1934 the Governors addressed the fact that neither boys nor masters had access to hot water. Among the larger items of expenditure came at last the installation of the Thermotank system for which Coleman Smith had asked almost as soon as he arrived at the school. The ventilation of the rooms on the top floor of the school was greatly improved, though the system was not entirely silent in operation and gave rise to a distinctive hum which was apt to puzzle visitors making their way for the first time to that remote region of the building.

The Rector meticulously consulted the Governors about all sorts of expenditure – £40 on a piano since none of the three in the school was satisfactory; on a safe; on thirteen new fire extinguishers since the number available was far too small; on furnishings for the new common room for staff in Colebrooke Terrace, for which he was instructed to enquire in a sale room. When in March 1939 Richards asked for a vacuum cleaner the Finance Committee did not think there were enough carpets in the school to warrant purchase of a new one, so he was told to endeavour to get a satisfactory reconditioned machine : if that failed he could get a new one 'of any first class make'.

The Rector even managed to control the flow of traffic outside the school. In October 1936 it was on his initiative that because of congestion in Colebrooke Street all wheeled traffic was asked to approach the Academy via Belmont Street and Colebrooke Place and to leave via Colebrooke Street. Additionally, a police officer would be on point duty at the junction of Colebrooke Street with Great Western Road at times when boys were leaving in the afternoons.

In Roydon Richards the Governors knew that, in the words of HMI, they had a man who while 'seeking to retain and enhance all that is good in the old traditions is sparing no pains to do full justice to modern demands'. Some of them were probably among those grateful for the English version of his school song which he offered in June 1935.

National events affected the Academy from time to time. The school celebrated the Silver Jubilee of King George V on Monday 6 May 1935. After his death, the Rector addressed the Upper School and Transitus on the lessons to be learned from his life and example, and the school was closed on the day of his funeral. On 22 January 1936 loudspeakers were installed in the Well for the Proclamation of King Edward VIII. 'Reception was excellent.' There was of course no coronation of Edward VIII but for the Coronation of King George VI and Queen Elizabeth the Preparatory School was gaily and tastefully decorated with bunting by the Janitor and the Senior School was floodlit. A party

went on the Corporation three day cruise to the Western Isles on the *Tuscania* and every boy received a souvenir box of chocolates. There was a single day's holiday on 12 May 1937 but leave of absence was given to boys 'whose parents desired their presence with them in London'.

Other boys visited London under the school's own auspices. During the spring of 1936 a party went to see the international match at Twickenham, the Houses of Parliament, Madame Tussaud's, Selfridge's and Westminster Abbey. 'A news-reel cinema and a revue at night completed the programme of a full but highly enjoyable day.' The following year another party had an even more adventurous trip on board the *Lancastria* which cruised to the Azores, Madeira, Tenerife, Casablanca and Gibraltar.

Joseph Carr retired from teaching Writing and Commercial Subjects in June 1936, following a very serious breakdown in his health which was in fact to lead to his death within three years. He had been at the school since 1911 but it was a measure of how much things had changed that the very title Writing Master now seemed to speak of another age. 'The tradition of a Writing Room with its broad benches somehow reminiscent of the bank and counting house for which they were training belongs properly to the last century. Schools can nowadays afford little time for the long tots and copper-plate hand which were once the passport to the "City".'

The Rector wished the Governors to make special arrangements for Cyril Engledow's salary, so that his maximum should be £600 and not £500. He was forty years old, had been at the school for sixteen years and took his work seriously – he had recently been awarded a grant of £20 by the Governors to enable him to attend a refresher course for schoolmasters arranged by the Oxford University Department for the Training of Teachers. He was an excellent teacher and disciplinarian who had been disappointed not to be promoted to Head of Department when Barrie retired.

Further changes concerned Jack Coleman Smith. It was agreed in January 1937 that he should occupy the Boarding House rent free. It was then decided that in September that year he should become Games Master in full control of the organisation of all the school's athletic activities.

He had the necessary personality and enthusiasm to perform the duties efficiently and the post would be 'a natural adjunct' to his existing duties, in which he would be assisted by the appointment of an assistant, first a temporary man and then, in 1938, Henry U'ren.

'Internal gymnastics' would be available to many boys in both the Senior School and the Prep School and during the week at least one class would leave for Anniesland each afternoon at 2.30. Boys who did not want to go would remain at school until 3.10 for extra PT. Teams of various kinds continued to do well. In 1938 the Shooting VIII won the Brock Shield, the Strathcona Cup and the London Scottish Cup,

First XI, 1938

while the First XI won the Western District Schools' Championship. The First XV for their part were Western Schools champions the following season. Golf enjoyed a revival and in 1936 was placed on the same footing as tennis : colours were introduced in 1937, but without the right to wear any distinctive dress.

E P Kaye, Head of Science, retired in 1938 and the Rector appointed to succeed him A J Mee from Cheltenham Grammar School. It was an appointment that he felt constrained to

First XV, 1938/39 - Master-in-charge, Mr Coleman Smith; Captain, H M Black.

defend to the Governors : he had placed advertisements in the *Glasgow Herald* and the *Scotsman* and done everything he could to obtain a man of Scottish upbringing but of the 54 applications only six had been from Scotsmen.

Paul Mallam also left in 1938, to take over a preparatory school at Tunbridge, having made for himself since 1919 a 'place in the school life which was peculiarly his own'. His eldest son, Lionel, had died in his seventeenth year earlier in 1938 and Mallam's fortunes did not really improve, for the war and its aftermath made it cripplingly difficult to make a success of the new venture. When he died in 1957, a colleague recalled that even in the mid twenties he was 'already happily and delightfully out of date. There was no means of knowing how much he taught of the Maths he came here to teach – "retreated in a silent valley" he and Geordie could sort that out, amicably and courteously as ever. He added to the pattern of Academy history a thread of gay colour that we should have been the poorer without'.

On Mallam's departure, R C Wylie took over command of the Cadet Corps, to which changes were agreed in the summer of 1939.

Membership of the OTC and the Cadet Corps was not compulsory, but almost everyone did join, and for the past eight years boys in the Second Form had joined the Cadet Corps, parading at the same time as the OTC – between 1.50 and 2.30 on Fridays. It was really possible to offer boys in the Cadet Corps only formal squad and platoon drill, as there were neither the officers nor the rifles available to do more, and without variety it was difficult to keep the boys keen. Besides, they seemed to grow out of their uniforms very quickly at the age of thirteen. It was agreed that in future boys should enter the Corps when they reached the Third Form, and that the Second Form should have an extra period of school work, which the Rector earmarked for French.

The OTC was not affected by these changes. It had put on its Entertainment as usual at Christmas 1938, but it had a new home and a new producer. Harvey Sheppard had taken over from Mallam and audiences were directed to the Athenaeum. This had the advantages that a charge could be made for tickets, only one performance was necessary and the upheaval in the Dining Hall could be avoided. The growth in the school of 'the dramatic spirit' was hailed as one of the remarkable features of the past twenty years. 'Pre-1914 it may have been there, but it was latent. Nowadays the number of really capable and imaginative producers on the staff is astonishing and the number of boys capable of benefiting by (and enjoying) histrionic opportunities most refreshing.' Another familiar function found yet another new home : the Prize Giving was held in June 1939 in the King's Theatre, as St Andrew's Halls was being redecorated.

By June 1939, too, the Governors had taken important decisions about the future of the school, decisions which had their roots in a meeting almost three years before when those present had their minds focused by three pieces of information. Firstly, the Rector pointed out that the science equipment was not suitable for scholarship work. He wanted to spend £100 on improving it : the Governors sanctioned £50 in the meantime. Secondly, the flat roof of the school, covered with zinc or lead, was leaking. It had been treated for many years during the holidays by an application of one composition or another but year by year the condition was getting less satisfactory. Thirdly, the foundations of the building had recently been opened up during construction work and the timbers upon which they rested were found to be very seriously decayed. A more thorough examination was authorised.

With these quite legitimate calls for expenditure fresh in their minds, the Governors were inclined to pay serious attention to one of their number, David Brand, when he brought to their notice his view that despite very encouraging numbers of pupils in the school there seemed to be no prospect of accumulating a substantial surplus – and yet it was apparent that many things required to be done to bring the school buildings up to modern standards.

The Governors recalled what they had written in 1934 and early in 1937 set up a committee to see what could be done about raising funds to bring to fruition the projects which had been mentioned then – the school hall, a new dining hall, a new gymnasium, a pavilion at Anniesland and the endowment of scholarships.

In the meantime, further reports were obtained on the remedial work which had become necessary. It would cost almost £1300 to repair the school foundations and another £1000 to put the roof right. The roof work proved to be not as urgent as had been feared, but a new problem arose when the boiler became so unreliable that during the autumn the Janitor was having to attend as late as 11 pm to keep the school heated. A new boiler was installed over the Christmas holidays, soon to be followed by one in the Science Building.

The Governors looked at rough plans which had been prepared for a school hall, gymnasium and dining hall on the site of the existing Dining Hall and the vacant ground to the north and approached a number of people in connection with the Building Fund : about £10000 was promised.

In January 1939 costings were considered and it was agreed that the assembly hall was a less pressing part of the scheme than the rest. It was decided to go ahead first with the gymnasium for which there was a particular need as it was proving necessary to supplement the present gymnasium by holding classes in the Well. The Trust was in a position to meet expenditure of about £5000 from its own resources.

By June 1939, the Building Fund Appeal had been launched, in the hope that a further £60000 could be raised. It was confirmed that the plan was to build first a gymnasium which could in due course be doubled in size, so making it possible to do without the present gymnasium altogether. When the Inspectors visited the school that summer, they were told that it was the Governors' intention to have the gymnasium erected 'forthwith' : that was not to be, though a start was made on the foundations.

As early as October 1938 the Governors had considered the course of action to be followed if war broke out. The school would be closed for at least a week to let things settle. Trenches to act as air raid shelters should be dug in the playgrounds by boys of the OTC, north of the Dining Hall and in the tennis court area on the Great Western Road frontage. The following February it was confirmed that in the event of an emergency the Governors' intention was that the school should be carried on at Kelvinbridge. During the spring it was agreed to make the playground and classrooms available as far as possible to Territorial Forces, including the Royal Army Medical Corps and the 52nd Lowland Divisional Signals.

The Rector sent out a circular on the question of evacuation and by April 1939 had received replies from the parents of 500 boys of whom 402 would, it was said, remain at the school. There had been just three letters criticising the Governors' policy. Before the end of the summer term an experimental air raid shelter was dug by members of the OTC, a trench some fifty five feet long on the piece of ground by the flagstaff.

Some eighteen months before war broke out, the *Glasgow Herald* had taken stock of the Academy and what it stood for. A 'highly-placed official at Glasgow University' had spoken about the boys of the Academy shortly after the war of 1914 - 1918 : 'They are respect-ful but without servility; they know your place; they know their own; they do not attempt to trespass. Moreover many of them are natural leaders, and take the lead without any fuss and unnecessary parade of authority.'

Another war was about to put the qualities of Academy boys to a fresh test.

War again

M asters and former pupils of the Academy went off to fight, just as they had done a quarter of a century earlier. 1646 served in the Second War, of whom 168 died, the first of them Sergeant-Pilot Sidney Hallas Newbigging on 11 December 1939.

The first two decorations of the war were gazetted on 10 October 1939 : one of the two recipients was Flying Officer Andrew McPherson, who was awarded the Distinguished Flying Cross. He was killed at Maastricht Bridge on 12 May 1940.

Flying Officer Andrew McPherson, DFC

The war memorial of Sherbrooke St Gilbert's Parish Church bears the names of seven men, very different from one another but with three things in common : all seven were members of that church, all seven were Academicals and all seven died on active service.

David Buchanan was 21 years old and a Sergeant Pilot in the RAF when late in the war he was killed in India. He had also served in South Africa, the Middle East, Burma and Japan. Robert Forsyth was 41 years old when he died

in Burma during 1945. He was a Lieutenant-Colonel in the Royal Corps of Signals and had also served in France. John Glen was killed in action in the Orkney Islands in 1944. He was 36 years old and serving as a Lieutenant in the Royal Naval Volunteer Reserve. He was survived by his wife and two daughters.

John Haddow had entered the Royal Navy as a midshipman in January 1938 and had the rank of Lieutenant at the time of his death on flying exercises. He had been awarded the Distinguished Service Cross for gallant and distinguished service while serving with the Mediterranean Fleet in 1942. John MacDonald was 21 years old when his aircraft crashed into the sea off the Bahamas during the summer of 1945. He was a Pilot Officer in the Royal Air Force Volunteer Reserve.

William Reid joined the Black Watch at first but soon transferred to the Royal Engineers. On 19 October 1943, little more than two years after he left school, he was killed while serving in Italy. He was 20 years old. John White was 32 when he was killed on 21 July 1940. He was an Aircraftman First Class in the Royal Air Force, serving with Coastal Command.

Three men who had taught at the Academy were killed. Two, Richard Rivaz and Aubrey Swan, had gone elsewhere by the outbreak of war but Michael Page was still on the staff when he joined the Black Watch in 1940. He was mentioned in despatches twice while fighting in Italy and at Arnhem and it was at Arnhem in September 1944 that he was killed in action with the Parachute Regiment.

Any selection of names leaves unmentioned too many whose service is, however, recorded elsewhere for posterity. In 1951 a Roll of Service was published to ensure that 'the memory of these gallant men, "wearing their wounds like stars", will not be allowed to die'. Walter Barradell-Smith wrote in his preface to that Roll of Service that 'to reflect on the contribution of those listed – to try to realise the mere geographical distances covered during their service – the long, drab periods when they were separated from their homes and their native land – to visualise the endurance of toil, hunger, thirst, captivity, and too often death – these are the sparks to kindle realisation of united and selfless endeavour'.

The Governors met very soon after war had been declared and on 4 September 1939 resolved to maintain their original policy : the school would be carried on in the usual way as soon as suitable provision had been made for the safety of the boys and staff. The architect did not think that an air raid shelter could be built under the site of the new gymnasium and suggested instead a series of trenches fitted with a concrete framework : it would, however, take months for these to be delivered. The Governors decided to carry on at once with the construction on the tennis courts of trenches revetted with timbers and within two days contractors had been engaged to undertake the work. It was clear, though, that the school would have to remain closed for longer than the week or two envisaged when contingency plans were drawn up. Work on the gymnasium was suspended and the contractors were told to secure the foundations.

The Rector was convinced that the Governors' policy should be directed towards the safety of the boys and the preservation of numbers in the school. It was an urgent priority, therefore, to resume school work in some shape or form as soon as possible.

Richards felt that since there was already accommodation in the shelters for fifty boys the Fifth Form should start their work for the Leaving Certificate at Kelvinbridge with little delay. This was not permitted by the authorities, but groups of boys did meet for Leaving Certificate work in masters' houses.

Arrangements were then made for other classes to meet under appropriate members of staff in private houses : the First and Second Forms from mid September, first of all in Milngavie and Bearsden and later in Giffnock and Whitecraigs as well, and the Third and Fourth Forms in the West End later in the month so that by 21 September about half of the boys who had been expected to enrol at the beginning of term were being taught – something over four hundred pupils.

The Rector consulted the Solicitor General in Edinburgh and was told that although local authority schools could not at that stage reopen, the Academy could do so provided air raid protection was available. It was envisaged that accommodation for five hundred boys would be available in the shelters by early October, allowing a length of two feet to seat each boy at a cost of about £2 per head to be recovered from parents. It was therefore decided to reopen for Forms III, IV, V and VI on 2 October and for Forms II, I and Transitus soon afterwards. Classes in outlying districts for younger boys would be continued until the end of the first quarter, after which they would return to the Academy. Shelters for the Preparatory School would be dug between the Dining Hall and the bank of the Kelvin. Arrangements were also made for the trenches to be lit. By December the boys had had so much practice in evacuating the building that it was possible for everyone to get into the shelters within three minutes.

The Rector believed that the Academy was the first school of its type in Glasgow or Edinburgh to resume normal working and the enrolment did include a number of boys from the High School and other schools who had joined the Academy temporarily. By the end of September there were 474 pupils attending, which had risen by Christmas to 641 and by the end of the session to some 700, about 85% of the normal total. The lower enrolment did have implications for the Governors and their management of the school. They knew that an arrangement existed for an overdraft of £5000 and that it might be necessary to use this. They knew, too, that there were too many teachers for the number of boys to be taught but in the event increasing numbers meant that only two had to leave. A further seven left for military service or work of national importance during the first year of the war and several temporary replacements were employed.

The nucleus of the Dining Hall staff was retained though at first only the Luncheon Bar was kept going. At the beginning of November, however, the Dining Hall was reopened for the service of a three course lunch and members of staff supervising tables were allowed a free lunch. In January 1945 Mrs Coleman Smith retired from the Dining Hall. She had taken over responsibility in 1933 and was succeeded by Miss Stark Brown.

As many as possible of the cleaning staff had been kept on by giving them half time work and to enable this to be done in the evenings blue varnish was painted on the cupola and the skylights in the main building. All the windows in the school were also fitted with black out curtains by Copland and Lye at a cost of £92. The Rector's Room and the Office had been equipped first, on the grounds that those were the rooms where late work was most likely to be done. Black-out restrictions meant that from November until the winter was over most classes stopped at 3.10. The Debating Society changed its meeting time from 7.15 on Fridays to 4.00 on Thursdays.

Charles Jones

There were other changes, of course. By November the Janitor had been called up, not surprisingly since in 1936, on the death of Thomas Winderam, Chief Petty Officer Charles Jones DSM had been appointed to the post. A replacement was appointed, but Mrs Jones was to be allowed to remain in Colebrooke Terrace with free light, coal and gas in exchange for small duties which she was at present doing. The iron fencing in the playground was taken away and sold for scrap but in May 1942 successful attempts were made to prevent the Ministry of Works from removing the rest of the school railings. The flag staff came down early in the war and was raised on supports to prevent it from decaying. When it was stepped and stayed in position again on 22 November 1944, those who saw it must have felt that the end was in sight.

Earlier in the war, wire was applied to all the windows and wire netting stretched across the top of the main building below the cupola, to protect boys in the event of glass being broken. Balloon barrages were stationed on the School ground at Anniesland and in the playground, and the Masters' Smokeroom in Colebrooke Terrace was commandeered as the detachment office. Members of the RAF were not always considerate guests of the school : their cookhouse caused a nuisance in the playground and complaints were made late in 1940 about the way in which the men used certain school facilities. In May 1941 fire in a heap of straw – packing for some of the RAF equipment – damaged a good deal of the woodwork in the shed on the east side of the school and in the Senior School lavatory. Repairs were very protracted. In 1943 more than £300 was received from the RAF authorities to pay for damage done during their occupancy of the houses in Colebrooke Terrace and the playground. By May 1944 the balloon at Anniesland had long been removed, but Air Force personnel were still billeted in the Lodge. It was hoped that, when the RAF finally left, the hut which they had installed might prove useful for extra changing accommodation, though it would have to be moved. A good deal of reconditioning would be needed as there had been twenty four balloon sites on the playing fields.

Although boys had started to prepare for the Leaving Certificate it soon became apparent that the Certificate as it had become established would not be available during the war, so great were the demands on the manpower of the Scottish Education Department. The Rector therefore suggested in October 1939 that candidates should be entered instead for the School Certificate Examination set by the University of London, which was the most appropriate form of external assessment that appeared to be available. As it happened, even this proposal had to be modified, since the School Certificate Examination papers were to be set in July, after the Academy's session had ended. Instead, Academy candidates would be entered for the broadly similar University Matriculation Examination. It transpired that they were also able to enter for the Scottish Education Department's Wartime Leaving Certificate which was based on the marking of scripts by candidates' own teachers.

Academic success continued. In 1940 four Academy boys won scholarships at Oxford or Cambridge and the record improved so that by 1944 the tally was four scholarships and three exhibitions.

School routine was varied to cope with blackout requirements : in November 1941 the solution was to work in 35 minute periods between 9.40 and 3.40. Clubs continued and some new ones started up or were revived. In March 1941 there was a Hobbies Club with its home in 3 Colebrooke Terrace, catering for boys in Forms One to Three. The eighty members met at lunchtimes or after school for all sorts of activities : model railways, aeroplanes, radio, Meccano, fretwork, woodwork, microscopy and photography. Later in the year a Chess Club was started. In 1943 the S C Society, a religious organisation, was established in the Academy. 'S C' stood for 'Schoolboys' Club' and the Society owed its origins to the Academy's long and firm connection with the Scottish Schoolboys' Club.

There were also changes to the Corps. The OTC soon became the Junior Training Corps and in 1941 the Governors agreed to the establishment in the school of an Air Training Corps. It was emphasised that the work of the Corps would be concerned with navigation, mathematics and signalling. In January 1945 it was agreed to comply with the requirement that the JTC should have three full day exercises each year. Partly to compensate there would in future be two Friday afternoon periods instead of three set aside for JTC work.

The Rector was anxious to establish the basis on which the Governors would treat masters who were away on war service. In April 1940 it was hoped that when they returned it would be possible to reinstate them at the rate of salary to which they would have been entitled had no war service intervened, but the future of the Academy was in the meantime so uncertain that it was not felt possible to give any definite undertaking. Later in the year, Richards tried in vain to get the Governors to agree that they would make up the difference between a master's service pay and what he would have been receiving had he remained at the Academy. He referred specifically to the savings which resulted from the employment of five masters on a temporary basis at salaries lower than normal and mentioned that he felt a particular responsibility towards those masters who had been called up because of the OTC work which they had been doing for the benefit of the school. The Governors decided that every case should be dealt with on its merits, promising that when hardship was proved, steps would be taken to meet the situation. The attitude of the Governors was to be explained by the fact that reduced numbers in the school appeared to be leading towards a deficit of some £2500 for the session.

Throughout the war there were considerable changes in the staff, some dictated by varying numbers in the school and others by the normal movement of teachers from one post to another. The Head of Mathematics left in the summer of 1940 to take up a headship in Warrington. The Rector felt that it was of the utmost importance to 'appoint a man of distinction outside the school' and did so, in the process gravely disappointing R W Runcieman. He maintained that he had a claim to the post based on his appointment to the staff by Temple in 1920 under the system whereby an assistant master ultimately achieved the senior post. Richards felt that the change of system fell hard on Runcieman and that his maximum salary should therefore be increased. The new Head of Maths did not stay long, but Runcieman did. When he retired in 1957 he was hailed as the school's first official Careers Master, but also as a man who had spent his time instructing those who, left to natural inertia would merit a label 'Lower', but – with goodwill on both sides and skill on the one – could achieve more.

Other appointments were made on a temporary basis, including in March 1940 that of Jimmy Scougall, a man who had played rugby for several English Counties and cricket for Essex Second XI and who was soon to demonstrate so many other talents useful to the Academy that as soon as circumstances permitted it, in December 1944, his appointment was made a permanent one.

Joe Ward Senior, 'Old Joe', returned to duty at Anniesland during his son's war service.

After a period of ill health early in the war, Miss Sloan, the Rector's Secretary, retired in 1943. The *Chronicle* reflected that all manner of things had increased the work load in the Office since it had first come into being little more than a decade before – the sets organisation, an annual timetable, more formal school examinations, the scholarship scheme and functions in St Andrew's Hall and the Cathedral.

These functions were interrupted by the war, in particular by the risk of air raids, and in the early years had to be held at school, where the Rector referred with regret to the consequent sacrifice of 'whatever measure of pomp and circumstance we have been able to achieve in recent years in St Andrew's Hall'. A full day Scientific Society Exhibition was also held in May. *School Pie*, the OTC entertainment for 1940, was again held in the Athenaeum, but the Well proved a suitable setting for *Romeo and Juliet* and subsequent school plays. By 1942 it was possible to return to St Andrew's Hall for the Prize Giving but difficulties with transport meant that the Commemoration Service was held in Lansdowne Church and not in the Cathedral. The functions did continue to move about : the Christmas entertainment for 1943 was held in the Dining Hall and the Prize Giving of 1944 returned to the King's Theatre.

In October 1942 the Rector brought before the Governors a scheme for extending opportunities for common worship, by holding three or four voluntary services a term in a church, to be conducted by the Rector with the assistance of ministers specially selected for their influence with boys. The idea originally was to have them on Sunday afternoons but this was ruled out and eventually the Rector decided that to have them at the beginning and end of each term would be best as this would not encroach on teaching time. So began a practice which continued for many years, with services held at first in Lansdowne Church and later at school.

In 1940 Miss Wilson inaugurated the Academy War Comforts Organisation and reported in the *Chronicle* – now appearing three instead of four times a year – that one of the classes in the Preparatory School had already sent 24 scarves and another had provided 'squares of all colours which a grannie would make up into blankets'. In the meanwhile Miss Walker continued her long-established Tin Foil Collection for the Orthopaedic Clinic. By 1944 the Comforts Organisation had sent off some seven thousand items.

Many boys also helped the war effort by attending a variety of camps. The first of these were forestry camps held at Braco in the summer of 1940, attended by about 90 boys in July and 50 in August who together put in 3812 days' work. The following year a similar camp was held at Roy Bridge. In 1942 there was a forestry camp near Alness in July and a fruit-picking camp near Cupar later in the holiday.

So significant were these camps and the assistance which the Government felt school pupils could give in gathering the harvest that in 1943 changes were made to the dates of the school holidays. Work was available for sixty senior boys near Hawick between 20 August and 20 September. There would also be three berry-picking camps and altogether 254 boys out of a possible 380 would be involved. Three weeks of school would be lost as a consequence. A fortnight could be made up by shortening the Christmas and Easter holidays by a week and the long weekend in October would also be cancelled. Boys whose parents had not made other arrangements would also be kept at school on the Autumn Holiday.

In 1944 310 boys and 12 staff went on various camps and the start of the new session was again delayed for the Senior School, though not for the Preparatory School. The younger boys did make their own contributions to the war effort. In 1942, for example, three from Form One and one from Transitus held an Exhibition of Relics from the Raids and raised over £8 which they sent to the Air Minister for the Spitfire Fund. Another contribution was made by Jack Coleman Smith whose name became a household word because of his nationwide broadcasts on physical exercises for men and the associated booklet which came out in March 1942 called *Ten Minutes a Day With Coleman Smith*. The games of the school continued and in 1940 the leavers included a young man who would later be remembered as perhaps the best all-round games player ever to have been educated at the Academy. Russell Andrew was the son of C W Andrew, first winner of the Indian Trophy. He won the boys' singles in the Scottish Hard Court Lawn Tennis Championships; in 1939 he had kept wicket for the First XI though the following year he appeared in the bowling averages – and topped the batting averages; he won three champion-ship events in the Athletics Sports; and he was 'outstanding in the three-quarter line' of the First XV.

The Academy's Building Fund was of course suspended during the war. Something over £5000 was left on deposit at the bank while the work done on the foundations and heating chamber of the new gymnasium, together with the stock of material on the site, was safe-guarded. The Governors did, however, acquire new property when in June 1940 they were offered 13 Belmont Crescent as a gift by Stanley and Douglas Smith, Academical sons of Sir William Smith, founder of the Boys' Brigade. The Boarding House had already extended into part of the house and to acquire the whole of it seemed a natural extension, although a good deal of work needed to be done to bring the property into first class order. The Drawing Room of 13 Belmont Crescent already had an important place in the hearts of many Academy boys since every Sunday afternoon for the twenty years between the two World Wars the Belmont Meeting of the Scottish Schoolboys' Club was held there, attended by between sixty and eighty boys, most of them from the Academy.

In January 1941 serious damage was done to the heating installation in all three areas of the school because the Janitor did not see to it that the fires were kept in and the pipes drained. He was deemed to have been guilty of an error of judgement rather than of negligence. Twenty radiators were damaged and the piping in the Art Room burst practically along its whole length so that the re-opening of the school after Christmas had to be postponed by a week.

The Academy suffered little from air raids. A bomb did fall in the field on the north side of Anniesland Road just opposite the Lodge at Jordanhill which was considerably damaged but at Kelvinbridge there was little to report apart from some badly cracked windows, even after the heavy raids of 13 and 14 March 1941. On the morning of 14 March only a few boys turned up for school and they were soon dismissed, only to hear a fresh alert. After ten or fifteen minutes in the shelters, they were sent home again. The Rector wrote to parents explaining what their sons were to do about attending school if there had been a raid : if the alert lasted less than an hour, they should attend school as usual; if it lasted between one and three hours, school would begin at 10 o'clock; if it lasted for more than three hours there would be no school, except that all available boys aged 16 and over should report at 10 o'clock in case they could be of use in clearing up glass, for example. The following month it was reported that 32 boys had been withdrawn from the school as a result of the raids.

Members of staff and pupils over 16 were among the fire-watchers who did duty at the Academy. Boys who did fire-watching were paid a breakfast allowance of 2/6 if they were unable to go home between the end of their watching duty and the start of their school day. In May 1941 two masters faced prosecution for leaving a light on in one of the classrooms while on fire-watching duty. The Trust agreed to pay the fine.

It had been agreed earlier that year that in order to keep 'undesirable people' out and to prevent pilferage of Red Cross equipment the shelters should be locked at night and a key left with the RAF Detachment. During the raids, though, as many as 600 people had come from as far afield as Maryhill to use the Academy trenches. There had been no supervision and the doors had not been shut when the lights were on. It was now accepted that it was futile to try to prevent the public from using the trenches but some supervision was essential. Six air raid marshals were therefore recruited and arrangements were made to issue tickets for the shelters to residents in the neighbourhood.

Clothing shortages early in the war led to difficulties in obtaining badges for blazers and caps. It also began to prove difficult to obtain items of sports kit and a scheme was therefore started in April 1942 to help get round the difficulties. The school purchased for resale a whole range of articles belonging to boys who were about to leave school : football shorts, shirts, boots and stockings, cricket boots, shirts, shorts and trousers, grey and white sweaters 'preferably with Academy colours', gym shoes, running shoes and shorts, and blazers.

Planning for a post-war Britain in which the political situation might be greatly changed began as early as 1941 when the Public Schools Governing Bodies Association was formed 'to protect the interests of public schools at the end of the war when it was anticipated that considerable changes might be proposed'. Only five schools in Scotland were entirely independent of any Government aid, and the Academy was the only day school : the others were Fettes, Merchiston, Loretto and Glenalmond. The only other school in Scotland invited to join was George Watson's College. During the summer of 1942 the Secretary of State asked each public school to outline how it could best be brought into co-operation with the national educational system.

For their part, the Governors of the Academy looked carefully at the way in which they managed the school. In the autumn of 1940 they had discussed the usefulness of Honorary Governors and agreed that the list of distinguished men did serve as a helpful guarantee of the standing of the school. From the Trust's inception the list had included eminent church-men, politicians, soldiers and academics. Members of the Trust expressed the view, however, in October 1943 that the elected and nominated Governors should include some younger men and a year later J W Dallachy was elected in response to this suggestion. At the same time, Sir Robert Mackenzie retired as Chairman. He had joined the Board of the Academy Company in 1896 and had thus been a member of the governing body for 48 years. He had been the first Chairman of the Trust and was now succeeded by Colonel David Brand,

David Brand

who had been a pupil at the school throughout his boyhood and had entered the legal profession after studying at Glasgow University. After distinguished service with the Highland Light Infantry in the First World War, he became a member of the committee which considered the formation of the War Memorial Trust and then one of the first Governors of the Trust. Active in the Red Cross and in the Territorial Association, he joined the Home Guard in the Second War and became Zone Commander for Lanarkshire.

It was also agreed by the Board in 1944 that there should be regular rotation of Governors, one or more retiring annually and not being immediately eligible for re-election. Furthermore, the Governors agreed that in future they should meet monthly.

Earlier in the war, the Board had decided to change the time-honoured practice of collecting the fees quarterly. There were now to be three dates for payment each year, in October, January and April.

The Board also agreed in January 1944 to pay a war bonus to the whole staff, permanent and temporary, £30 for men and £24 for women. The initial approach had been made by Walter Barradell-Smith, whose arguments found an ally in the Rector. Richards was able to point out to the Governors that the Academy required the same number of teachers as it had in 1939 but actually had four fewer, with the result that teachers were taking larger classes and teaching more hours. In the Senior School the permanent staff accounted for barely 50% of the teaching body and the heads of department, with assistants barely qualified for the highest work, were hard put to it to maintain standards. There were fourteen temporary teachers. Of the men responsible for subjects three served in the JTC or the ATC and one commanded the ATC. In 1939 ten men had actively assisted Coleman Smith with the games whereas now there were three, all of whom had many other commitments, in the JTC, in the Home Guard, as head of a department or in keeping the school's dramatic activities going.

The bonus would be welcome not simply to acknowledge the increased load on the staff of the school, but as compensation for the fact that the ordinary teacher's salary had fallen behind what was being paid by the authority, though principal teachers, paid £675 at the Academy, remained better off than their Glasgow counterparts. The Rector's salary at this time was £1600.

A full staff was required because numbers had continued to increase. In 1942 there were 763 boys on the roll, almost a hundred more than in the previous year. In July 1943 it was anticipated that the new session would begin with 800 boys – there turned out to be 801 – and there had already been 150 applications for the session after that. That number continued to rise : by January there had been 290 applications and the Rector knew that he would have to turn down two out of three. He wrote to the Scottish Education Department about the matter since he shared with officials there a belief that the sudden surge in applications had to do with the Glasgow authority's decision to alter the status of the High School. The *Chronicle* at the time noted with pleasure that Kelvinside Academy was to return to its own buildings that September : 'no less hearty are our good wishes for the Glasgow High School alumni in their gallant efforts to preserve intact their long and honourable traditions in the service of education'.

There were 840 boys on the roll in September 1944. Two new classes had been started, all accommodation was being used and the Academy was clearly in a strong position to meet the challenges of the peace. The end of the war in Europe was marked by holidays on VE Day and VE+1 and a service in Lansdowne Church on 10 May. As the school's centenary approached, it was time to look back over a hundred years and arrangements were made to bring out a commemorative book, edited by Professor Charles Arthur Campbell, himself perhaps a symbol of the best that the Academy stood for. Arthur Campbell had been Captain of the School and of Rugby, Dux of the School, and winner of the Hardy Tennis Cup, the Masters'

Arthur Campbell, Captain of the Academy in 1914

Prize and the Indian Trophy. When he left in 1914 it was to serve with the Border Regiment in Egypt : but two years later he was invalided out and returned home, taking up a temporary position on the staff of his old school. In time he went on to Glasgow University and then Oxford, before taking up an academic career which culminated in his holding the Chair of Logic at Glasgow University. He continued to give unstintingly of his time to the Academy, serving as a Governor from 1938 – as it transpired until 1962.

1945-1954

A centenary celebrated

The centenary was also an opportunity to look forward : a Centenary Memorial Buildings Fund Committee was set up to resume the work which the war had interrupted. It met in December 1945 and decided that the commemorations should include a service in the Cathedral, a luncheon or dinner, a Past v Present cricket match or a special feature added to the Sports Day programme and, after the Prize Giving, a meeting with speeches. Although it was not at all clear when building might start, plans for the Hall and Dining Room were submitted and approved : the cost would be £50000, twice what had been estimated before

the war. A brochure was to be prepared, publicising the Appeal, which would have a target of £100000, and drawings of the new buildings would be included.

In March 1946 the Governors heard that a donation of £20000 over seven years had been promised to the Hall if it could be named after the benefactor's family. This was agreed, even though the donation would not cover the whole cost of the building : hence the Cargill Hall. William Cargill, the benefactor, had been at the Academy between 1891 and 1897, the youngest son of David Sime Cargill, who had become a Director of the Academy when the school moved to Kelvinbridge and whose principal business interest had been the Burmah Oil Company. The success of the company allowed the family to develop a tradition of benefaction which worked greatly to the benefit of the City of Glasgow : Sir John, himself one of the original Governors of the War Memorial Trust, endowed a Chair in Natural Philosophy at the University, David gave pictures to the Art Gallery at Kelvingrove while William, who lived the life of a gentleman of independent means without ever being actively concerned with any of the family businesses, enriched with its new Assembly Hall the school which he and his brothers had attended.

The Centenary Dinner on 18 June in the Grosvenor Restaurant was attended by some 360 and St Andrew's Hall was well filled for the Prize Giving next day, and for the meeting addressed by Principal Sir William Hamilton Fyfe, Aberdeen University, and Walter Elliot, one of the most distinguished political figures to have been educated at the Academy. He came to the school in 1898 and went on to qualify in medicine at the University of Glasgow, but at the end of the First World War he entered the House of Commons, representing first of all the constituency of South Lanark. In 1924 he was elected as the Member for Kelvingrove and two years later began his career in government, a career which encompassed such posts as Financial Secretary to the Treasury, Minister of Agriculture, Minister of Health and Secretary of State for Scotland. He was eventually made a Companion of Honour, which as the *Chronicle* noted is 'one of the highest marks of royal favour that any commoner can earn'. Speaking at the Centenary Prize Giving, he urged support for the Academy Appeal : Glasgow, he said, had

a nine hundred years old tradition of scholastic life and was famous for scholars long before it was famous for iron and steel. It was famous for education in the highest sense of the word. Such a tradition should be cherished and encouraged for indeed it was one of the great glories of Glasgow and of Scotland as a whole.

Later in the evening, Sir Tennant Sloan spoke of the four loyalties displayed in the Academy's coat of arms – loyalty to country, to city, to school and to the dead 'by whose sacrifice we live'. Sir Tennant himself had recently returned to Scotland from India : his renewed connection with the Academy was soon to become even closer.

Various fund-raising methods were adopted. There was the direct appeal; there was a special edition of the *Chronicle* in November 1946 which reminded readers that for 75 years the school had been a dividend-earning institution and that 'men do not endow limited companies'; blotters carrying a sketch of the Hall were issued as Christmas cards to all those on the appeal list, 5000 blotters altogether. By the end of 1946 the total promised to or received for the Building Fund was a little more than £40000. The following year for the first time a Dinner Dance was held to add further to the Fund.

In the meantime the school's existing property had to be cared for and in some cases restored after wartime use. Although the Preparatory School air raid shelters had been removed by the summer of 1945, the Senior School trenches between the Academy and Great Western Road were not dealt with until September 1946 and it was another year before the Governors accepted a quotation for re-conditioning the part of the playground which had been affected. Six years later the Rector was still lamenting the fact that two tennis courts had not been replaced : the following year they were restored in blaes.

During 1946 it was agreed to re-glaze the cupola of the main building with wired glass rather than try to remove the black-out paint. A new boiler and automatic stoker were provided for the Science Building. Repairs to the fire damaged shed and lavatories were undertaken at last and the play shed in the junior playground which had become very dilapidated was also seen to. The capital of one of the pillars on the south frontage fell on to the roof of the shed, fortunately without causing any damage to property or person. It seemed to be an isolated case of frost damage.

In June 1946 the Rector asked for equipment for the Dining Hall to allow 450 meals to be provided each day, rather than 350. He maintained that it was the school's duty to provide meals for all who wanted them but as things were, some boys had to be permitted to have their lunch in a restaurant (Hubbard's) in Great Western Road or bring it with them, which was 'detrimental to discipline'. It was not until the boarders started having their lunch in the Boarding House in 1953 that it was possible to reinstate the old rule which insisted that only boys going home for lunch were allowed to eat lunch out of school.

Other renewals gradually became possible and part of the playground was put under tarmac. The heavy embossed gates at the entrances to the two playgrounds were both in a serious state of decay : when they were taken away they were not replaced. Facilities were gradually provided for the practice of various sports, including tennis, cricket and even rugby :

in 1949 a short set of goal posts was put up.

Although a number of boys had started coming by motorbike and even in their own cars, many still rode bicycles to school and stored them during the day in the shed on the east side of the school, where they were liable to theft. As part of a major reconstruction of sheds and lavatories undertaken in 1952, space for eighteen cycles under lock and key was provided to the north of the main building. It was suggested that a further eighteen could be kept in the shed facing the gymnasium, but as this was used occasionally for 'ceremonial purposes' the suggestion was not implemented. Improved facilities for washing were at last provided during this renewal.

Planning for the erection of a memorial to those killed in the Second War began in December 1948 and in preparation the museum cases were removed late in 1951. The war memorial was unveiled opposite its First War counterpart on 22 February 1952 after a Commemoration Service in Lansdowne Church at which the names of the dead were read by the Rector. A guard of honour was inspected by Major-General Douglas Graham CB, CBE, DSO, MC who had commanded the 50th Division and held the highest rank achieved by an Academical. He was one of the first British officers to land in France in 1914 and again in 1939 he was one of the first in France with the British Expeditionary Force. Major-General Graham then unveiled the Memorial which was dedicated by Dr Warr, Dean of the Thistle.

Eighteen members of the staff as it had been in 1939 had served in the war and their gradual demobilisation allowed things to return to normal. Walter Barradell-Smith had joined the school in 1907 – 'the stern old days when the junior masters' metal was tested by a lengthy probation among those who least wanted to imbibe knowledge' – and had been due to retire at the end of August 1945 but he continued to work for some weeks at the beginning of the following session until Ben Aston was free to succeed him. His labours on behalf of the school were not over, however, since he had accepted the task of compiling the Roll of Service. There were also changes at the head of the Mathematics Department at this time, with new men being appointed in 1945 and 1947. Miss Sloan returned briefly as Rector's Secretary but retired finally in 1947. In that year, Miss Wilson retired from her post as Head of the Preparatory School. She had been a teacher for 45 years and had spent 29 of them at the Academy. There were 65 applicants for the post, which the advertisements made clear was open to men as well as to women. None of the men was suitable, however, and Miss Agnes McEwan was appointed. She had for 23 years been

mistress of First English Senior – Prep Three – and her place as a class teacher was taken by Miss Jean Ritchie.

There were other changes in the staff as well, so numerous in fact that the Rector expressed concern to the Governors. In January 1947 it was agreed to pay substantial increases to D D Ogilvie, who had succeeded Kelley, and George Preston as heads of Geography and History, both Leaving Certificate subjects. They were not, however, to be classed as principal teachers. Both men had been offered headships and Richards was keen to encourage them to stay. The Rector's own salary had recently been increased to £1750. At the end of 1945 the five members of staff who were still paid quarterly joined the rest of their colleagues in being paid each month : another link with time-honoured practice was broken, after one hundred years. (Some practices continued which really seemed to belong to a bygone age : when in 1949 one of the lady teachers was married she was required to resign and be re-appointed as a temporary teacher.)

To attract teaching staff, as well as to retain them, it proved helpful to offer incentives. When a vacancy arose for a teacher to be in charge of Chemistry within the Science Department it was necessary to pay Eric Walker a partial responsibility allowance to induce him to accept the post. Accommodation in Glasgow was also a problem. One man was thinking of moving to a post in Edinburgh since he could get a house there : while teaching at the Academy he was living in Carluke. The Trust had already taken over the tenancy of houses in Wilton Crescent and Colebrooke Street which were occupied by their employees. In May 1947 the Governors went a stage further and began to

Miss Christian Wilson greets Sandy Mackintosh — the first "John Ross"

buy property. The first purchase was a top flat house with three rooms and a kitchen in a 'comparatively modern tenement' at 10 Garrioch Drive, for which they paid £1050. Members of the Academy staff were to live in this flat for over forty years.

The Rector even found the ability to offer a free lunch helpful in recruiting staff. When it was discovered that the Dining Hall had incurred a loss of over £1000 during a single year some thought was given to the possibility of charging masters for their meals, but the Rector held out against a change, on the grounds that it had always been hoped that the staff could be paid more than the national (or 'Teviot') Scale. Since this had not been possible, a free meal was a helpful incentive.

In June 1947 Moreton Black joined the ranks of Academicals who had returned to teach at their old school when he was appointed to the Modern Languages Department. Captain of the School in 1938/39, he had won the Indian Trophy and the Mowat Scholarship, and had served during the war in the Seaforth Highlanders. In 1951 he left the Academy for a second time after his first stint on the staff and moved to Tasmania, but in 1954 he returned to Scotland, trained at Jordanhill and resumed his service at the Academy the following year.

Gordon Carruthers was appointed to teach Science in May 1948. 'He does not play games but as there is absolutely no field of choice of Science Masters this cannot be avoided.'

An important change of responsibility occurred at the end of 1946, when Frank Parkes, who had been teaching Mathematics at the Academy since 1930, took over from Cyril Engledow as Officer Commanding the JTC.

Gordon Carruthers

Engledow had served in the Corps for 25 years and had been OC for ten of them. At the very end of the war it had been announced that the age for entering the JTC had been lowered : it was therefore no longer necessary to run a separate Cadet Corps. A year later it was agreed to disband the Air Training Corps, which had only 14 members, apparently because boys' expectations of flying experience had not been satisfied. In 1947 the appointment of an Assistant Janitor made it possible to release Petty Officer Jones, the Head Janitor, to devote six hours a week to the Corps. Accommodation was later provided in Colebrooke Terrace for the Assistant Janitor.

In 1948 the JTC became the Combined Cadet Force but for the time being only an Army

Unit was formed in the Academy. Forms Three and Four formed the Basic Unit and after that boys entered the Army Unit. Steps were taken in 1949 and 1951 to establish Air Force and Naval Sections.

In June 1948 the Academy Band won the Glasgow Highland Club Pipe Band competition for schools in the West of Scotland which had just been revived. Some time later the question of providing suitable uniform for members of the band was discussed and it was agreed that they should wear a Glengarry, a battle dress top, a Mackenzie tartan kilt, a hair sporran and white spats with tartan hose for pipers or red and white dice hose for drummers. To kit out the entire CCF in kilts would cost £1000, so that was out of the question.

Attempts were made in 1949 and again in 1953 to find a suitable Permanent Staff Instructor. In 1950 Frank Parkes handed command of the CCF to J T Ainslie, who in turn was succeeded in 1952 by Gordon Carruthers. Carruthers – known universally as 'Jock' – had already established himself as a leading light in the CCF Christmas Entertainment, which from 1950 became more or less firmly established as a pantomime. The first was *Aladdin* : Carruthers wrote it and appeared as Dame, a pattern which was to be repeated over many years.

The CCF Entertainment took its place in a pattern of productions which in the years immediately after the war continued to be held in the Dining Hall. The stage was a sectional arrangement, the pieces being brought over from one of the basements in Colebrooke Terrace. Stage lighting was the responsibility of a team of three boys under the overall supervision of a master. Normally there was one boy from each of Forms Four, Five and Six to ensure continuity but Gordon Bannerman recalls being drafted in at short notice when his predecessor was summarily relieved of his responsibilities. 'He had become over-ambitious and wanted to achieve special effects which overloaded the fuses. We had one main switch located near the stage to which the lights were connected and this had a 30 amp fuse. This blew and was replaced but it blew again and my predecessor doubled up the fuse and tried again.

'The result was that the main fuse serving the Dining Hall which was also 30 amp also blew and was also doubled up. Then the 50 amp fuse in the Science Block went and was also dealt with. When the janitor found my predecessor trying to double up the main fuse for the whole school action was taken rather rapidly and I found myself with a new job.

'The installation was crude but remarkably effective. Lights were not white but a mixture of red, yellow and blue – the three together giving the white effect – and other colours were obtained by selective dimming. The switchboard was mounted at the side of the stage and consisted of a board with six banks of four switches, each controlling a block of lights. Below the board was a pivot rod carrying six wooden levers, one for each bank of switches. To dim the lights in a block the operator pushed down the appropriate lever while for a black-out all six could be depressed by using the forearm across them.

'To the inner end of each lever was attached a string with a lead weight and the string carried with it a wire attached to the circuit. The strings, weights and wires went down through the stage to earthenware pipes on end whose bottom ends had been plugged with cement through which a terminal was bored. The pipes were filled with salt water and when the handle end of a lever was up the back end was down so that the weight and the terminal touched and full current flowed. When the handle was depressed the weight and wire went up, leaving the current to flow through the resistance of water and dimming the lights.

'The amount of salt needed depended upon the amount of current used in the circuit. This was a trial and error process – salt was added gradually until the right effect was achieved. If too much went in, the lights would not dim completely and we had to siphon out some of the salt water and dilute the remainder with fresh. This was one of the duties of the Fourth Former – he had to suck out the salt water!

'Naturally some was spilt and if it was not dried up there could be spectacular effects – flying sparks streaking across the floor. I discovered that the system I had inherited was so designed that the switches and dimmers were on the same side of the mains – which meant that either the whole circuit was at mains voltage even when switched off or the dimmers were live and it was this which was the cause of the sparks. The first thing I did on taking over was a complete rewiring of the switchboard.'

Clubs, societies and extra-curricular activities of all sorts flourished in the Academy at this time. Though the production of *The Taming of the Shrew* planned for the summer of 1947 had to be cancelled when a leading member of the cast became ill, the school had a notable visitor the following autumn when Dame Sybil Thorndike performed for the Fourth, Fifth and Sixth Forms, 'introducing them to two vivid and exciting personalities, the other being Lady Macbeth'. The Globe Players

The choir at the Carol Service in Lansdowne Church, 1953

Camp at Brinsop Court, 1954

broke from their Shakespearean tradition by choosing *St Joan* by George Bernard Shaw to present in 1952. The Scientific Society was revived; an Aquarium Society, a Philatelic Society, an Ornithological Group, a Wireless and Television Club, a Classical Society, an Auto-mobile Club and a Sixth Form Table Tennis Club were all formed. The Academy Fellowship was established as a common meeting ground for all the religious organisations that had in the past worked separately in the school. There were reckoned to be 180 members of the Scripture Union meeting with the Fellowship in the Senior School. The Orchestra met every Friday at the lunch hour and the choir grew to eighty voices, meeting in room L where a piano was again installed. An innovation in 1947 was a Carol Service in Lansdowne Church.

The Debating Society found in 1951 that its gavel was missing. It was no ordinary gavel for it had been presented to the Society by Edwin Temple in 1915 and was made of oak taken from the roof of Glasgow Cathedral and five hundred years before that from the Forest of Luss. A new one from the same wood as the original one was later presented as a replacement.

In 1952 Jimmy Scougall was given a printing machine and some type and started the Printing Club which operated in Colebrooke Terrace and printed the cricket fixture card and the programmes for the concert and the swimming and athletics sports.

During the war 1150 boys had attended camps of one sort or another – forestry, berry-picking or harvesting – and it was Scougall once more who thought that the school should continue to organise camps during the holidays. Early in 1946 he sounded out opinion amongst the boys and discovered that well over one hundred would be interested. During the summer, over a period of three weeks, a camp was held at North Berwick : groups of up to 36 attended at one time, representing all classes from Transitus to the Sixth Form. The camp in 1948 was held at Keppoch House, Roy Bridge, revisiting haunts of one of the early wartime camps in the summer of 1941. The same site was revisited for two weeks in 1951. One participant wrote with relief that 'yet again

Lochaber failed to live up to its reputation as the wettest part of Great Britain. The barn served as a combined dining-cum-games room, the river for bathing and (occasional) ablutions, the cottages for kitchen and shop, the area between the cottages and river for tenniquoits and volley-ball, and the field near the railway for games. The tents were pitched near the house. An innovation was the installation of a gas cooker and boiler equipped with portable gas cylinders. This was a great success, making for regular mealtimes, quicker and cleaner washing up and an immaculate kitchen. More experienced campers, though, felt the kitchen incomplete without its usual reek, and breakfast was hardly in the right tradition without smoked porridge, while camp officers were somewhat dis-appointed that they were deprived of their usual privilege of getting up at 5 a.m. once a week to light an unwilling fire. Routine was as usual, with cycling, fishing and hill climbing for the more hardy members. The teams for organised evening games were named, as usual, after former camps – Dairsie, Portpatrick, Yetholm and Garlieston.'

The culmination of the school's wartime fund-raising came when a mobile canteen was presented to the Church of Scotland, who stationed it in Germany. Fund-raising continued, however. The Corps Entertainment helped to defray the expense of sending a team to Bisley, but the proceeds of the school concert and the play in the summer were devoted to the Building Fund. The surplus from Sports Day was also given to the Building Fund and in 1948 it was agreed that Governors and other friends of the school should be asked for subscriptions so that the pre-war practice could be resumed of giving replica trophies to the winners of some of the events.

A major contribution to the Building Fund came from a bazaar organised by Mrs Richards and Miss Wilson and held in the school on the afternoon of Saturday 22 March 1947 : it raised £460. In 1947, too, some boys in Form Two started a magazine which they called *Searchlight*. It survived into their time in the Third Form and profits from its production were devoted to the Building Fund. Its senior contemporary, the *Chronicle*, did not make a profit and, in an effort to defray the cost of printing, advertisements were accepted for the first time in 1949. In 1952 a permanent reduction was made in the number of issues of the magazine published each year, from four to three. Boys who took it were charged five shillings a year. Later there were two issues, in June and November, and eventually the magazine, in a very different format, became an annual production.

A chronicle of a different form emerged in 1947 in the shape of a documentary film called *John Ross of Glasgow Academy*, produced by Jimmy Scougall and shown every Thursday

Dr. Richards bids farewell to Colin Macdonald as "John Ross" leaves the Academy

evening between February and May the following year. Over 2500 people saw the film, which followed the career of an Academy boy growing up and passing through the various stages of school life in the Preparatory School and the Senior School. John Ross was portrayed by four different boys of various ages, Sandy Mackintosh (5 years old), Hector Kirsop (10), Graham Snell (14) and Colin Macdonald (18).

The buildings which the Fund would make possible were urgently needed and in particular the gymnasium. Inspectors were openly critical of the present arrangements, in particular the limitations imposed by there being classrooms beneath the gym at the top of the school. There was no dressing room and it was desirable to 'improve the atmosphere and general cleanliness of the gymnasium by providing a floor covering'. The Governors also learned that the recommended size for a gym had increased since the foundations were laid, from 40 feet by 60 to 40 feet by 70. It was therefore agreed in May 1949 that construction of the gymnasium, extended by 10 feet, was a priority and early the following year the Governors accepted an offer by Messrs Robert Gilchrist and Son to build it for just over £12000. Sir Hector Hetherington performed the opening ceremony on 20 October 1951 and a bazaar held at the same time was a resounding success, raising just under £2500.

It was soon decided that provision should be made for fitting the gym with a stage, protecting the floor and buying stacking chairs so that it could be used instead of the Dining Hall for school productions. It was also decided to install a telephone, the first 'extension' fitted in the school. The old gymnasium continued to be used, though when repairs to the equipment there were authorised in 1954 ropes were not included : it could be arranged for all 'rope work' to be done in the new gym.

It was agreed in June 1950 to proceed with the Dining Hall and Pavilion if licences could be obtained. No immediate progress was made, and the following summer, when the Building Fund stood at just under £57500 it was decided to have a further appeal. Detailed planning for a Dining Hall to accommodate 450 began in July 1953 and early the following year the long-awaited licence was granted. It was still necessary to raise extra funds and yet another appeal was launched, with the result

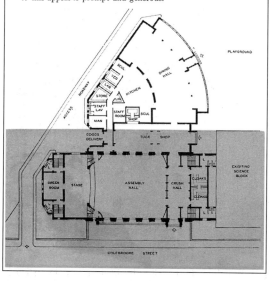

PROGRESS

By the end of the present year the extension and alterations to the pavilion at Anniesland will have been completed, and the new dining hall will be ready for occupancy. It will then be possible to clear the site for the new Assembly Hall but the hall cannot be built without additional funds.

The shaded portion can only be financed if your response to this appeal is prompt and generous.

that by November the Fund stood at £73000. During the summer the Governors learned that William Cargill would add a further £10000 to the Fund, provided that by the end of 1955 at least £90000 had been raised.

The Dining Hall, and the tuck shop which would later be built on the site of the old Dining Hall, would together cost a little over £40000. The contractors employed for the work were Thaw and Campbell. Work began in October 1954, by which time work had also been started on the extension to the pavilion at Anniesland which was to cost just under £9000.

The whole question of accommodation at Anniesland and what went on there proved to be extremely contentious and difficult in the post-war years. In June 1947 a protracted search began for additional playing fields, preferably enough for four or five pitches. The Governors eventually expressed an interest in ground to the west of their existing field, owned by the Jordanhill Estate, but were thwarted when in December 1951 after many months' negotiations, the Estate withdrew their offer to sell. In May 1953 the Governors were dismayed to learn that the ground in question had apparently been offered to Jordanhill College. They wrote to the Estate making clear their interest in the land which lay between Anniesland Road, Ryvra Road and the proposed line of Helensburgh Drive and heard the following month that the Estate was prepared to sell. Negotiations continued in the hope that the authorities would agree not to continue Helensburgh Drive west of Ryvra Road but for four years there was no progress to report.

In the meantime steps had been taken to ease the shortage of changing accommodation at Anniesland by bringing a hut from Banchory on Deeside and installing it at right angles to Great Western Road, immediately to the east of the groundsman's house. Hamish Dallachy recommended that instead of having lots of sprays and wash hand basins there should be 'one good sized tank with only one spray and one wash hand basin', advice which the Governors accepted in view of Dallachy's 'knowledge and more recent experience'.

The school continued to use the Club ground a good deal more than the Club did and the Trust's contribution towards the running costs was substantially increased. Both Club and school mourned the death in 1952 of 'Old Joe' Ward, who had come to Old Anniesland as groundsman in 1902 and retired in 1938, returning to duty during the war years when his son, who succeeded him, was directed to war work.

Club and school were not so unanimous, though, when it came to discussing the standard of rugby played by the boys : members of the Club expressed their disquiet in 1948 and suggested that Academicals should once more help with the coaching on Wednesdays, which in 1945 had once again become the senior games afternoon.

The following year the school took steps of its own to increase interest in rugby, by returning the number of houses to four. This was intended to make it possible to select teams for the senior and junior house league matches which would be more evenly matched in terms of weight and age. The four names retained were those which had a closer association with the school's history. When it came to competing at Sports Day the House colours now became chocolate for Albany, dark blue for Arthur, orange for Morrison and green for Temple.

During 1949 there was also a suggestion from the Club that rugby should be compulsory for all boys from the First Form in the Senior School upwards. The Rector felt that there were not enough staff or pitches to make this possible. He was however prepared to introduce a rule that all boys should on the appropriate games afternoon take such exercise as the school might prescribe, either at school or at Anniesland. This was introduced progressively, beginning with the boys who entered Form One that September. It was also made easier for boys to get to Anniesland, by reintroducing special buses from the school at a charge of 3d per journey.

There were other more delicate negotiations which led in 1949 to the appointment of Henry U'ren to take charge of games, leaving Coleman Smith in charge of Physical Training.

Members of the Club and of the Trust continued to express dissatisfaction. In November 1950 one speaker at the Trust's AGM maintained that 'the reputation of the Academy had been built up on its success as a nursery of rugby football players'. The Club had suggested that there was a lack of genuine enthusiasm on the part of the staff responsible for rugby.

The Rector replied robustly when these matters were raised by the Governors. It was his belief that 'a good school must be good at work and as good at games as it is at work'. He acknowledged that touch line attendance was falling, but nothing could be taken for granted in a new age when parents were conscious that their children's success depended upon work, examinations and so forth. It took considerable effort to bring the claims of rugby to their notice.

But the Rector reminded the Governors that this situation had arisen before and caused much anxiety to his predecessor. An attempt had been made to recruit a Games Master from outside but it had failed because the candidate had discovered what the relationship between the Games Master and the Academicals was liable to be from time to time.

Coleman Smith's hopes for the games of the school had been shattered by the war : too much had been left in the hands of too few for real progress to be made. Now U'ren had been in charge for one and a half terms of rugby and an attempt was being made to oust him. The Rector's anger was plain : it was not only the Games Master who was criticised when games were criticised, but the volunteer masters who included two pre-war men and seven others whose rugby had been of Club, County, College or University standard. 'Those who think the short cut to greatness is to look for a head on a charger simply have no notion of what keen, devoted and knowledgeable men were daily doing in the school.'

Two men who had been intimately connected with rugby and a third who had built up the school's shooting retired at this time.

Frank Reid

Mr and Mrs Coleman Smith with the boarders in 1948

Frank Reid, always known by the boys as 'Freddie', retired in 1950 after 40 years' service. Educated at Watson's and Edinburgh University he had spent three years in Perth and Arbroath before coming to the Academy. He won the Military Cross during the First War and on returning took charge of games for fifteen years, during which the First XV won 178 matches, lost 94 and drew 23. A R Munday was appointed as Senior Classical Master in his place.

Frank Batchelor was not appointed since he, too, was shortly to retire. He had given up his responsibility for shooting in 1949 and in 1954 his career at the Academy ended after 35 years' service, all of them spent in Room P. He had come to the school after service in the Black Watch and had 'by unflagging enthusiasm and lavish consumption of his leisure made rifle shooting an integral part of the Academy'. The Masters' Room had been 'enriched by his

constant acts of kindness and consideration' and on his retirement he had presented the school with two lecterns, for use at Prayers in the Well and – in due course – in the new Assembly Hall. He had been the senior member of the Common Room and on his retirement Cyril Engledow became the Second Master .

Preparations for the retirement of Jack Coleman Smith began in 1950 when the Governors agreed that on his departure they would take over responsibility for the Boarding House. There were then 38 boys in the House, of whom 7 were from Scotland, 8 from England and 23 from overseas. When Coleman Smith had taken it over, there had only been three : he had sold all the furniture for less than £20 and started with an unfurnished house. When he retired in 1953, responsibility for the Boarding House passed to Frank Parkes and for Physical Training to Henry U'ren.

Coleman Smith had joined the Indian Army after the First World War and retired with the rank of Captain, coming to the Academy in 1924 as successor to Samuel Stewart. In 1937 he had been appointed to the newly created post of Head of the Department of Games and Physical Education. Two years later a start had been made on his new gymnasium, but for twelve years until it was completed in 1951 its foundations had been known as 'Coley's Folly'.

He had been a great organiser – of the unveiling of the War Memorial, for example, or the hectic trench-digging of June 1939, before the professionals took over – and he had become known the world over for his early morning broadcasts. Mrs Coleman Smith's roles as wife of the Boarding Housemaster and Superintendent of the Dining Hall had assured her of a vital place in the school community.

Changes were made in the Science Department, reflecting the greater autonomy of the three sciences. There would be one Head of Science, Eric Walker, but Jimmy Scougall would be Head of the Biological Section and would report directly to the Rector.

Inspectors who saw the work of the staff praised what they saw, though they did continue to express 'doubt as to the complete suitability of the courses for boys whose natural endowments are less strong'. The academic continued to shine, however : in 1950 the Rector reported that the tally of open scholarships and exhibitions at Oxford and Cambridge had risen to 44. In 1951 the University of London's arrangements for school examinations changed and the Rector decided that boys should be entered for the Advanced Level of the Oxford and Cambridge Schools Examination Board. This had the advantage of a Scholarship paper which would be a useful preliminary for boys intending to compete at Oxford and Cambridge. At the other end of the scale, there were improvements to the facilities in the Preparatory School which Miss McEwan was anxious to make, in particular the provision of a small library of books. She also noted that the Prep School did not have a wireless or a gramophone.

The school was full : in 1950 there were 849 boys on the roll. It was agreed in 1947 not to adopt a suggestion that at the beginning of each session there should be a meeting at which parents could address questions and criticism to the Rector and some Governors. In November 1949 the Rector asked for and received the backing of the Board in dealing with parents who unreasonably asked for leave of absence for their children.

A highly controversial issue arose in December 1952. The Governors had enquired in 1947 about the number of Jewish boys in the school and had decided in 1949 to include a question on the application form about the applicant's religion but the case then arose of a boy whose parents were of 'pure African extraction'. The father was a graduate of Glasgow University and worked in the West African Civil service. The Board decided that there should be no question of refusing the boy on account of his colour. Three Governors dissented, however, from the view that there should be no colour bar and the matter was raised again the following month. Six Governors then expressed the view that coloured boys should be treated in the same way as any other non-priority candidate; six believed that a coloured boy should be considered only if there was no white boy who was an acceptable candidate. The Chairman gave his casting vote for the first which he believed confirmed the existing practice.

Sir Tennant Sloan

The Chairman by now was Sir Tennant Sloan, who had been elected after the death in March 1948 of Colonel David E Brand. Sir Tennant was the youngest of the six Sloan brothers who were at the school in relays between 1878 and 1901. From the Academy, where every year he occupied one of the first three places of his year, Tennant Sloan went on to Glasgow University and eventually to Oxford. As a young man he excelled at both rugby and cricket, playing rugby for Scotland on seven occasions. Entering the Indian Civil Service in 1909, Sloan held a variety of appointments of increasing importance over the thirty six years which he devoted to the sub-continent. Their titles have the ring of another age – Deputy Secretary to the Government of the United Provinces and the Government of India; Special Reforms Officer and Secretary to the Government of the United Provinces; Joint Secretary to the Home Department of the Government of India – but they give a clear enough indication of the mettle of the man who in 'retirement' offered so much to his old school.

The eldest of the Sloan brothers died on 8 January 1953. D Norman Sloan entered the Academy in 1878 and, like his younger brother, gained honours of one sort or another each year until in his last he was Captain of the School and one of eight Academy boys in the top fifty of the Glasgow University Bursary List.

Norman Sloan

He was intimately associated with the Academical Club and in 1918 became Secretary to the Glasgow Academy Company, having been its auditor. In due course he became one of the first Governors of the War Memorial Trust but after two years relinquished that position to become Secretary and Treasurer of the Trust. For fifty years a member of the Glasgow Stock Exchange, he was also Secretary of the Institute of Accountants and Actuaries in Glasgow. In 1944 he was Lord Dean of Guild.

Hamish Dallachy

J W Dallachy became Secretary and Treasurer in place of a man whose connection with the Academy had begun in 1878 and whose last act of business, some 74 years later, had been a conference in the Rector's room. Hamish Dallachy's connection with the Academy, already well established, was to become scarcely less remarkable than Norman Sloan's.

The Governors continued to pay attention to their responsibilities towards the staff. They put on record in October 1948 the principle that in the event of sickness full pay would be given for three months followed by half pay for three months. They agreed to continue the practice of paying Heads of Departments on the basis of maximum responsibility allowances. In 1951 they awarded the Rector an increase in his salary to £1850 and bought him an 8 hp Morris Minor with an allowance for its maintenance.

The Board also kept an eye on the day-to-day life of the school about which the Rector ensured that they were informed. In 1950 discussions took place with Pettigrew and Stephen in the hope that the firm would supply woollen goods such as pullovers and stockings in Academy colours. Before that only the blazer and cap had been supplied in official colours. In 1953 a prefect's badge was devised for the first time, in the form of a bar of light blue ribbon worn along the upper edge of the blazer pocket.

After a succession of special holidays at the end of the war, the school was closed again on 20 November 1947 to mark the wedding of Princess Elizabeth and for half a day to commemorate the Silver Wedding of the King and Queen the following April. Following the death of King George VI, plans were made to celebrate the Coronation of Queen Elizabeth II. The cost of bunting would be too great to warrant decorating the school in that way and since the Coronation was to be held in June, there would be no point in floodlighting the building. Instead, it was decided to plant flowering trees and small flowering shrubs on each side of the main steps and young oak trees on the Kelvin banks outside the boundary fence. Shrubs were also planted in front of the houses in Colebrooke Terrace. The school had three days' holiday at the very beginning of June to mark the Coronation.

At the beginning of a new era, though, the reality and poignancy of war remained vivid at the Academy. The annual commemoration of Armistice Day at the War Memorial was a moving occasion and did not pass unnoticed by the wider public of Glasgow.

'Through a window overlooking a school war memorial yesterday morning were heard shouts of command. The act of remembrance was over, but there on the rain swept corner stood the mixed forces of the school corps, soldiers, sailors and airmen once a week and on special occasions, slight, dedicate, rigidly at attention. A woman, bulky in boots, in plastic waterproof and hood, and with a shopping bag, stood watching from the other side of the road.

'At the word of command the parade left-turned and marched off to reveal the khaki-wet stone of the memorial with two poppy wreaths now on its steps. In front of it stood their officer and the head master, his black gown slashed as he turned by a crimson hood. As the parade disappeared he replaced his mortar board, took an umbrella from where it leant against the wall of the memorial and, opening it, side a large area of the roof between the outer edge and the cupola had been destroyed. The cupola itself, virtually resting on charred sticks, had to be removed within 48 hours and by mid January a temporary roof had been erected just below the ceilings of the second floor class rooms.

Richards quickly made arrangements to house the 550 boys of the Transitus and Upper School classes from 11 January until they could return to the school building. Accommodation was provided in the Accountants' Hall, St Vincent Street, the Scottish Schoolboys' Club, Lansdowne Crescent, the West Princes Street and Jardine Street Drill Halls, the Reith Hall and the Stevenson Memorial and Lansdowne Church Halls. Desks were brought from the school and blackboards borrowed from the Education Department in response to their offer of help. Each day's work was organised into three sessions and boys fitted in visits to the Academy for Science, Art, Music and PE.

On 14 February the classrooms on the first and second floors were restored to use. Accommodation had been found in 19 Belmont Crescent, so it was possible to discontinue the use of the various halls. As a token of their thanks to the Scottish Schoolboys' Club, whose premises at Lansdowne Crescent had been given without charge, the Governors bought them a ping-pong table.

The cost of the fire was in excess of £40000 and was met by insurance. Plans for rebuilding began immediately, with modifications to the structure so that the rooms on the top floor would be improved. The roof over the centre of the Well was lowered to the level of the ceilings of the second floor, which would allow through ventilation, and dormer windows were

fitted, so that the top floor rooms would no longer be lit through skylights. It was decided that the art room should be housed on the top floor, together with the subsidiary gymnasium.

Work on the rebuilding started on 4 July, after the school had broken up for the summer, and the new rooms were available for use the following February, making it possible for the classrooms below to be reconditioned. Giving the art room a new home allowed the old room to be used as an additional science laboratory. Consideration was given to installing a new rifle range on the top floor but it was later agreed to build a range behind the new gymnasium, the cost to be met by the War Office.

In the meantime work continued on the new building projects. By October 1955 the Building Fund had passed £80000 and still another appeal was issued to ensure that by the end of the year £90000 had been raised. The target was met and the Trust therefore qualified for the additional donation offered by William Cargill. The extension to the pavilion was ready by mid September 1955. The Dining Hall came into use, rather behind schedule, on 11 January 1956 and was formally opened and dedicated by the Dean of the Thistle the following month.

During the autumn of 1955 the Governors considered plans for the new Assembly Hall, which at a cost of some £40000 exclusive of furnishings would seat 600 with a large entrance hall capable of being opened up to seat an additional 100. Since the steel that was needed would take six months to obtain, the architect advised that an early start should be made and the Board agreed to go ahead as soon as the site could be cleared. By the following summer a start had been made on putting down the concrete raft for the new Hall and rather more than a year later plans were made for the formal opening of the building.

Basil Holden presides over an assembly in the Cargill Hall

A service of dedication was held in the Cargill Hall on 8 November 1957, conducted once more by Dr Charles Warr. Accompanied by the newly installed Compton organ, the congregation and choir sang music which included The Old Hundredth and Paraphrase 59 to the tune 'Glasgow'.

The following day an At Home was held, attended by some 1400 parents and Academicals who were able to see the school buildings, old and new, and some of the work that went on in them. In addressing the guests Sir Tennant Sloan recalled that it had been at the Prize Giving in 1933 that the Rector had first voiced the need for an assembly hall. Now it would be possible to have the Prize Giving at the school itself, a Preparatory School ceremony on the last Wednesday of the session, followed by the Senior School Prize Giving next day.

The Globe Players, too, were able to take full advantage of the new Hall. Their first production there was *King Henry V* : it had last been tackled in the Academy 'some twenty years ago, almost on this very patch of ground – But oh, how changed! – the four or five most vile and ragged foils were more concerned with keeping their weapons out of the curtains and the tie-beams of the old Dining Hall than with the prestige of Agincourt; but now, if we were still called on, as the text demands, merely to imagine horses printing their proud hoofs in the receiving earth, it was by choice of the producers rather than for lack of room'.

In the meantime, thoughts had turned to modernising the laboratories and equipping the new one to be housed in the old art room. An approach was made late in November 1955 to the Industrial Fund for the Advancement of Scientific Education in Schools which rapidly resulted in an altogether more ambitious project. In February of the following year the first drawings were discussed of a new building to be sited between the dining hall and the gymnasium. At a cost of some £15500 including fittings it would house a general physics laboratory and a Sixth Form physics laboratory. The

Chemistry laboratory in the old Science Building would remain, but Chemistry would also be taught in the small laboratory downstairs. The old Art Room would be converted into a Biology laboratory and the old Physics laboratory would become a general purpose one. In 1955 the Academy had had three laboratories : soon there would be six and a Science lecture room.

One of the new Physics laboratories

The Fund would provide not less than half and not more than two thirds of the cost, on condition that an additional science teacher was appointed : the Governors committed themselves to finding the balance. In this they had the help of a benefactor, Gilbert Innes, who made available either directly or through the Kilgarth Trust several sums of money which enabled them to ensure completion of the new single-storey building by January 1958. Gilbert Innes also gifted to the Trust Gartaneaglais, his property at Killearn, and money to assist with its conversion into a number of separate dwellings.

In December 1955 Jimmy Scougall left the Academy to take up a headmastership in New Zealand. It was he who had created the school's first Biology laboratory out of the old lecture room, but he would be remembered for much else during his comparatively short time at the school : *John Ross of Glasgow Academy*, the summer holiday camps which had grown out of the war-time camps, the arrangements for selling second hand kit, the cricket net he contrived in the playground during the war, the Printing Club. When he left he presented a cup which is still awarded to the best all-round athlete in the school. Scougall had also been a stalwart of the Academical Club, for whom he turned out to play both rugby and cricket.

A newcomer to the Physical Education Department in 1957 was Ian MacGregor. The *Chronicle* remarked on his appointment that 'it is hardly necessary to remind followers of Rugby that Mr MacGregor has played for the Barbarians and for Scotland'. John Plowman was appointed at the same time to assist with the teaching of Physics and Chemistry. Carruthers assumed charge of Biology, but the subject was not taught in the Fourth and Fifth Forms. In June 1958 James Jope was appointed to the Mathematics department. Until his application was received, the position seemed set to go to a Dutchman.

In 1958 John Peebles Conn gave up the visits which he had been making to the Academy to teach violin under five separate Music Masters. Henry U'ren, another violinist and indeed leader of the school orchestra, also resigned in 1958 on his appointment as Director of Physical Education and Recreation at Aberdeen University and it was agreed that the Games Mastership need not necessarily go to the master in charge of Physical Education. Ken Waine was therefore appointed to take charge of PE and Ian MacGregor became Games Master, having been obliged by an injury to exchange his post in the PE Department for one teaching in the Preparatory School. George Preston resumed responsibility for cricket.

15 November 1952 — Academy 8, Fettes 8

The whole question of games continued to exercise the Governors, especially when in 1955 there were further claims at the Academical Club that boys coming to the football section were lacking in knowledge of the game. Some of the masters questioned whether the policy of making games compulsory was actually achieving the desired effect and it was agreed the following year to withdraw the compulsion to play rugby for boys in the Third Form and above. Boys who did not go to Anniesland would instead take a period of physical training at school. The Governors also agreed to accept some financial responsibility for the provision of transport between the school and Anniesland which was estimated to cost about £600 a year. It was accepted that parents laid more stress than they had in the past upon academic achievement, being especially anxious that their sons should have the Leaving Certificate before going off on National Service, that compulsory two-year period in the armed forces which came to an end only in 1962.

There was still the problem of a shortage of pitches. In 1956 the maximum number of boys wishing to play rugby on Wednesdays was 222 : they could be accommodated when five pitches were available but not when weather conditions restricted the number of pitches to three. Negotiations over the purchase of additional ground continued until it was at last agreed in October 1958 that the Trust would buy the ground between Anniesland Road, Ryvra Road and Jordanhill Drive which later became known as Windyedge.

Whether or not its reputation in rugby circles had really declined, the Academy remained a popular school. In 1955 there were almost 500 candidates for 93 places. The sons of Academicals and boys with brothers in the school were deemed to be priority cases and of these there were 133. Except in the Third Form, the number of priority candidates exceeded the number of vacancies. In March 1956 the Governors accepted that the system of priority admissions should continue, despite the possibility that it denied entrance to a significant number of boys of quality and merit. The Rector did have discretion to admit a limited number of specially suitable non-priority candidates in preference to priority candidates when he considered this to be in the larger interests of the school.

In 1958 the Governors asked still more radical questions, spurred on by a wish to know whether there were steps which they could take to strengthen the position of the Academy against the possibility of action being taken against independent schools by a future government. Was it desirable that places should be found for a restricted number of boys nominated by the Scottish Education Department or a similar body, who would be responsible for their fees? If so, to what extent should the admission of priority candidates be limited? Under what conditions were boys admitted to 'assisted places' at other schools?

A good deal of research was undertaken to provide answers to such questions. Some 30% of the boys admitted were Academicals' sons, and younger brothers, the other priority case, brought the total to 45% – but the Rector did not feel that any significant number of quality candidates was being excluded. As far as grant aid was concerned, there seemed to be three possibilities for the Academy : admission of a limited number of scholars with fees paid by the local authority; grant aid in some form or another which would attract representation from the local authority on the Board and some form of possible control; or independence. Towards the end of the year the Labour Party indicated that it was not its intention to interfere with the independent schools but would take action over grant-aided schools. The Governors unanimously agreed that it was not a time to change the school policy and that a position of complete independence should be maintained.

Early in 1956 the Governors outlined their policy on salaries : the Academy should certainly not lag behind the scale laid down for state-aided schools and it was in fact desirable to maintain a salary scale in excess of the state scale. The Board was, however, concerned about the effect of raising the fees in order to pay higher salaries and particularly wished to avoid doing anything which might change the nature of the school, making it too expensive for 'a very desirable class of pupil, those drawn from the professional and university classes'.

In March 1956 proposals were made to establish a salary structure for the Academy which would allow £100 more than the state scale to teachers at the bottom of the scale and £40 to those who had reached the maximum after 15 years. Heads of Department would receive an allowance of £350 rather than £240 as in state schools, reflecting the practice in England. Women's pay would be adjusted over six years so as to become equal. After listening to certain observations from the staff, the Governors put forward modified proposals which required a fee increase of 15%. The matter was raised again when a further increase was made to the state scale and the Governors agreed to maintain the Academy scale at not less than £25 ahead of the authority scale. In March 1956 the salaries bill was £38000. The increase awarded in April added £9000 and the further increase in November another £3000. Further substantial fee increases were inevitable but in October 1958 the practice of charging extra for athletics, the library, stationery, the CCF and Science ceased : the *Chronicle*, though, continued to be charged for separately.

Salaries and superannuation accounted for nearly 80% of the Academy's total expenditure and as they continued to rise, so fees would continue to rise. The Governors felt themselves to be in a dilemma, but concluded that complete independence even if coupled with the exclusion for financial reasons of certain boys was a lesser evil than taking some form of State assistance.

The Governors did not spend all their time debating such weighty and difficult matters. They noted with pleasure the gift of a grandfather clock in 1955, to be placed in the Rector's Room. They agreed that five sets of bagpipes were not really enough for the pipe band and sanctioned the purchase of two more. They learned with interest that in the autumn of

1955 some thirty members of the staff wished to use the gymnasium for Scottish country dancing on Wednesday evenings. They heard that the Albany Academical Club was being wound up in 1955 but that money would be available to perpetuate the memory of James N McRaith, through the annual award of a medal. In due course this became a prize, awarded for the last time in 1961.

The Governors will have known that the Glasgow Academy Circle of the Scottish Children's League was raising useful sums of money for that worthwhile charity. They may have read in the *Chronicle* of the activities of the Field Studies group, newly constituted in 1957, which over the spring and summer terms had trained itself in the arts of hill-walking, outdoor cooking and the conquest of difficult routes. They had camped for three days at Glen Massan and spent time surveying a new forest road, climbing Ben Mhor and studying forestry matters.

There were always practical matters to be considered. In 1956 Miss McEwan specially asked that the junior playground should be asphalted. The Governors agreed to look into the matter and also to consider resurfacing the parts of the senior playground which were still only gravelled. In January 1957 difficulties experienced with the lighting in Room D led to removal of the tiered seating which had survived there some time after being removed from other classrooms. There was a risk that year that Colebrooke Street might become an official car park and the Governors agreed to contest the proposal as strongly as possible. The following summer it was agreed to clean down the stonework at the front entrance of the Academy and in doing so to remove the old carved crest

above the doorway which was in very poor repair.

During 1957 the Rector asked that the clothing rules printed in the prospectus should be extended. For many years they had stipulated only that 'all boys are required to wear an Academy Cap, and a Tie of the School colours' but from September 1958 the uniform regulations were much more explicit. They included the strong recommendation that parents should arrange for their boys always to wear Academy uniform in public and also insisted that 'the wearing of duffle coats is not permitted'.

On 3 June 1956, Roydon Richards suffered a heart attack. Cyril Engledow as the senior member of staff acted as Rector until Richards was fit enough to resume his duties, part time, mid way through October. In July it was reported that the Rector acknowledged that for some years there had been a need for a Second Master, although he had hesitated to bring the matter before the Governors. He did not wish to make a recommendation at the

Cyril Engledow plays his part in a mock trial held in Room LL in January 1952

moment but the Governors approved in principle of making such an appointment. Later, when Richards was able to join fully in the discussion, it was agreed that Engledow should become the Rector's Administrative Deputy, with status and salary equal to those of a Head of a Department. In the Rector's absence he would be responsible for the discipline of the school. Varley, who was the senior Head of Department, was quite happy with this arrangement : the Rector suggested that he should have the status and title of Senior Head of Department and in the absence of the Rector would deal with matters of an academic nature. No precedent for the future was being established as this was an appointment personal to Engledow who would teach half time. Room C became Engledow's office and classroom, but all that was needed to equip it for its new role was a filing cabinet, a Yale lock and a telephone extension.

At the Annual General Meeting of the Trust in November 1957, Sir Tennant Sloan retired as Chairman, remarking that it was 107 years since his father had entered the school as a pupil and that Lady Sloan's grandfather had been William Campbell of Tullichewan, who had convened the meeting at which the decision to found the Academy had been taken.

Thomas G Robinson was elected as the next Chairman of the Trust. At the Academy in the years immediately preceding the First World War, he entered the family timber business and took on a wide variety of other responsibilities – President of the Glasgow Chamber of Commerce, Lord Dean of Guild, Chairman of the Clyde Navigation Trust, Director of the Scottish Amicable Life Assurance Society, Session Clerk of St Luke's Church, Milngavie. He was, too, an enthusiastic mountaineer, yachtsman, curler,

golfer and angler, and had been Convener of the Academy's Buildings Committee at the time when the programme of work financed by the Centenary Building Fund was being carried out.

T G Robinson

In April 1958, the month in which it was announced that the University of Glasgow was to confer the degree of Doctor of Laws upon him, Roydon Richards made it known to the Governors that he wished to retire in March or August 1959.

The Board quickly decided the terms on which his successor would be appointed. A salary of £2200 or upwards would be paid : Richards had been awarded an increase to £2400 in 1956. No one over 45 need apply. After some hesitation, the Governors decided to indicate that they would provide a house rent free.

Three of the 21 applicants were interviewed on 29 July and Basil M Holden was then invited to become the fifth Rector of Glasgow Academy. Housemaster and Senior Mathematics Master at Oundle School and

Basil Holden

himself educated at Queen Elizabeth's Grammar School, Blackburn, and King's College, Cambridge, he would be the first Rector not to be a classicist. The search for a suitable house for the Holdens was a protracted one but in March 1959 the Trust bought 98 Southbrae Drive.

Dr and Mrs Richards, meanwhile, planned to move to Arntemplar, one of the houses at Killearn which had been given to the Trust by Gilbert Innes. The Academy said its farewells to them at the end of March. Presentations were made and the portrait for which the Rector had sat was unveiled. The artist was David Donaldson, who was able to depict Richards in the robes of his doctorate. Many tributes were paid to Dr Richards, one of the most telling by a member of the Board who remarked that 'it didn't matter what sort of questions cropped up at our meetings, on any subject connected with the school, from pedagogies to plumbing, the Rector appeared to

carry in his mind the complete dossier'. Roydon Richards had demonstrated his grasp of detail at the very beginning of his Rectorship and had maintained it unabated for almost 27 years.

When Roydon Richards died in 1978 he was remembered above all as the Rector who had encouraged the cleverest boys in the school 'to show their paces under the most exacting conditions'. But he was remembered too as a man who loved music and who had stimulated its growth within the school : he had nurtured it as a subject within the curriculum and he had encouraged the development of the choir and the orchestra. Richards was a Rector devoted to high standards : he encouraged them in others and expected them of himself. It is fitting that when the Academy's library found a new home in the Well, Michael Richards – an Academical – gave furniture for it in memory of his late father, to whose heart the provision within his school of an adequate library had been so dear.

1959-1975

Basil Holden

Dr Morrison, Dr Temple and Dr Richards had between them been Rector of the Academy for 98 years. The portraits of Temple and Richards were hung in the Cargill Hall where on 14 April 1959 Basil Holden was introduced to the school for the first time.

During 1959 the Governors realised that the money raised by the Appeal Fund would not be sufficient to meet the costs of the building work which had been undertaken and other urgent calls on the Trust's funds. It was decided during the spring to go ahead with laying out the ground which had been acquired at Ryvra Road and to put up a new Pavilion on the Academy's own ground. Fees would be increased to meet increases in staff salaries, which continued to allow for a modest premium over the government's scale, and in the allowances paid to those with particular responsibilities – the Senior Master and the heads of Modern Languages, English, Mathematics, Science, Classics and the Prep School were each paid £1890 compared with the Rector's £2200. To assist with the costs of building and other projects it was agreed to charge £5 as a levy for capital purposes from the beginning of the following session. The Governors were soon asked whether £5 was sufficient : they did not wish to pitch it any higher, however, since they recognised that the burden of school fees was a considerable one for some parents. They continued to feel anxious that the level of fees should not debar 'certain groups of parents whose boys it was desirable to have at the school'.

It was agreed in December 1959 to launch a further Appeal, for Buildings and Playing Fields, with a target of £35000. An illustrated brochure was printed, and it was hoped particularly to interest in the Appeal some of the industrialists of the city who would be reminded that the Academy had made a considerable contribution to the industrial life of the city and was the only independent school in Glasgow.

The Appeal got off to a slow start : by June 1960 it had raised just short of £2500 and since this total included two individual donations of £1000 and £400 there was a feeling of disappointment. There had been just two responses from Glasgow firms, contributing £350. As the year went by, however, matters improved so that by the autumn the number of subscribers had risen to 200 or so, who between them had given some £12000. The Appeal remained open for several years, during which the total naturally increased still further, though the original target remained elusive.

One fund-raising activity which was revived early in 1961 as a result of the Appeal was a Dance in the Cargill Hall. This soon regained its place as a recognised Academy tradition and has continued to raise substantial sums for various projects ever since. For many years the name of Mrs Belle Mitchell was inextricably linked with its organisation.

By the summer of 1960 the grass on the new playing field had been mown for the first time and hopes were high that before long the new pitches and the new Pavilion would help to reduce the number of senior boys who were disappointed at not being able to play at Anniesland on Wednesday afternoons, when the shortage of accommodation still meant that numbers had to be seriously restricted.

The hut which had been imported from Banchory was still in place but it scarcely represented a long-term solution and just before

Christmas 1960 discussions took place about the siting of the new pavilion. Planning went ahead on the basis that it would be built on the north side of the ground at the entrance in Anniesland Road and that it would contain an assistant groundsman's house, changing accommodation for 150 boys and provision for serving tea. Several suggestions from masters were incorporated into the design. The pavilion was built at a cost of some £30000 by Messrs John A Russell and was ready for inspection by the Governors after the Prize Giving on 27 June 1963. Joe Ward, the groundsman, was among those who had waited many years for this addition to the facilities at Anniesland. There had been a great expansion since he first took over from his father in 1938, so that where once there had been a single ground and some extra pitches on the Alps, latterly he had charge of three separate fields. He died on Christmas Eve 1967 and was greatly missed, not just for his skills as a groundsman but also for his excellence as an umpire – 'not in the least afraid of giving decisions against Academical cricketers'. Between them 'Old Joe' and 'Young Joe' had ensured that for almost 66 years there had been a Joe Ward in charge at Anniesland.

During Holden's Rectorship much was also done at Kelvinbridge to improve the Academy's amenities. One of the most remarkable features was the steady acquisition of houses in Colebrooke Terrace and their imaginative conversion to a wide variety of uses. The first house to come to the Governors' attention, in October 1961, was No 11. It was decided not to buy it, because of problems with subsidence, but the Board did record that they would consider the possibility of purchasing any house in the Terrace which came on the market.

For some years nothing happened but in November 1965 the Governors considered the school's accommodation requirements and came to the conclusion that the Preparatory School needed a storage room, playground space, a library big enough for 30 boys, a handicraft room and an assembly hall for 270 boys : an estimate had been obtained for erecting a wooden building to the rear of one of the houses in Colebrooke Terrace.

For the Senior School, the Governors envisaged a building of two or possibly three storeys which might house the library, the music room, some classrooms and possibly some workshops : just over a year later they considered plans for a rectangular building extending southwards from the south gable of the gymnasium. In September 1967, however, they received such a discouraging report about the reliability of foundations there that no further progress was made.

This was not the only front on which the Governors had hoped to move forward. At the same time as they first turned their thoughts to a new building they had written to the owners of 5 - 9 Colebrooke Terrace to express an interest in buying the houses.

In May 1967 the Trust acquired 8 Colebrooke Terrace from North Kelvinside Church, followed in September by No 7. In each house two sizeable classrooms were created and it was also possible to provide a Junior Library, a handicraft room, space to leave large projects undisturbed from one day to another and a television and projection room, large enough to hold three classes at once. Holden enthused about the possibilities for younger boys – those 'whose ages have not reached double figures thrive in classrooms which have

space enough to allow frequent rearrangement of desks, space enough in which to enjoy free expression in arts and crafts, and space enough really to enjoy living'.

Between 1969 and 1971 the Trust bought Houses 6, 9 and – after all – 11, acquisitions which meant that from September 1971 Nos 1 to 4 could be devoted entirely to the Prep School, though after a spell in the Terrace Transitus returned to the main building. In Houses 6 and 7 were to be found the Senior School Library and teaching rooms for Classics and Music. A Fine Arts Centre was built in Houses 8 and 9 with Painting and Drawing Studios on the first floor and beneath them accommodation for Pottery and Printing and a workshop fitted with woodwork benches and with lathes to enable three dimensional designs to be fashioned in wood, metal, plastic and other modern materials. This represented a major expansion of Art and a second member of the Department was appointed to enable it to happen. House 11 was devoted to the Sixth Form, who had private study rooms there.

During 1971 and 1972 the Trust bought the two flats which made up 10 Colebrooke Terrace and were bequeathed No 5 by Mrs H J Craig, the widow of an Academical. The following year 12 Colebrooke Terrace came on the market but was reported to have a serious fracture which might well become dangerous. If the Trust acquired the property, it would only be to prevent it from falling into other hands.

The school did, however, own Houses 1 to 11 and by 1975 a further reorganisation had been implemented. The Prep School continued to occupy 1 to 4; House 5 became the Sixth Form House; House 6 was home to the Library, which in 1974 received a handsome gift from Dr Barbara McGeachy in memory of her brother; there was a language laboratory and audio visual centre in House 7; Houses 8 and 9 continued as the Fine Arts Centre; House 10 contained two residential flats and the Music Department took over House 11.

On the night of 20/21 July 1975, the roofs of Houses 8, 9 and 10 were destroyed by fire which also damaged the roof of No 11. The buildings also suffered very considerably from water damage. The Art Department had to move back to its old home at the top of the main building and into the junior gymnasium next to it. Senior School Music had to be taught in the Cargill Hall and two staff flats were also affected.

The Rector reported in the summer of 1976 that 'out of the ashes of the fire were arising new purpose-built Fine Arts and Music facilities and facilities for classwork in Drama'. The cost of the work was some £106000 of which about half was recovered through insurance. The balance was paid for out of the proceeds of the sale of some of the Killearn property which had been put on the market before the fire. Dr and Mrs Richards had moved to a flat in Edinburgh and there was considerable difficulty in finding tenants for the houses who had the Academy connections which Gilbert Innes had wished. He himself had died some four years previously.

Amidst all the changes in Colebrooke Terrace was an important one in the main building. In 1971 the former Masters' Room became a classroom and the staff moved to Room D. The staff itself changed, too, as was inevitable.

In June 1960 Cyril Engledow retired. Christopher Varley succeeded him as Second Master and Moreton Black became Head of Modern Languages. Engledow had taught only at the Academy where he was appointed in 1922, to teach History and French at first and later French and German, when the second language was reintroduced. Nothing ever flustered him : 'he enjoyed an imperturbability which was a constant tonic to colleagues less proof against adversity'.

A year later another senior figure retired. Miss Agnes McEwan had been Head-mistress of the Preparatory School since 1947 and a teacher there since 1924. Miss Doris Mackintosh was appointed to succeed her. In November 1981 Miss McEwan was elected an Honorary Governor of the Academy, the first – and to date the only – lady to be so honoured.

Yet another Head of the Academy's Mathematics Department died in office on 3 June 1962. George Allman had come to the school in 1947. Frank Parkes acted as Head of the department until at Easter 1963 E B C. Thornton came from Radley College to take

Miss Nan McEwan

over. Ironically, Parkes also died before reaching the age for retirement, in 1967. He had been at the school since 1930 and had contributed much through his command of the Corps and his Housemastership. Gordon Carruthers took over the Boarding House in the emergency and Jim Cowper took over permanently in September.

Ben Aston reached his sixty-fifth birthday in May 1967. Almost a year earlier he asked the Governors if he could continue as Head of English for a further year but it was felt that all staff should retire at 65. G B Payman was appointed to succeed Aston, who had been on the staff for 42 years, including his years of war service – a remarkable record for any man, but especially for one who purported to dislike the city so much : 'if you open the window the air will move in in a block'. He was a man of forthright opinions who did not believe that it was really possible to teach a boy English until he was mature enough to have taste. The boys invariably called him 'Baggy' – either because of his initials or because when he first came to the school he wore the then fashionable wide trousers known as Oxford bags. In 1992, after Ben Aston's death, William Crosbie presented to the school one of his paintings, in memory of a man to whom he – and many other Academicals – felt enormous gratitude. Crosbie had been born in China and when he came to the school in 1924 his Mandarin was better than his English. This meant that there were those who did not make his life easy, but Aston befriended him and Crosbie never forgot it. Noted at school as 'good at drawing' he went on to become a Royal Scottish Academician and perhaps the doyen of Scottish artists : his gift was therefore an especially significant tribute.

D D Ogilvie retired at the same time as Aston : by comparison he was a newcomer, for he had joined only in April 1936, teaching Arithmetic to Transitus and Commercial Subjects to the Senior School but soon taking charge of Geography when Kelley left to fight in the war. Ogilvie's successor in 1967, David Humberstone, had made it plain that if he came he would insist on developing the work of the Department still further, in particular extending it into the Sixth Form.

Despite the Governors' decision to insist that Ben Aston should retire, they accepted that it was possible that ladies teaching in the Preparatory School might reach the age of 60 without having taught for the 40 years necessary to qualify for a full pension. Such cases would be treated sympathetically and teachers might be allowed to remain beyond the official age of retirement. The Governors, indeed, encouraged Miss Mackintosh to consider staying on as Headmistress of the Preparatory School until she was 65 – and she did so.

Men had the advantage for pension purposes of the additional five years and when the Rector suggested that Christopher Varley should remain for two years beyond his sixty-fifth birthday the Governors were cautious. In the event, after Holden had taken soundings, it was agreed that he should after all retire at the due time but that he would remain on a part-time basis for scholarship teaching. Gordon Carruthers took over as Senior Master in September 1969.

Chris Varley – Sixth Form French

Varley had been at the school for 33 years, succeeding Barrie in 1936. He taught first in Room G and then took over Room K which since time immemorial had been the room of the Head of Maths. Now the pupils became convinced that they were being taught there by a real live Frenchman since at times he seemed to speak no English words. He filled his pupils to the brim with vocabulary and expected them to remember it, even if it was the word for an itinerant scissors grinder : 'Now then, young man, you ought to know that – we had it four weeks ago!' Norman Stone, who became Professor of Modern History at Oxford and a well-known figure on television and in the press, recalled gratefully that Varley's pupils were infected with 'a mad enthusiasm for the dictionary that left competition standing'. Varley, whose first love among languages was in fact Spanish, finally retired at Christmas 1973.

Archie Foster died in 1969 after 34 years, first in Transitus and later in the Mathematics Department. He had been Careers Master, a post for which he was well equipped by his 'unusual understanding of the late adolescent who has not yet come to terms with some sides of school life'.

The following summer George Preston retired after 42 years. The History Department had been one of the most successful in the school, certainly in terms of preparing boys for Open Awards at Oxford and Cambridge, and he had been at its head since 1945. He had also been master in charge of games between 1934 and 1937, had coached the last undefeated First XV in 1935/36 and had been responsible for cricket as a whole and the First XI in particular until 1963. Cricket for him was a real passion : he became a regular member of the Academical XI in 1929 and, with a break for war service, continued until 1953 when he transferred for a further ten years to the Second XI. For some, though, his greatest distinction remained the fact that in 1950 it was he who had spoken the first words in the first Academy pantomime : 'I am Fairy Blossom'.

Two Heads of Department who retired in 1970 and 1971, E B C Thornton, Head of Maths, and Eric Walker, Head of Science, had been at the forefront of developing new teaching methods in their subjects. Thornton had been a contributor to the Scottish Mathematics Group developing the new course 'Modern Mathematics for Schools' and Walker had served on a number of committees producing alternative syllabuses first in Physics and then in Chemistry.

Eric Walker – Third Form Chemistry

He had seen the accommodation for science grow over his 24 years at the school from one building with three laboratories to two buildings with eight laboratories, a lecture room and several preparation rooms. So extensive had the Science Department become that on his departure it was agreed to pay separate responsibility payments for Physics and for Chemistry. In 1974 the next step was taken with the appointment of Ian Shirley as the first Head of Biology : the Governors had for some years cherished the hope that the subject might be taught to a more advanced level. In the same year, in another area of the curriculum, Alan Hutchinson was appointed as the first Head of German.

As some areas grew, others contracted. In 1970 Classics was taught by three full-time teachers, with help from two others. In 1971 the three specialists sufficed but when one of them left during 1972 not a single application was received for the vacant post. When E E Peters retired after 18 years as Head of Department in 1974 it was decided that no new appointment should be made : one full-time teacher of the subject, with part-time help, was all that was required.

There were also significant changes outside the classroom. In June 1964 T G Robinson indicated his wish to retire. Maxwell Simmers, who had come to the Academy as a twelve year old in 1916, was appointed as Chairman in his place. An accountant by profession and Chairman of Scottish Highland Hotels, Simmers was intimately involved in the work of organisations such as the Red Cross, the Boys' Brigade, the Scottish Schoolboys' Club and the Church of Scotland. He was, too, an outstanding athlete who won 28 Scottish caps at both centre and wing three-quarter and served as President of the Scottish Rugby Union. He had also been President of the Academical Club.

Maxwell Simmers

When Simmers died, suddenly, in November 1972 he was succeeded by William Leggat Smith. Leggat Smith, a member of the undefeated First XV of 1936, went from the Academy to Oxford and after the War, during which he was awarded the Military Cross, entered the legal profession. He became the senior member of a leading law firm in Glasgow and a prominent citizen – at various times Deacon Convener of the Trades of Glasgow, Dean of the Royal Faculty of Procurators and Chairman of Governors of the Glasgow School of Art.

William Leggat Smith

In 1960 the Janitor, Charles Jones, died and was succeeded by Donald MacRae, who for three years had been Assistant Janitor. Jones had been at the Academy since 1936 and was extremely highly regarded both in the school, which he was said to regard as a ship to be kept spick and span, and in the wider community – he was, for example, an elder of Lansdowne Church.

In 1967 Miss Stark Brown retired from the Dining Hall after 22 years, leaving behind memories of Academy Delight and Westmoreland

Soup. Her successor as cook/supervisor was Mrs O' Hara. Two years later Mrs Ford and Mrs Leven, better known to their customers as Jean and Ina, retired after 30 years in the Tuck Shop, latterly in new premises near the Dining Hall but originally in the Well.

There were numerous improvements, large and small, to the fabric of the school. The Dining Hall had proved to be a rather noisy place and acoustic tiling was therefore fitted to the ceiling there during the Easter holidays of 1960. A system was also installed so that sound could be relayed from the Cargill Hall to adjacent areas. Some years later the Governors took further decisions about the Cargill Hall when they met, as was their habit, after the Prize Giving : they came to the conclusion that some form of amplification was essential – and that there should be a clock on the wall facing the platform!

Two of the tennis courts were re-surfaced in 1961 and a third one provided. Early in 1963 an all-weather bitu-turf cricket net and wicket were placed between the tennis courts and Great Western Road. During the

course of its construction, the flagpole was broken away from its foundations and fell towards Great Western Road, breaking when it hit the boundary wall. Also during 1963 the part of the playground at the south end which was still ash and gravel was finally given an asphalt surface. In 1965 consideration was given to refurbishing the lavatories completely and at last providing hot water.

Part of the RN Section at work in the newly-surfaced playground

Facilities for the staff in the Prep School still left something to be desired. Miss Mackintosh had nowhere to interview parents, so a ground floor cloakroom was converted during 1962 into an office. Her staff were also short of space and had to do their cutting out on the floor of the staff room until extra accommodation was acquired. This naturally inhibited the development of handicraft work, which was an area which the new Headmistress was eager to promote.

Early in 1964 a committee which had been looking into the teaching of science reported that requirements included better qualified technicians, an additional Physics laboratory and another member of the teaching staff. The Rector was authorised to obtain a senior and two trainee technicians to replace the present part-time staff and architects were commissioned to investigate the possibility of adding a laboratory to the Physics Building. Their report indicated that a second storey of light construction could be added at a cost of £13400 and the work went ahead, though by 1980 the roof was leaking and major upgrading was undertaken during 1996, at a cost of £100000.

It was the turn of the Chemistry Building in 1972. Work began during the Easter holidays with the intention of upgrading the accommodation but a builders' strike during the summer meant that the work was delayed and arrangements had to be made at the beginning of the next session for Sixth Form boys to have the use of a laboratory at Strathclyde University on Thursday afternoons.

Another major project was carried out during the summer of 1975 when £20000 was spent on screens and doors to meet the require-ments of the Firemaster.

The purpose of spending money on the buildings and the facilities of the Academy was of course to help the teaching become more effective and in this, too, the Governors and the Rector continued to respond to a changing world.

After Holden had had some months to examine the ways of the school, he began to make proposals to the Governors to be implemented in September 1960. The most far-reaching stemmed from the Rector's belief that it should be wholly exceptional for boys to repeat classes in their earlier years at the Academy : instead, the Fifth Form would be sub-divided into two sections, to cater for the different levels of attainment that might be encountered there. Steps would be taken to keep a close eye on boys' progress and to identify early any who might be experiencing difficulty with their work. When they reached the Second Form, each boy would be allocated a Director of Studies, or tutor, with whom he would remain for the rest of his school career. The Rector was clearly anxious to help the boy who was not able to progress as quickly as his fellows, and the intention was to devise a timetable adjusted to his ability. This change of practice attracted some attention in the press and was seen as a departure from Scottish custom which had always insisted on a boy successfully completing one year of his course before proceeding to the next. 'Always' was not quite accurate : the practice had not been at all widespread before Donald Morrison brought the idea back with him from Germany in 1875.

To help make the new arrangements work, Holden gave parents the opportunity to meet their sons' tutors at evening meetings. The first such occasion was organised with consider-able success early in the 1961/62 session.

The school rules, too, changed with the times. The exhortation to parents that they should encourage their sons to wear uniform 'always in public' was dropped in 1970, to be replaced by strictures about keeping hair tidy. At that stage, too, the school cap became compulsory only in the Prep School and Forms I and II in the Senior School. On other matters the authorities stood firm : boys would not be excused from school in order to sit a driving test. The General School of Motoring had in 1961 written to the Rector to let him know that Academy boys were more successful in passing their driving tests than boys from any other school. As a result, the School wished to present a cheque for £25 to the Academy, together with a trophy. The Governors realised what was afoot and did not relish the idea of the handing-over ceremony that was also suggested : in fact, they thought that it would be an embarrassment to the Academy. Their reservations did not prevent them from pointing out to the Driving School that there was a Building Fund for which contributions were always welcome.

The Rector was glad to have the backing of the Governors over particularly thorny matters of discipline. He asked for, and received, their support in a case where he had refused permission for a boy to attend the wedding of someone who was not a relative, but the boy had been taken anyway. 'The parent realised now that he was in error.' There were other much more serious breaches : in May 1971 the Rector had to deal with a boarding house pupil who had been found in possession of drugs.

The Boarding House gave cause for concern in a number of ways during the second half of Basil Holden's Rectorship. A serious outbreak of dry rot had to be dealt with in 1967 and there was serious storm damage in January 1968 when a chimney head fell through a roof into a dormitory injuring one of the eight boys sleeping there. Much more fundamentally, however, the Governors began in 1967 to question the whole future of boarding at the school, particularly in view of what was then called 'the changing nature of the applicants for admission to the Boarding House'. It was agreed the following spring that the Boarding House should be continued, though the situation was to be reviewed annually and the Boarding House must be financially self-supporting.

Early in 1975 difficulty was still being experienced in keeping the Boarding House full and the financial results continued to be poor : indeed there had been a deficiency on revenue every year except one for the previous ten years. It was also quite clear that boys who would not have been accepted as day boys had been accepted as boarders. The decision was taken in February that year that the Boarding House should be phased out and the projected numbers were such that in June it was announced that no boarding facilities would be offered after June 1976. The final year of the Academy's Boarding House began with 13 boys in residence and the following summer a tradition which had become somewhat anomalous came to an end.

The whole question of admissions to the school continued to offer the Rector and the Governors a good deal of food for thought. For the first time a registration fee of £1 was charged in 1961 : it must have brought in a useful sum since there was a huge demand for places. In 1962 there were 322 applications for the 51 places available from Prep 1 to Prep 4; 77 applications for the 26 places in Prep 5 and 149 applications for the 16 places on offer between Transitus and Form III. Priority candidates again outnumbered the places available in some classes, but the Governors upheld the principle that 5% or 10% of the places could be allocated by the Rector to boys who were not priority candidates, even if this meant excluding some who were. Priority candidates who were younger brothers of existing pupils were often admitted at considerably reduced fees. In 1966 there were 24 third brothers at half fees, four fourth brothers for whom no fees were charged and one fifth brother who was also educated for nothing. It was decided that in new cases all brothers after the second should be charged 75%.

A significant advance was made possible in 1962 when John A Rose, who had been at the school between 1902 and 1909, transferred to the Trust investments worth some £20000, to be used to fund scholarships. The Governors agreed that they would also assist the parents of boys awarded scholarships with the cost of uniform and so on, if assistance was not available elsewhere. During 1964, when the Board was concerned about the effect on the Academy of a government opposed to independent schools, the Scholarship Fund was transferred to separate Trustees and constituted as the Montrose Educational Trust. Prudent investment increased the Montrose Fund from John Rose's original £20000 in 1962 to over £600000 in 1996. As for the scholarships awarded to boys leaving the school, it was reported in 1970 that for some time the winners of the War Memorial and Temple Scholarships had been awarded a prize and not an annual scholarship because an annual award would have reduced the grant they were entitled to receive from government sources. Mowat Scholars had continued to receive £150 because that figure was available from the investment of the Mowat Bequest but all winners would in future receive prizes of between £75 and £50.

In 1964 the Rector recommended that the intake into Prep 1 should be confined mainly to priority candidates but that assurances should be given to approximately fifteen of the best non-priority candidates that they would be accepted a year later for Prep 2. Miss Mackintosh thought she had a better chance of judging a

The first floor in 1964

boy at the age of 5, when she interviewed all the candidates, than after they had had a year's schooling elsewhere. The Rector admitted 12 boys that year into the First Form of the Senior School and had to turn down a number of good candidates : that meant there were three divisions of 34 boys each. The best boys continued to do well. The *Sunday Times* calculated that as far as awards to Oxford and Cambridge were concerned the Academy was the most successful school in Britain in 1964 and the second most successful in 1966. Another measure on which the Rector reported in 1969 was the percentage going on to university : 76.6% of the Academy's leavers did so, which placed the school third, after Winchester (87%) and Manchester Grammar School (77%). A Scottish Education Department report on the school in 1965 did, however, suggest that there was too much pressure on the less gifted boy. It also felt that there were shortcomings in class room accommodation : this was scarcely surprising since numbers had increased so much that three new teachers had been engaged in 1962 and teaching accommodation found for two of them by forming classrooms in the CCF Hut.

The school did work hard to keep abreast of modern developments. Two members of the Modern Languages Department attended a conference in 1961 about audio-visual methods and money was spent on equipment for that purpose; the SED asked the Academy in 1964 to take part in an experimental scheme for the teaching of Mathematics; the same department began to buy calculating machines a year later; reading laboratories were introduced by the English Department; the first overhead projectors were bought for the school in December 1970; in 1971 a Latin course was introduced which involved the use of a tape recorder. During the summer of 1971, too, a conference on 'The Challenge of Industry' was held at the school by the Industrial Society.

Several important decisions about the work and organisation of the school took place between 1971 and 1975. Firstly, the division of Prep 4 and Prep 5 into two groups according to ability stopped in 1971. This coincided with an increased emphasis on working in groups and being able to move freely in the classroom. Two years later, the curriculum for the Second Form was reorganised so that those who did not wish to continue with more than one foreign language, a quarter of the boys, followed instead a course which included Chemistry and Modern Studies. In 1973 it was agreed to approach the ABC Educational Co with a view to operating a book exchange scheme within the school for a week at the end of each session. Then in 1975 the Governors considered a request that a girl (from Laurel Bank) should be allowed to attend classes in Advanced Level Chemistry and

Physics. This was the first time since 1846 that the question of co-education had been considered. The Governors had no objection in principle but the idea came to nothing.

Outside the classroom, the growth of extra-curricular activities continued. A Film Society started in 1960 : its first three films were *Whisky Galore*, *Pickwick Papers* and *Hamlet*. Coincidentally, the school was placed first out of eight in a *Hamlet* competition held in connection with the Junior Citizens' Theatre. The Gavel Club was formed in September 1960 to encourage public speaking.

A change in the management of the Globe Players saw it renamed the Glasgow Academy Dramatic Society. In June 1968 it gave the first amateur production on any stage of Peter Shaffer's *The Royal Hunt of the Sun*, described at the time as 'an exotic and interesting play which marks a new episode in the artistic life of the school'. In 1969 the school play was moved to the end of the Easter Term – examinations made the Summer Term very difficult – and the concert to the middle of the Easter Term. A junior play was to be put on in June instead, so that the programme for 1969 was *Billy Budd* in March and *Jungle Jungle* in June : that was the first work written by G B Payman for the Academy Junior Players. The following year four girls from Park School joined the senior boys to perform *Romanoff and Juliet*. In a 1972 production of *A Man for all Seasons* members of Westbourne School took part and *The Tempest* in the following year involved Park. Musical activities included a Madrigal Group, a Folk Society and joint concerts with Westbourne School

An Art Club was started in 1968 and later in the year the *Chronicle* included a School

The dramatic production in March 1975 was 'Hamlet'

Supplement, containing original contributions by pupils. This in turn was superseded in 1970 by a separate magazine for creative work called SAGA. Other clubs included a Model Flying Club, a Mathematical Society, a French Club, a Zoological Society, a reborn Philatelic Society and a Curling Club. Some of these lasted longer than others.

The summer camps had by now been discontinued, but tours to the Continent of one sort or another continued. In July 1961, for example, a party of thirty six boys with three masters travelled by train from Glasgow to London, then on to Harwich and across by steamer to the Hook of Holland. From there an overnight train took them by way of a train ferry to Denmark. The party stayed at Vapnagaard for a week of intensive sightseeing. More informally, a group went youth hostelling in Germany during 1972. In 1971 the first French exchange visit was organised between a group of Transitus boys and a party from the Lycée Claude Bernard in Paris, who arrived on the very evening when the crucial vote on Britain's entry to the Common Market was taken at Westminster.

The CCF continued to be an activity of major significance and in September 1962 it was laid down that exemption from participation would be granted only on grounds of physical disability or conscientious objection. The CCF was seen as an important part of character training as well as to some extent making up for the lack of technical education within the Academy which outside observers had commented upon from time to time. It was argued that in the signals section, for instance, a boy could get some acquaintance with equipment which elsewhere he would get in a school workshop. The CCF also provided adventure training and other activities like ski-ing and hill-walking that helped a boy's development. It also became possible for boys to undertake community service, at first under the auspices of the CCF but later independently. In 1969 the school badge in metal was issued to cadets in the Army section replacing the HLI badge which had been worn for many years. In the same year John Plowman became Officer Commanding. He was succeeded in 1972 by Ken Waine who continued as Head of PE with general supervision of Games : he did, however, have assistance in the organisation and administration of Games from another member of the PE Department, from 1973 Rob Littlefield. Command of the CCF reverted to John Plowman in 1981, when membership was made compulsory for two years rather than three.

During the spring of 1974 Basil Holden was taken ill and Gordon Carruthers deputised for him. In August it became clear that the Rector wished to retire. A committee of

Roy Chapman inspects the CCF in 1976. Ken Waine stands behind him.

Governors met on 12 December and interviewed seven candidates to succeed him. Three were selected to meet the Governors a week later when the decision was taken to offer the post of Rector to Roy deC Chapman.

Chapman would come to the Academy in September 1975 as the school's sixth Rector. Born in India in 1936, he had attended Dollar Academy and then St Andrews University. His first teaching appointment was at Glenalmond, after which he went to Marlborough and became Head of Modern Languages. He also had command of the CCF.

Gordon Carruthers, who had been Acting Rector for eighteen months, became the Academy's first Deputy Rector in September 1975.

Wallace Orr, who had been at the Academy as a boy and then as Art Master, painted Basil Holden's portrait. It was unveiled at a ceremony on 19 April 1975 at which the Chairman paid tribute to the Rector's 'constant concern to bring on the average boy and to develop in every boy whatever talent each one had'. No longer could it be said of the Academy, as it had on occasion in the past, that it was fine for the bright boy but the average or slightly less than average was sometimes left to sink or swim. The Trust soon marked its appreciation of Basil Holden's services to the Academy by appointing him an Honorary Governor.

1975-1982

Roy Chapman

Two major building projects occurred during Roy Chapman's seven years as Rector. He identified the priorities early on : new accommodation for the Preparatory School, a Sixth Form block, an improved library, additional classrooms and, echoing a suggestion made some two years earlier by Ken Waine, a Sports Hall. At the end of his first year at the Academy Chapman reported that he sensed that the school was ready to accept the challenge of change both in the physical structure of the school and in the development of the curriculum. He had in mind particularly the introduction for the Sixth Form of a General Studies programme the following September. At that time, too, the school would be offering places in the Sixth Form to boys and girls who had completed their SCE and wished to follow the Academy's established one year course to Advanced Level and possibly beyond to Oxford and Cambridge entrance. The Governors had identified the possibility of accommodating more pupils at that level and believed that the girls' schools had difficulty in meeting the requirements of a comparatively small number of pupils. The SED had agreed that up to twenty girls could be accommodated in the school without adding to the present facilities. No girls were, in fact, admitted at that time and it was not until September 1981 that Gill Peters, Jane Singleton, Louise Dron and Ranu Roy entered the Sixth Form and ensured, as one of them put it, that 'gone were the days when a teacher could begin the lesson without fear of contradiction "Now gentlemen!"'

There was no real demand, however, for girls to be admitted to what was still in essence an all-boys' school and in 1984 it agreed to discontinue all reference to the admission of girls in the prospectus.

More definite progress was made, however, with building plans. A scheme for an extension at the rear of the Preparatory School was laid before the Governors at the beginning of 1976 and a possible site for the Sports Hall was identified. Fund-raisers were appointed and their representative given an office in 12 Belmont Crescent, confident of raising £400000 over a 15 month campaign. In fact this target was achieved by January 1978 and in order to keep the momentum going it was agreed to publicise the third object of the appeal, the provision of scholarships.

Investigations late in 1976 suggested that the site beneath Colebrooke Terrace was far from good because of various underground coal seams. There was also concern about the condition of the old buildings, but the feeling was that any settlement there would not affect the new construction. A start was made in September 1977 on a new two-storey building at the back of the houses in the Terrace : the Preparatory School would have classrooms and

A special occasion in the Prep School Assembly Hall

its own Assembly Hall on the ground floor, with a Senior School Library above.

Despite the success of the appeal it became clear that interest charges would mean that work on the Sports Hall would have to await further successful fund-raising. The active appeal stopped on 12 May 1978 when £527000 had been raised. The new buildings were inspected by the Governors just under two weeks later. Their total cost was £282366.

Attention did then turn to the Sports Hall and in September 1978 plans became available which included changing accommodation and three playing areas side by side, but not the swimming pool which had at first been envisaged. The estimated cost kept climbing and when tenders were received the Governors were shocked to discover that the lowest figure was well over £400000. This was reduced to £380000 by excluding CCF accommodation. Some years later with financial assistance from the Ministry of Defence this was provided in what had been the gym changing rooms.

A supplementary appeal to raise money for the Sports Hall was launched in 1979, generating £100000, and the building was formally opened during an Open Day on 28 March 1981. The new buildings meant that the old gymnasium became redundant and Transitus could return to the Prep School side of Colebrooke Terrace. The Rector earmarked the accommodation which had been released for re-housing the Biology and Geography Departments but detailed estimates for installing Biology on the top floor proved to be so costly that it was decided instead to convert the Chemistry lecture room into a Sixth Form Biology laboratory. The ground floor room in the south-west corner of the main building became a Science lecture room and the Geography Department moved to the top floor. Across the road in Colebrooke Terrace Sixth Form study rooms were fitted with carrels and the attics in Houses 4 to 7 were assigned to the CCF, the Careers Department, the Printing Club, the technicians and residential accommodation.

Along with its new accommodation, the Preparatory School had a new Headmistress in September 1978. Miss Katherine Ferguson came from Haldane Primary School, Balloch, to succeed Miss Doris Mackintosh on her retirement after 17 years at the Academy. Jim Cowper retired at the same time. He had been the last Housemaster in Belmont Crescent where as it happened the two houses were sold for £36000 shortly before the end of that summer term. A second flat was bought in Garrioch Drive, but one in Belmont Street was sold. 12 Colebrooke Terrace came on the market, but not at a price which the Governors were prepared to pay.

The Academy did, however, interest itself in property elsewhere. In April 1977 the Rector had mooted the idea of acquiring a base for outdoor activities, a cottage or outbuilding which could be improved by the boys themselves, and a start was made on accumulating funds for the purpose – there were, for example, six performances of the CCF Entertainment in 1977 and after the expenses of the production and sending the shooting team to Bisley in 1978 had been met, the surplus was handed over to the Outdoor Activities Centre Fund. The search for suitable property took some time but by the spring of 1979 a house and barn in Glen Etive had been identified, the property of the Forestry Commission. The Academy took possession of Invercharnan during June, with John Plowman in charge of its use and development. Planning permission for the reconstruction of outbuildings was received in January 1980. Some improvements were made, the Centre was used from time to time by small groups and the property was in fact purchased outright from the Forestry Commission some years later, but without very considerable investment in its improvement it did not offer enough facilities for large parties. It was also somewhat inaccessible. As a consequence it was sold in 1993.

One of the users of Invercharnan was the Sub-Aqua Club which had been founded in 1981. Other organisations which sprang up included a Horticultural Society, which organised marrow and gladioli competitions, a War Games Club, a Basketball Club, a Ski Club, a Numismatic Society, a Photographic Society (again), an Aero-Modelling and Flying Club, a Computer Club and a Rock Climbing Club. These activities naturally reflected the interests of members of staff as well as of boys and were more or less ephemeral. Others seemed to have acquired a degree of permanence : in 1977 the Christmas Entertainment was the twenty fifth for which Gordon Carruthers had been responsible, in the old Dining Hall, the Gym or the Cargill Hall – and as it turned out it was the last, for the following year Gary Gray, the Head of Art, took over. In 1980 there was a production of *Oliver* in which girls from Westbourne School joined Academy boys for the first musical of its kind to be put on in the school.

On 11 June 1977 an Open Day was held. During the proceedings a Canadian maple tree was planted in honour of Queen Elizabeth II's Silver Jubilee. There was also an Art Exhibition and this became an annual occasion. The Commemoration Service and the Carol Service continued to be held in Glasgow Cathedral : the

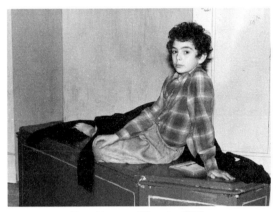

Rory Day as Oliver in 1980

Minister, the Revd Dr W J Morris, became the first Chaplain to the school in December 1975. A Chaplain to the Queen in Scotland since 1969, Dr Morris became Dean of the Chapel Royal in Scotland in 1991 and in recognition of his service to the Academy was appointed an Honorary Governor of the Trust in 1995.

Another new post for which Chapman argued was that of Bursar. For many years in the past the Academy had called on the services of a part time Master of Works : it was now proposed that a full-time appointment should be made to see to this and the oversight of other ancillary matters, though the administration of fees and salaries remained in the hands of the Secretary and Treasurer of the Trust. In August 1977 Wing Commander Roy Schofield took up the position. Four years later Donald MacRae died. He had been at the Academy since 1958, as Head Janitor since September 1960. A Scots Guardsman, a Company Sergeant Major of the Glasgow Highlanders, a member of the Guild of Professional Toastmasters and a freeman of the City of Glasgow, his dignified presence added much to Academy occasions.

The staff in the early 1980's:
sitting on the front row, from left to right, are Mr Waine, Miss Johnston, Messrs Black, Carruthers, Chapman,
Miss Ferguson and Messrs Robertson, Humberstone and Payman.

Early on in his Rectorship Chapman addressed a number of administrative matters. He felt that at all levels communication should be improved, suggesting that more Governors' meetings should be held at school and that Governors should lunch from time to time with the Rector and meet a number of members of staff. He suggested that an internal telephone system should be installed and that extra outside lines should be provided for the CCF and Janitors' offices. He also subjected the contracts for teaching staff, technicians, janitors and administrative staff to close scrutiny. One effect of this was abandonment of the practice of employing women teachers in the Senior School only on a year to year basis. In 1972 it was only 'in the absence of a suitable male applicant' for a post in one department that a lady teacher had been appointed for a year.

There were other modernising moves. From 1976 the cap was to be worn only by boys in the Preparatory School; two years later caps and shorts were to be worn only up to and including Prep 5. An even more radical change in the Preparatory School occurred in 1979 when a Prep 6 stage was introduced for most boys, giving most pupils a full seven year primary course before they moved into the

Senior School. A Transitus X class continued to omit Prep 6 until Session 1983/84.

In the Senior School, the Rector made it clear in 1975 that sitting 'O' Grade in the Fourth Form should be phased out. Only boys not proceeding to Higher in a particular subject should be presented in it at 'O' Grade. At the same time it was agreed that membership of the Independent Schools Careers Organisation should be available to parents who paid a once only charge at the beginning of the Fourth Form.

In 1977 special courses of a practical rather than an academic nature were provided at the end of the Summer Term for boys who had completed their SCE examinations. A number of pupils also began to spend a week on work experience in the business world. Biology at last became an Advanced Level subject in 1976 and three years later was made available as an option in the Fourth Form. In 1979 the Governors felt that the Rector might wish to appoint an additional PE teacher because of the difficulty of getting teachers sufficiently qualified to coach games : Chapman felt, however, that a more important priority was to reduce the size of science classes.

A scholarship funded by money from the appeal was made available in September 1979 to a boy entering the First Form. During 1978 the Governors had decided that the only type of external grant acceptable to them would be one made to parents and not to the school. It was therefore open to them to agree two years later to take part in the Assisted Places Scheme, offering at least five and at most ten places with full remission of fees.

School equipment continued to be brought up to date. Photocopying facilities were introduced in 1976 and three years later the Rector proposed that the school's first mini-computer should be bought : at the beginning of the Spring Term in 1980 it arrived, a Commodore Business Machines 'Pet'. The cost was just over £600 and software cost a further £200 : but the Governors did not at first sanction the purchase of a printer. A Resource Centre for the new equipment was provided by partitioning off part of Room LL. Funds for another machine were provided from the proceeds of the Parents' Dance in 1981, which also raised money for the Pipe Band and for lighting in the Well for Art Exhibitions. This was the first Dance for which Mrs Lorna McNaught was responsible, taking over from Mrs Belle Mitchell whose final Dance the previous year had provided equipment for the Sports Hall.

There were other improvements. A medical room was provided in Colebrooke Terrace and a time clock was installed in 1978 so that the bell did not have to be rung by hand at the end of each period of the day. At the same time the Preparatory School timetable was rationalised so that the women and the men who taught there worked equal hours. Planning for a new type of prospectus, advertising the facilities and benefits offered by the school, also began in 1978. In 1982 the Governors agreed to allow the payment of fees by instalments.

Other changes proposed made slow progress : it was some time after a change to cafeteria service in the Dining Hall was first mooted before the system was actually introduced – and it took even longer to dispose of corporal punishment. In 1982, almost a century after Donald Morrison had expressed the conviction that it could be banished from the classroom, Roy Chapman told the Governors that discipline could be maintained perfectly well without it, but it was not until 1987 that the use of the belt – the 'biff' in Academy parlance between the wars – was finally abolished.

Despite changes to the constitution of the Club admitting to certain categories of membership individuals who had not been pupils at the Academy, the Trust and the Club continued to enjoy a close relationship, particularly in connection with shared use of the facilities at Anniesland. During 1979 the Governors agreed to increase the annual amount made available by the Trust to the Club in order that life membership of the Club would be given in due time to all boys leaving the school. The two bodies also funded jointly the employment of a cricket professional. Part-time help had been given in the past by such men as Brian Edmeades, formerly of Essex, and two Pakistani Test cricketers, Intikhab Alam and Sadeq Mohammed, but when Phil Cooper took over the post in 1981 he transformed Academy cricket. His coaching over the next eleven years resulted in a number of boys from the school achieving international recognition at junior level and indeed in 1995 three young men who had been his protegés, Douglas Lockhart, Euan Stubbs and Jonathon Graham, all played for their country in the same under 19 side.

In 1978 the Club was added to the list of bodies which were able to nominate Governors to serve on the Board. Strathclyde University was added at the same time. At the Trust's Annual General Meeting in November 1980 William Leggat Smith intimated that he was retiring as Chairman, after eight years. He was succeeded by Alastair D S Rolland. Rolland, the son of an Academical and himself the father of Academicals, became a Chartered Accountant

Alastair Rolland

on leaving the school in 1947. He was Treasurer of the Royal College of Physicians and Surgeons of Glasgow and Deputy Chairman of the Edinburgh and Paisley Building Society.

Long-serving members of the staff inevitably retired from time to time, including Miss Jean Ritchie in 1979 after 32 years in the Prep School, demonstrating 'her faith in the capabilities of small boys to respond to the stimulus of carefully prepared work' and Lachlan Robertson three years later. Appointed in October 1950 on the retirement of Miss Kate Gentles, he too had served for 32 years, teaching Transitus – for much of the time in Room E. He had been Chairman of the Common Room and much else besides, both within the school and outside it – CO of the 15th Para and a Deputy Lieutenant of the City of Glasgow, to give just two examples. The Chairman of the Common Room represented the views of his colleagues to the Rector and it was accepted that the proper channel of communication between Common Room and Governors was through the Rector. A system of more direct liaison was proposed in 1982, though, when it was agreed that two Governors would from time to time meet representatives of the staff to discuss matters which had already been submitted to the Governors by the Rector. The Governors had by then revised the salary scale offered to staff at the Academy by doing away with the fixed supplements which in the past had been added at various stages of the scale. Instead a percentage was added to the salary which would have been paid if the national scale had been in force.

At the beginning of April 1982 the Governors learned that Roy Chapman had been appointed Headmaster of Malvern College with effect from the beginning of January 1983. On 9 June Colin W Turner was selected to become the seventh Rector. He had graduated from King's College, London, in Geography and had then become a teacher of Mathematics at the Edinburgh Academy. He was Head of Maths there and then, in 1975, became a Housemaster. He had also commanded the CCF for several years.

Colin Turner

1983-1994

Colin Turner

Roy Chapman's last school functions were the Carol Services – and the perennial Christmas Entertainment, now written and produced by Gary Gray and in 1982 entitled *Colebrooke*, a school story about a new boy encountering nine or ten different facets of life in a school which bore only the faintest resemblance to the Academy.

Among Colin Turner's first functions were performances of *Macbeth* during March 1983. He inherited a well-established annual routine of events and activities at school and further afield. The Christmas Entertainment and two Carol Services, for the Prep School and the Senior School, gave musical and dramatic opportunities in December and the Senior School staged a play or a musical during the Spring Term – *Guys and Dolls*, *My Fair Lady* and *The Gondoliers* are examples of the ambitious productions that were undertaken and in 1991 *Orpheus in the Underworld* was staged at Christmas in place of the traditional pantomime. Junior pupils continued to be given the opportunity to take part in a play of their own, such as *Treasure Island* in 1988, and the Prep School played to appreciative audiences each March. Their concert developed ambitiously : in 1986 it concluded with a musical play, *The Burning Bush*, and eventually the whole evening was given over to a full-length show, such as *Rats* or *Babylon Times*.

One change was made in December 1984 when for the first time the school's Carol Service was held on a Sunday evening in the Cargill Hall instead of in Glasgow Cathedral. A new electronic organ was installed in the Cargill Hall during 1984 and the musical life of the school also benefited from the gift of Roydon Richards' grand piano which found a new home in the Cargill Hall during the same year.

A wide variety of opportunities was on offer during school holidays. At Easter 1988 a party of twenty boys visited the Collège Victor Hugo at Tarbes. Correspondence had been going on for eight years but this was the first actual exchange. The arrangement continued happily over the next few years. Ski-ing trips went to Switzerland, France and Austria and other holidays to such destinations as Crete, the USSR, Italy, France, Corsica, the Dolomites, the Mont Blanc region and East Africa. The CCF, too, organised many activities, very different from the Annual Camp at Gailes which was so familiar to an earlier generation : there were hill-walking trips in Glen Etive and Torridon, Junior Leadership courses on Arran, camps at Cultybraggan, at Garelochhead and on Orkney, Fleet Tender cruises on the Clyde, RAF camps in Lincolnshire, Buckinghamshire, Bedfordshire, a Naval Air Acquaintance course at Yeovilton – and much else besides. Cadets were also able to travel abroad – to Canada, Gibraltar, Germany.

Boys from the Prep School began to spend time at the Abernethy Outdoor Centre, at first during the holidays but later during the

A First Form group in Glencoe, with David Gray

Summer Term, and in May 1989 for the first time the whole of the First Form went to Glencoe in groups for a programme of Field Studies based in the Youth Hostel there. New extra-curricular activities continued to be added to the already lengthy list : a Sailing Club started in 1984 and so, too, did the Duke of Edinburgh's Award Scheme, which was soon to grow into the most popular of all the activities on offer at the school. In June 1988 the first Academy boys to win the Gold Award visited Holyrood Palace.

The lists of sporting fixtures arranged against other schools embraced an ever-widening field of activity : to rugby and cricket, so long established, had been added over the years swimming, curling, golf, athletics, tennis, cross-country, squash, even football (the Association variety once so roundly decried in the pages of the *Chronicle*).

There were changes within the classroom. In 1989 the school took over responsibility for text books and parents no longer had to buy them for their children. A new system of examinations led to the demise in 1990 of the arrangement under which many boys had bypassed 'O' Grade. Instead, all pupils were presented for eight subjects in the new Standard Grade, a system which laid unfamiliar stress on coursework and internal assessment.

For many years, the administration of external examinations had been in the hands of Gordon Carruthers as Deputy Rector but during the spring of 1985 the Governors heard that it was his intention to retire at the end of the year. He had joined the Academy in 1948 to teach Chemistry and Physics but later taught Chemistry with some Biology. He had commanded the CCF – and he had masterminded the CCF

Christmas Entertainment. Under his guidance those who took part and those who watched had had tremendous fun – but the whole undertaking was carried on with characteristic concern for high standards and discipline. In later years Carruthers rather ruefully reflected that it was this activity more than any other which Academicals remembered about him. He resigned as Contingent Commander when he became Senior Master in 1969. During the difficult period between the onset of Basil Holden's illness and Roy Chapman's assumption of the Rectorship – between May 1974 and September 1975 – Carruthers was Acting Rector of the Academy. It was a time when there were staffing difficulties to be dealt with but also exciting prospects for the future, since plans were being made for the use of the houses in Colebrooke Terrace and the construction of a Sports Hall had been mooted.

After Chapman's arrival, Carruthers became Deputy Rector : on retiring from that post in January 1986 he was succeeded by John Davidson Kelly, who had been a Housemaster at Epsom and Deputy Headmaster at Christ

John Davidson Kelly with a group of senior pupils

College, Brecon. He immediately and successfully set about the re-invigoration of the Pipe Band and immersed himself enthusiastically in school rugby and cricket. He also became a well-known figure amongst Academicals at Anniesland.

When Gordon Carruthers retired, a new post was introduced : Ken Waine became Senior Master with administrative duties including responsibility for discipline. Rob Littlefield was appointed Head of Physical Education and Games. In June 1988 Waine himself retired after thirty years' service, first as Head of Physical Education but soon with responsibility also for Games. He introduced the system of continuity by which a member of staff coached a team throughout its first three years in the Senior School. He also commanded the RAF Section and in due course the entire CCF and was, too, an enthusiastic member of the Academical Club, of which he was President in 1985, the first serving member of staff to be accorded that honour.

Ken Waine was succeeded as Senior Master for three years by Tony Richards, who had joined the English Department in 1960.

In the classroom he quickly established for himself a reputation as a meticulous teacher whose insistence on accuracy and conciseness produced for many boys results far beyond their expectations. Richards also involved himself in the CCF, in cricket, in preparing maps of the cross-country course at Mugdock, in the Christmas Show and in helping with other dramatic activities. On his retirement in 1991, the post of Senior Master was taken by David Humberstone, who had been Head of Geography.

Miss Doris Johnston retired from the Preparatory School in 1983 after twenty five years. She had put much time and care into the organisation of the Prep School Library : her pupils, though, would probably remember singing *Silent Night* in German and going on what was an annual class picnic to Kilmacolm. Two years later, Jimmy Jope retired after teaching Mathematics for 27 years : the Gavel Club, still going strong, was his creation in 1960.

Moreton Black had an even more remarkable connection with the Academy than any of those long-serving teachers. He had joined the school as a pupil in 1931, in the last months of Dr Temple's Rectorship, and had been

Captain of the School and Captain of the First XV. He had been awarded cricket colours and a Mowat Scholarship. After the war and completion of his degree at St Andrews he returned to his old school to teach Modern Languages and, with an interlude in Tasmania, continued to do so until his retirement in 1986, from 1959 as Head of the Department. He established the Naval Section of the CCF, re-established the Stamp Club, looked after tennis and captained the masters against the boys at cricket. He also took no fewer than 42 trips to the continent – and it was his modest boast that he never lost a single boy.

Another member of the staff who had attended the Academy as a boy was Pat Silvey, who had returned to teach Mathematics and in 1985 was appointed the school's first Head of Computing. By then computers had become well established in the school : there was a teaching set of 13 BBC B machines and the departments of Mathematics, Physics, Chemistry, Biology and Geography each had their own. Other new subjects were added to the range on offer : in 1987 Economics and in 1988 Craft and Design.

In 1989 a computerised administrative system was installed both in the School Office and in the Trust Office which had moved to the school itself the previous year. Since 1953 the Trust's work had been carried out in the office of J W Dallachy who had succeeded Norman Sloan as Secretary and Treasurer in January that year. After 36 years of remarkable service, Hamish Dallachy handed over his duties in 1988 to Ian McNaught.

Hamish Dallachy had come to the Academy as a pupil in 1916 and remembered

clearly being taught in Room A by William Melven who himself had been appointed to the school in 1881. On leaving school, Dallachy qualified as a chartered accountant and at once became thoroughly immersed in the activities of the Academical Club. He was Captain of the Academical XI in 1932 and 1933 and in 1935 became Secretary of the Club, a post which he held until 1960. He served also as Vice-President of the Club between 1933 and 1935. He also gave great service to the Scottish Cricket Union, as Secretary and Treasurer for many years and then as Vice-President and President. He was President, too, of the Institute of Chartered Accountants of Scotland.

His election as a Governor of the War Memorial Trust in 1944 coincided with the succession to the chair of David Brand. When Dallachy became Secretary and Treasurer to the Trust in 1953, the Chairman was Sir Tennant Sloan – and then a succession of Chairmen and Rectors had cause to be grateful for Dallachy's shrewd advice and unremitting loyalty to his school. Sir Tennant was followed by Thomas Robinson, Maxwell Simmers, William Leggat Smith, Alastair Rolland and – in 1985 – Forrest McLelland. Dallachy had been a pupil at the Academy under Edwin Temple : as Secretary he worked with four other Rectors, Roydon Richards, Basil Holden, Roy Chapman and Colin Turner and saw the annual income of the Trust grow from £50000 to £1700000.

To mark the occasion of Dallachy's retirement a dinner was held in his honour early in 1989, attended by 46 past and present Governors. During the summer of that year the redecoration and carpeting of the first floor of the school's main building was undertaken, following an appeal to Academicals for contributions in recognition of Dallachy's remarkable service to the Academy. Hamish Dallachy was appointed an Honorary Governor from 1 January 1989.

In 1989 it was agreed that all school leavers should automatically become members of the Trust and the nominal life membership fee disappeared.

Forrest McLelland, the eighth Chairman of the Trust, retired from the post in 1990. He had come to the Academy as a boy just after the First World War : after the Second, during which he served in Africa, he went to work with Brownlee and Company, a firm founded by his great-great-great-uncle just three years after the Academy had opened its doors in Elmbank Street. He was thoroughly involved in many organisations ranging from the Order of St John to Glasgow College, of which he was Vice-Chairman, and Glasgow Caledonian University, into which the College was eventually trans-formed. The Academy and the Academical Club were extremely close to his heart : he played in

the Academical First XV and served a term as Club President, and was Chairman of the Governors of the Trust in historic times for the school. If he had a special interest within the school, it was probably the Pipe Band.

Forrest McLelland with Pipe Major Robin Lane in 1988

Forrest McLelland was succeeded as Chairman by Bill Mann. He attended the Academy between 1944 and 1952, qualified as a chartered accountant and then established his own company. Although he played rugby for the Academicals his first love was cricket, and

Bill Mann

he captained the Academical XI in 1963 and 1964, serving also as President of the Scottish Cricket Union. He was involved in the establishment of the squash section of the Academical Club and in the introduction of mini-rugby at Anniesland, and, as Secretary, he was responsible for saving the Western Baths Club from closure.

In 1990, too, Miss Katherine Ferguson retired as Headmistress of the Preparatory School : Mrs Helen Fortune was appointed to succeed her. In 1991 Ian MacGregor retired after 34 years' service, mainly with the boys of Transitus where his talents in story-telling and acting, in particular, made him a gifted teacher. As the senior member of the Prep School's staff he had been right hand man to two Head-mistresses, but the niche which he made most especially his own was in the world of rugby, to which he gave great service – Academy rugby, Academical rugby and Scottish rugby. He was an internationalist, Convenor of the SRU's Laws Committee, Manager of teams touring to France and to Australia, and Convenor of the Selectors for four years, including the Grand Slam year of 1984.

Although none of these established teachers was affected by the change, it had been agreed in October 1983 that members of staff employed at the Academy after that date should retire when they reached the age of 60.

Two young members of the teaching staff for whom retirement had seemed some-thing entirely remote and distant were tragically taken from the Academy on 3 February 1991 when Ian Jeffery and Alex Tysen were killed whilst climbing on Creag Meagaidh. Alex Tysen had been a teacher in the Prep School and then in the Mathematics Department of the Senior School. Ian Jeffery had taught Biology : a travelling scholarship in his memory was funded from his estate. Both men had arrived at the Academy on the same day in September 1980 and Colin Turner paid moving tribute at a Service of Remembrance in the Cargill Hall to what they had achieved in their ten years at the school.

Biology was a subject to which the Governors had for some years paid a good deal of attention. They had agreed in 1985 that the most urgent capital requirement at the school was accommodation to teach it in and that autumn they approved a plan to provide laboratory space on the first floor of 5, 6 and 7 Colebrooke Terrace, with rooms for teaching History on the ground floor. This scheme received a severe setback when the Governors were advised to spend a very large sum on infilling so as to avoid mineral subsidence in the future, that is the collapse of the old mine workings which ran beneath Colebrooke Terrace. All work on the project was suspended.

Elsewhere in the school another scheme hatched at the same time made better progress. The cloakroom accommodation around the Well had for many years been largely unused and was now fitted out to provide a careers library, a number of small offices, a kitchen, a medical room and accommodation for secretarial work. This work was completed in time for the beginning of the session in September 1986 and was so successful that the even bolder step was taken of commissioning plans to install the school library in the Well itself. When this had been done, late in 1987, Miss Susan Clark was employed as the school's first qualified librarian and a substantial sum of money was provided by the Governors for new books.

The Library in the Well

In addition a Book Fair was held on 11 March 1988 at which parents and friends of the school were able to purchase books for the library after listening to a number of distinguished speakers giving their views on the sort of books that were, for them, required reading. The school's visitors that evening included two who were not Academicals – Sir Andrew Gilchrist who spoke on biography and travel and Tom Weir who spoke on natural history and the countryside – and two who were, Norman Stone on history and politics and John Beattie on sport and

recreation, fittingly since he was the most recent Academical rugby internationalist.

Further upgrading was carried out in the main building at the same time : the former science lecture room was equipped as an audio-visual room with tiered seating to accommodate just over 50 pupils.

An even more startling transformation took place to the outside of the main building and the houses in Colebrooke Terrace. Like most of the Victorian buildings in Glasgow they had acquired a layer of grime which concealed the natural colour of the sandstone and it was agreed that the stonework should be cleaned. Part of the funding for this was provided by the sale of flats, including the two in Garrioch Drive which had been used for temporary staff accommodation. Once the building had been cleaned, floodlighting was installed and the Academy again became a particularly striking sight from Great Western Road, especially when seen under the floodlighting. The appearance of the houses in Colebrooke Terrace was further improved during 1987 and 1988 when the gardens in front of them were remodelled by Community Service volunteers who made imaginative use of stone slabs and also built stone-walled raised beds for shrubs and flowers. Alterations were made to the rear of Houses 10 and 11 including the provision of accommodation for CCF boats and in October 1988 12 Colebrooke Terrace was purchased for £35000. The first floor was eventually upgraded for residential purposes and the basement converted into premises for the school outfitter but the first priority in 1992 was to turn the ground floor into office accommodation for the Bursar and his staff.

In 1993, after five years, Ian McNaught retired, having successfully brought together two posts which previously had been quite distinct – Bursar of the School and Secretary to the Trust. Ian McNaught's connection with the Academy was probably unique and spanned over sixty years : he had been a pupil at the school, a leading light in the Academical Club, a parent, a prominent Governor and then – having retired from his professional career – Secretary to the Trust, a post in which his friendly courtesy and meticulous attention to detail did much to assist those with whom he was working.

Ian McNaught

The needs of Biology had not been forgotten and early in 1987 it was agreed that an entirely new building should be put up between the Physics Building and the Gymnasium. This, too, required the consolidation of mine workings and the overall cost approached £250000. The building was opened on 2 March 1989 by an Academical, Professor Sir Malcolm Macnaughton. Professor of Obstetrics and Gynaecology at Glasgow University and President of the Royal College of Obstetricians and Gynaecologists, Sir Malcolm was also a Governor of his old school and later an Honorary Governor. Accommodation was provided in the new building for the three Biology teachers who were then on the staff : thanks to a new appointment at the beginning of the session Biology was, after many years, staffed in exactly the same way as Chemistry and Physics. There were two large laboratories, together with a lecture room and a greenhouse.

Following the refurbishment of the first floor of the main building, work was undertaken to improve the classrooms on the second floor. Modern Languages classrooms on the west side were equipped with up-to-date listening posts, which had superseded the Language Laboratory, and Mathematics classrooms on the east and south sides were also modernised. This work included the permanent division of the former Writing Room, which for over fifty years had been 'temporarily' divided into Rooms L and LL, into three new classrooms. When it became part of the curriculum, computing found a home at the top of the main building, in part of what had been the Gymnasium. In 1990 it was moved downstairs to Room P, one of the rooms on the north side, and Geography took over the whole of the old Gym. A major refurbishment of this area was undertaken during 1994. The Chemistry Laboratories were also substantially upgraded over a number of years. Planning to convert the tennis courts to an all-weather surface all-purpose games area began in the spring of 1988.

There were other improvements to the facilities for games. A conditioning room was fitted in the Sports Hall during 1986 and better equipment for athletics – together with storage – was provided at Anniesland.

In November 1988 the Governors met to consider the unpalatable but undeniable fact that for a number of years the numbers in the school had been falling : in September 1985 there had been 899 boys on the roll, falling to 880 in 1986, to 869 in 1987 and then to 825. The Board recognised that the Academy's reputation was perhaps not as pre-eminent as it had been and the school's location no longer the advantage it had been. Public relations needed to be improved – it had already been decided that an improved prospectus should be prepared – and a committee was established with that remit. The question of co-education was raised, but it was agreed that a number of ways of increasing the roll should be examined and given a fair trial before it was considered further : there might, for instance, be the possibility of specialisation in one particular niche – remedial work and music were cited as possible examples.

Early the following year it was agreed to commission a market research project and to take positive steps to promote the school. It was a year before the project bore fruit but the Board's discussions continued in the meantime. There was a feeling that if more assistance were available through scholarships the roll would increase, since boys would come to the school who would otherwise be unable to do so. Two sub-groups of the public relations committee were established during the autumn of 1989, one to examine marketing, the other to consider the possibility of co-education.

On 12 February 1990 the Board examined the conclusions of the market research project, which had identified a continued and possibly increasing demand for co-education in the Glasgow area. In 1960 only two of the 18 Headmasters' Conference schools in Scotland

had been co-educational, whereas in 1990 just three accepted only boys. The report reiterated that there had been a falling roll at the Academy in recent years and concluded that this might in the long term pose a problem. Co-education could certainly improve the potential intake to the school. In discussion, members of the Board accepted that one possibility to achieve co-education would be to amalgamate with a girls' school.

On 22 February a further meeting was held and a number of issues aired – action which might be taken to attract more boys to a boys' only school, the practical problems of becoming a co-educational school, the effect of a falling birth rate on numbers at the school – but when the Chairman tabled the motion that 'This Board agrees to produce proposals to put before members of the Glasgow Academicals' War Memorial Trust for co-education at Glasgow Academy' it was carried by a very substantial majority.

On 29 March it was agreed that since one route by which co-educational status could be achieved was amalgamation with a girls' school, the Chairman should write to his counterparts in Park, Laurel Bank and Westbourne to enquire 'whether the Governing Body of any of the three West End girls' schools is interested in combining two schools to form one co-educational establishment'. On 21 May it was reported that the Chairman of Westbourne School for Girls, Alistair Struthers, had suggested a meeting to pursue the points made in the Chairman's letter : a meeting was held and the Westbourne Board appointed a small committee to continue joint discussions.

From the Academy's point of view, it was stressed that amalgamation was still only one of a number of possible ways ahead – the Governors had, for example, appointed a part-time public relations specialist who continued to advise them until 1992. The Board's objective was to create a better Glasgow Academy, and not an altogether new school. The name of the school would be retained after any merger, the Trust would continue to manage it, Colin Turner would be Rector, and whilst there would for as short a time as possible be a two site arrangement ultimately the whole school would be at Colebrooke Street. The possibility was considered of acquiring the plot of ground bounded by Belmont Street, Great Western Road and Colebrooke Street for a new Preparatory School, to be financed by selling a girls' school's property, but this was soon ruled out. The Academy's Board noted that Westbourne had no playing fields, but felt that within the Academy's property there would be sufficient space for games.

On 28 June it was reported that the Westbourne Governors had accepted the Academy's principal points, although they hoped that it would be possible to retain some reference to their school, perhaps on letter headings or in the name of a building. The Board of Governors of Glasgow Academy then voted in favour of an amalgamation with Westbourne, provided that a proper scheme of incorporation could be achieved.

Westbourne School for Girls had been born as the Westbourne Gardens School in September 1877. William Levack purchased 34 Westbourne Gardens (No 33 was soon acquired, too) and each of his six daughters had an association with the school in its earliest days, five as teachers, the sixth in charge of the housekeeping. The two eldest were the school's Headmistresses until they were married and in 1887 Miss Madge Levack took over. She had taught in the school since its inception and was to remain at its head for thirty years until she was succeeded in 1917 by Miss Annie Neilson.

In the early years of Miss Madge's Headship the school had just over one hundred pupils in eight classes, the largest of which consisted of fourteen girls. Boys were admitted to the youngest classes. After a lesson in arithmetic first thing in the morning, the whole school assembled in the drawing room for prayers. It was in the drawing room, too, that dancing lessons were given. The school was famous for the beautiful sewing achieved by the girls and one pupil recalled of her days at the school just after the turn of the century that what Miss Madge really wanted 'was to produce young women with as much good influence in matters of morals, speech and elegant living as seemed possible'. Other schools moved ahead earlier than Westbourne Gardens School into the teaching of science, though one teacher did make a gesture in that direction: 'with only a kettle on the fire and a number of bottles with tubes inserted sealed in the necks, she demonstrated the effect of boiling water on the various fluids contained – but with no laboratory nor tools of the science she could not carry us very far'. Although there was a gymnasium no games were played until about 1915 when a concession was made in favour of netball, badminton and cricket – but hockey had to wait until 1918. Tennis courts appeared shortly after the school moved, in 1920, to new premises – Kelvinside House.

Kelvinside House had been built as Beaconsfield House in 1875, by James Brown Fleming who in 1846 had been one of the first

Kelvinside House

pupils of Glasgow Academy. Increasing numbers at Westbourne Gardens School – there were by now some 150 pupils – meant that new premises had to be found and the mansion house was ideal, providing as it did space for classrooms and living accommodation for Miss Neilson, the Headmistress, together with her mother – and her sister, Miss Jetnie Neilson, who continued a Westbourne tradition of excellent French teaching initiated by Mlle Eugenie Ceccaldi. 'The basic skills of social competence' continued to be imparted : one former pupil recalled being 'taught to open a bazaar and to write a reference for my cook'.

There was no school uniform until 1902 when a red flannel blouse was introduced with a navy blue tunic. The tunic was later combined with a red wool jumper, a navy tie with red crest, a red girdle and black three-quarter socks, a white shirt replacing the jumper in summer.

When Miss Neilson retired in 1931, Miss Muir became Headmistress, followed four years later by Miss Rose Harris – Mrs Henderson after her marriage in 1953.

In September 1939 the school – known as Westbourne School for Girls since the move to Kelvinside House – was evacuated to Symington House, near Biggar, the country house of a family whose girls had been at the school before the war. It was thought necessary for the future of the school that it should return to Glasgow as soon as it was safe to do so, but in 1944 Kelvinside House was still occupied by the military authorities. It was therefore decided to rent No 1 Winton Drive, nearby, and so greatly had the numbers increased that the lease was maintained even after Kelvinside House became available again. At first the Senior School was housed in Kelvinside House and the Junior

Winton Drive

School in Winton Drive but the situation was reversed in 1952 when No 3 Winton Drive was acquired. Science laboratories were formed from the billiards rooms of the Winton Drive houses and a dining hall built in what had been the back gardens.

A substantial addition was made to the school's buildings in 1956 when the Ann Fraser Hall was erected in the grounds of Kelvinside

House and equipped as a gymnasium. 5 Winton Drive was eventually added and a new Laboratory, Art Room and Home Economics Room were housed in a building which linked Houses 3 and 5. Two of the teachers ran a boarding house for weekly boarders in No 15 Winton Drive until 1965 and for some time the school owned 17 Beaconsfield Road where it had classrooms for the older girls in the Preparatory School.

The school continued to be privately owned until 1951 but in that year it became a limited company with a Board of Governors. The first Chairman was Hugh Fraser, a parent, who became successively Sir Hugh Fraser and Lord Fraser of Allander. Westbourne benefited hugely from 'his genuine interest, his time, his business acumen and experience and his kindly humanity and personal insight'. Lord Fraser was a Glasgow Academical whose life encompassed both his business interests as Chairman and Managing Director of House of Fraser Ltd and a wide range of other commitments, as a Director of the National Bank of Scotland, a member of the Scottish Tourist Board and an interested supporter of the Salvation Army. He was succeeded as Chairman of the Westbourne Board by another distinguished Academical, John Donald Kelly, who was in fact a Governor of his old school. Kelly was by profession an accountant, but he was much else besides : he served as a member of Glasgow Corporation for some thirty years, received the St Mungo Prize, was President of the Royal Glasgow Institute of Fine Arts, chaired the Governors of the Glasgow School of Art, convened the committee charged with housing the Burrell Collection and served as a Director of the Scottish National Orchestra.

The Westbourne uniform was changed in 1953 when the navy and red of the previous half century gave way to a navy pinafore, navy blazer, navy jumper, lilac shirt, striped tie and black tights. This in turn was replaced after twenty years or so by a lilac skirt, a lilac and white checked blouse with 'Peter Pan' collar – and thus no tie, a purple jumper and a purple blazer.

Miss S L McKillop became Headmistress in 1964, and after her Miss Elizabeth K Henderson, who was Headmistress between 1969 and her retirement in 1988, when the Governors appointed Westbourne's first Head-master, John N Cross. He came to a school whose pupils enjoyed a wide academic curriculum embracing all three levels of the SCE, a proud record in all manner of athletic activities and an enthusiastic commitment to every sort of extra-curricular activity.

During the summer of 1976 Westbourne had combined for the purposes of financial management with Laurel Bank, Park and St Columba's under the auspices of the West of Scotland School Company Limited in an arrangement which allowed each of the schools to retain its individuality and traditions.

Discussions between Westbourne and the Academy continued during the summer of 1990 and the conclusion was reached that amalgamation was indeed a practical proposition. On 25 October it was reported to the Academy's Governors that the Westbourne Board had met the previous evening and had agreed in principle to the merger. The War Memorial Trust held its 71st Annual General Meeting on 29 November 1990 and overwhelmingly agreed that an amendment should be made to the Trust's Memorandum of Association, allowing girls to be educated at the Academy. Members were told that it was hoped that Glasgow Academy would become a family school at which brothers and sisters would be able to benefit from the same educational experience. Architects had already prepared a scheme which would transform Houses 1 to 7 in Colebrooke Terrace into a first class Preparatory School building. While the work was going on, Prep 1, Prep 2 and Prep 3 would be housed in Kelvinside House.

After the Trust's AGM, Westbourne representatives began to take part in the planning meetings of the Academy Board and early in 1991 the staffs of the two schools met to discuss curricular matters arising from the amalgamation. Thoughts turned to a new uniform and to the constitution of a new Governing Body : there would be sixteen Governors, of whom thirteen would be elected and three nominated, by the Glasgow Chamber of Commerce representing business interests, the Universities of Glasgow and Strathclyde representing the academic world, and the Glasgow Academical Club. Some of the existing nominating bodies no longer had the strong Academical links of years past. It was proposed that four of the sixteen Governors need not be former pupils of either school.

The changes to the constitution of the Board were approved at an Extraordinary General Meeting of the Trust in July 1991 and the way was therefore opened for the first ladies to become Governors of the Academy and for the assets of the Westbourne School for Girls Ltd to be transferred to the Trust on 1 August 1991. The first lady Governors of the War Memorial Trust were Mrs Alison Bruce, Mrs Inez Murray and Mrs Alison

Thompson. They were later joined by Miss Betty Henderson.

At the Trust's meeting it was also announced that the refurbished Preparatory School building would be known as Westbourne House. The budget for this major building development was some £675000 and by September that year twelve classrooms were available in what had been the first three houses. The whole building was finished in time for the three junior classes to exchange Kelvinside House for Westbourne House at the beginning of the summer term and the Secretary of State for Scotland, the Rt Hon Ian Lang, performed the formal opening ceremony on 5 June 1992.

Ian Lang with Jane Crawford and David Howie in the new Academy uniform

There are eighteen classrooms in the refurbished building, together with the Assembly Hall, an Art and Science Room, an Audio-Visual Room and accommodation for learning support. There is also the McEwan Library, named in honour of Miss Agnes McEwan and opened in February 1992 by George Macdonald Fraser, an Academical author well known for the 'Flashman' books which began to appear in 1969. Over £3000 was donated by Academicals to a Library Appeal in Miss McEwan's memory.

The Senior School also needed more accommodation. In September 1991 the Rector reported that two more laboratories were required : one would be provided in the Chemistry Building where a ground floor room was in use as a Sixth Form Common Room and a second could be formed by joining the Physics and Biology Buildings. Accommodation for Home Economics would be needed, together with a number of additional classrooms. A new home should also be found for Music.

The laboratory which was developed between the Physics and Biology Buildings was opened by Alistair Struthers in January 1993 and named the Levack Laboratory in honour of the Misses Levack of Westbourne Gardens School and in recognition of the fact that the Trustees of the Westbourne Appeal had contributed £50000 towards the cost of providing what was to be the fourth Biology laboratory in the Academy. The merged school opened with eleven laboratories in its three science buildings.

An entirely new development for the Academy began to emerge late in 1991 when the Preparatory School committee of Governors and staff unanimously recommended that the school should offer Kindergarten facilities, a well established feature of Westbourne. The Governors of the Academy had in 1983 themselves looked into a proposal to have a nursery school associated with the school but had decided to take no further action. A site for the Kindergarten at Kelvinbridge was eventually identified to the rear of Houses 8 and 9 and construction was undertaken during 1993. Children were admitted to the Kindergarten on the understanding that this would not mean automatic acceptance into Prep 1.

At the end of 1992 a scheme was devised to provide accommodation for the English Department, Home Economics and the Sixth Form by reconstructing Houses 10 and 11. This would mean that enough classrooms would be available for the fully merged school by September 1993, except that Music would have to be provided with makeshift accommodation in the meantime. The work was done during the summer holiday of 1993 when it was also found possible to provide new computing facilities, in Room A, and changing facilities for girls in the Sports Hall.

After some deliberation as to where it should actually be situated, it was decided in November 1993 to go ahead during the following summer with the construction of a new Music building next to the Sports Hall and the tennis courts. As well as two sizeable classrooms, one of them equipped with computerised keyboards, there are small practice rooms, teaching rooms for small groups and a magnificent recital room with a new grand piano, overlooking Great Western Road but soundproofed from it. The Westbourne Appeal again contributed to the cost of equipping the new building : it also made funds available to purchase equipment for the Duke of Edinburgh's Award Scheme.

Young musicians perform in the new recital room

The move of Preparatory School children to Kelvinbridge during 1992 and the merging of the Senior Schools the following year meant that Kelvinside House and the houses in Winton Drive could be put on the market. It was not an easy time to sell property and with Kelvinside House in particular there were disappointments. It was nevertheless the first of the buildings to be sold, followed by 5 Winton Drive and then the two semi-detached houses. The sale of the Westbourne properties realised close on £900000, which helped to finance the major developments at Kelvinbridge and allowed £250000 to be added to the Scholarship Fund.

This Fund had been established in 1984 after the school had received a number of legacies and it continued to benefit enormously from money received in the same way. The Governors undertook in particular to name a scholarship after Miss Kate Gentles who had taught in the Prep School and who had left almost £40000 to the Academy. Other bene-factors included John McGaw, Loudon McQueen and Andrew Wilson, whose bequest was a particularly handsome one, in excess of £125000. The generosity in the past of Gilbert Innes was brought to mind again with the sale in 1984 of the last remaining Killearn property : and in April 1985 a legacy of £2000 was received from a lady who had received fee rebates between 1975 and 1979 following the death of her husband.

When the proceeds of the Winton Drive sales were added to the Scholarship and Bursary Fund and the Montrose Trust Fund was also taken into consideration something approaching £1000000 was available to assist parents who might not otherwise be able to send their children to the school. For the benefit of pupils in the Sixth Form there was an annual grant of some £4500 from the W A Cargill Trust, used to fund two or three scholarships. The Academy continued to take part in the Assisted Places Scheme, though the number of pupils involved, which had increased after the amalgamation, was being reduced. In addition discounts were still available where three or more members of a family were in attendance. The arrangements for educating the children of teachers at the school were re-negotiated.

In September 1989 there was virtually the same number of boys in the school as in the previous year, but in 1990 there was a substantial drop to 773. That number then climbed to 786 and there were in addition 254 girls, making a combined roll in 1991/92 of 1040. This was somewhat more than the optimum number for which accommodation was available and subsequent sessions saw the roll fall to just below 1000, excluding children in the Kindergarten and Nursery.

The changing nature of the school meant that the Governors had to consider its staffing very carefully. Amalgamating two schools meant amalgamating two staffs as well as two bodies of pupils and it was necessary to ensure that the various departments of the co-educational Academy had the number of teachers they needed to deliver the curriculum to a school of just under 1000. Mrs Joan Deane, who had been Headmistress of the Junior School at Westbourne, became Deputy Head of the Preparatory School. John Cross retired and his Deputy, Mrs Rae Murphy, became an Assistant Rector at the Academy, together with Iain MacLeod who had been Head of English since G B Payman's retirement in 1984. In addition to Home Economics, the study of Accounting and Finance was added to the Academy's curriculum and provision was made for Learning Support.

Facilities had also to be planned for girls' games, in particular hockey, and in 1991 it was decided that an all-weather hockey pitch should be located at Windyedge and a grass pitch at the Club Ground. It was decided to retain four Houses. Three of them kept names with Academy connections – Temple, Morrison and Arthur – and the fourth took a 'Westbourne' name, Fraser.

In 1991 a termly newsletter was produced for the first time and called *Newslines*, whilst in 1992 there appeared the first issue of a redesigned *Chronicle* in A4 format to be produced annually – and issued to all pupils free of charge, as it had been since 1983. The first Editor was Mrs Margaret Dow who also became the first lady to head a major department at the Academy when she succeeded Iain MacLeod in 1993.

Work was also undertaken to achieve a new corporate image for the school, to be used on letter headings, advertisements and so on. The Academy's motto was retained but the badge was subtly altered with the addition of some purple – Westbourne's distinctive colour. The uniform for both boys and girls was redesigned to reflect the fact that the school colours had changed. The tie, in particular, became dark blue, light blue and purple. All boys were to wear the same tie – the Governors had rejected the idea of a special 'colours' tie in 1988. The blazer became slightly bluer and a tartan was designed for the girls' skirts or pinafore dresses in the new colours.

Pupils of the Academy had continued to excel in activities both sporting and academic. It was not uncommon for upwards of half a dozen each year to represent their country in an increasingly wide variety of sports – no longer just rugby and cricket, now, but tennis, lacrosse, athletics, shooting, wind-surfing, cross country, squash, amongst others. Iain Higgins played both chess and badminton for Scotland in 1991. In the same year Richard Good was awarded prizes by the Scottish Geography Teachers' Association and the Institute of Physics for producing the best Higher papers in Scotland in those two subjects. The following year Omar Khan, who in the end went to Cambridge, was placed first in the Glasgow Bursary Competition in the final year of its existence. The Advanced Level results were so excellent in 1992 that the Academy was placed 21st in Britain in a league table produced by the *Sunday Times*.

In 1993 Miss E K Henderson donated a Dux Medal to be awarded in the Preparatory School. The first recipient was Michael Atkinson. At the same time it was decided once more to award a Dux Medal in the Senior School and Iain G Macfarlane was chosen as the Dux Medallist for 1993.

The co-educational school involved itself wholeheartedly in a range of activities which reflected the interests of all the pupils. The Art Department organised trips to destinations such as Paris, Barcelona and Amsterdam and the annual Art Exhibition was revived. Pipers under the watchful eye of John Davidson Kelly did well in a variety of competitions. Pupils won awards in several writing competitions, perhaps most notably the W H Smith Young Writers' Competition in which the Academy was the only Scottish school to win a School Award in 1994 for the high overall quality of its entry. The *Chronicle* collected a number of prizes in *The Scotsman* School Magazine Awards. Debating and public speaking went from strength to strength and a remarkable range of musical and dramatic events continued to take place, involving pupils from the earliest stages of the Preparatory School right up to the Sixth Form in the Senior School. Rugby, hockey and cricket players went on tour and pupils from the Academy continued to win international honours in many sports. The Young Enterprise Scheme was introduced to give its members a taste of running a business and each year an imaginative range of 'products' was marketed – Christmas cards and decorations, discos, cushions for use in the Cargill Hall, a fashion show. Fund-raising for various charities continued unabated.

Colin Turner retired in June 1994. He had been Rector of the Academy at a time when the school experienced what he – and others – believed to be the most exciting development in its history. As well as co-education, though, the Academy had embraced many other changes during Colin Turner's eleven years and more at its head : major building works, the addition of

Colin Turner opens the building named in his honour

new subjects to the curriculum, the change to new methods of examination. To all this he had brought qualities of faith and vision.

Colin Turner has two tangible memorials within the Academy : a portrait by Norman Edgar was unveiled shortly before the end of his last term and in September 1995 he returned from retirement to declare open the new music school, which the Governors decided to call the Turner Building in his honour.

The planning to find a successor to Colin Turner had begun in 1992 and on 8 November 1993 the Governors decided to appoint David Comins as the eighth Rector of the Academy. A Yorkshireman, he had read Mathematics at Downing College, Cambridge, and then embarked upon a teaching career which was to take him, as it had taken Edwin Temple, to Glenalmond. David Comins became Head of Mathematics at Glenalmond and then Director of Studies, but he came to the Academy after a period as Deputy Headmaster of Queen's College, Taunton.

From 1994
into a new era: *David Comins*

When Bill Mann became Chairman of the Governors, Colin Turner took the opportunity at Prize Giving to express his confidence that the financial control of the school could be in no better hands. That confidence was well placed : at the first AGM of the Trust which David Comins attended after taking up his post it was reported that a deficit of almost £55000 in 1991 had gradually been turned into a surplus in 1994 of well over £120000 before crediting the capital levy of some £75000 and charging depreciation of £65000. Progress continued to be made, so that in the three years to March 1996 the cashflow surplus before any extraordinary income and before charging major capital expenditure such as the Turner Building and the hockey pitch at Windyedge amounted to £932000.

The emphasis in recent years on the transition to co-education and on matters of finance had ensured a firm foundation on which the eighth Rector could build. There was, inevitably, still some way to go before girls and boys were equally represented on the school roll: in September 1995 31.5% of the pupils were girls, though the proportion in the Prep School was higher, poised soon to reach 40%.

Two long-serving members who had joined the Academy when thoughts of co-education would have been laughed out of court retired from the teaching staff just before the school celebrated its sesquicentennial. John Plowman had served for 37 years, principally as a teacher of Physics and as an apparently essential component of the CCF in which he was involved for over thirty years, with two separate spells as Contingent Commander : he finally retired from that post in 1988 when he handed over command to Ian Wright. Latterly, John Plowman's invaluable function in the school was to act as the timetabler, a responsibility which he combined with a number of other administrative tasks in which his remarkable talent for finding solutions to seemingly intractable problems came once again to the fore.

David Humberstone retired in June 1995. For four years he had been Senior Master, dealing with a whole raft of administrative matters and generally overseeing the discipline of the school : his room was well known to latecomers reporting with their ingenious excuses, to persistent offenders turning up for detention, to the absent-minded and careless whose school bags had been 'stolen'. Humberstone had been appointed in 1967 as a reforming Head of Geography with a clear view of his subject's rightful place in the Academy. He had also been for many years Chairman of the Common Room, a mark of the respect in which his colleagues held him and of their confidence in his ability to represent them effectively. His sense of humour and what a

John Plowman

colleague described as his 'forthright common sense' ranked high among his hallmarks.

Other long-serving members of the Academy community who continued their service as the school approached its sesquicentennial included Mrs Margaret Tindall, who as Miss McNeill had been appointed in 1965 to teach the boys of Prep 3 and who had made a particular mark as a devoted fund-raiser for the RSSPCC. Miss Rachel Teggart had been appointed Rector's Secretary in 1970. Miss Teggart's encyclopædic knowledge of Academy families was only one of the invaluable qualities from which four Rectors were to benefit, and after the amalgamation of the Academy with Westbourne School for Girls she was able to add her knowledge of that school's families, too : she had been Head Girl of the Academy's new partner and, somewhat later, a Governor. She retired from her full-time post in 1996 but continued in a part-time capacity.

The session beginning at the end of August 1995 was marked as The Glasgow Academy's 150th Birthday. Every pupil in the school had the opportunity to join in a range of special events, many of which also involved parents, Governors and Academicals as well as members of staff. Foremost among these activities was the raising of money – but not for the Academy itself. The intention was to raise £50000 to refurbish and re-equip accommodation for teenage girls with disabilities living at East Park in Maryhill Road. Academy pupils had been visiting East Park for several years as part of the Community Service programme and were used to contributing towards its funds through collections at Carol Services and similar events. The 150th Anniversary of the Academy seemed an opportune occasion on which to strengthen the connection. Each class in the school was given a target – appropriately £150 – which it was hoped they would raise through activities of their own devising; a selection of commemorative items was produced for sale – golf balls, chocolates, wines, sweaters; a raffle was organised; a Summer Ball was held towards the end of June 1996 for which the playground at the school was magically tented over. The target was reached and at the start of the following session a cheque was presented to East Park on behalf of the Academy by John Beattie.

John Beattie opens The Courtyard at East Park

Many other events commemorated the anniversary. There was a sixteen-team rugby tournament at Anniesland in September 1995, a hockey tournament at Windyedge the following November which also celebrated the opening of the all-weather playing surface there, a squash tournament in December, and a cricket match against the MCC in May which the Academy team won. During the holiday week in October 1995 two ambitious foreign trips were organised : senior hockey and rugby players enjoyed a successful tour to Canada while the most ambitious Art Trip to date offered pupils the opportunity to experience the attractions of New York. Later in the year, the annual Art Exhibition was opened by Angus Grossart, who left the Academy in 1955 and eventually became the first chartered accountant to be called to the Scottish Bar and, in time, the founder of a merchant bank. It was as Chairman of the National Galleries of Scotland, though, that he was invited back to the Academy in 1996.

Another ambitious plan for the 150th year was for groups of pupils, parents, members of staff and Academicals to climb at least 150 Munros – Scottish mountains over 3000 feet – on the same day, 26 May 1996. In the event 151 peaks were climbed in an endeavour which did have links with the Academy's history : the first man ever to climb all the Munros, Aeneas Robertson, was an Academical and completed the task in 1901. Later, in August, a group of past and present pupils and two teachers set out to climb in the Himalayas and mounted a successful assault on the 18600 feet of Gondoro Peak. One of the group, Claire Walker, was the youngest girl ever to have reached the summit.

The Academy's strengths in debating and public speaking were marked during the anniversary year by two special functions. There was first a special 'Question Time' in the Cargill Hall during February when a number of prominent Academicals, at the school in the 1940s, 50s and 60s, returned to give their views on a wide variety of topics. In the chair was Sir Michael Hirst, Chairman of the Scottish Conservative Party. Norman Stone flew from Oxford for the occasion. Three other political viewpoints were represented by a pair of Academicals and a former member of staff : Robert Maclennan, President of the Liberal Democrats and MP for Caithness and Sutherland; Douglas Crawford, former Scottish Nationalist

MP for Perth and East Perthshire; and John Maxton, the Labour MP for Glasgow, Cathcart, who taught History at the Academy in the 1960s. Perhaps not surprisingly, in view of his later career, the comment was made when he left for another post that his teaching had 'paved the way for the discussion of the world's social and economic problems'.

Later, in May, there was a debate on the motion that 'William Wallace would be proud of Scotland'. With another in the chair, three young Academicals were joined in the cut and thrust of debate by David Gray, who was shortly to retire from the English Department after serving the school since 1972, not only as a teacher but as a rugby coach, a leader of the CCF's RAF Section and an enthusiastic organiser and promoter of debating. In 1983 his team, Paul Sinclair and Anthony Frieze, had won the Scottish Schools Debating Trophy and a whole succession of accomplished debaters had gone on from the Academy to the debating chambers of various universities : the return of four of them made for a happy occasion.

The Prep School celebrated the Academy's Birthday with a party at the Academical Club's ground on the gloriously sunny afternoon of their Sports Day in June. There had been another, perhaps grander, party much earlier in the session – on 15 September 1995 – when after the opening by Colin Turner of the new music building in the morning the Academy was honoured in the evening by the City of Glasgow. A Civic Reception was held in the City Chambers at which 350 representatives of the Academy community were entertained to dinner : there were speeches and there was music, provided by pupils, Academicals and members of the music staff.

Perhaps the most moving acknowledgement of the Academy's 150th year, however, came in November. The Academical Club's Dinner was held in the Cargill Hall and the principal speaker was Sir Iain Vallance, in 1961/62 School Captain, Captain of the First XV and regular member of the First XI – and in 1996 Chairman of British Telecom. There was also an exhibition of Academy memorabilia in the library and there were various reunion sports fixtures – but on Friday 10 November the entire school, from the Nursery to the Sixth Form, witnessed in dignified silence a Service of Remembrance at the War Memorial in Great Western Road. On that day, certainly, there can have been few members of the school who did not recall to themselves the fact that the Academy was a 'living and enduring memorial to the former members of the school who served in the war of 1914-1918'.

That November morning's Act of Remembrance was all the more poignant because the Academy had so recently suffered the shocking loss of two young members of its community. Mark Scott, a Fifth Year pupil, had been murdered in the streets of Glasgow and Andrew Reid, who had just begun his studies at Edinburgh University, had fallen into a diabetic coma from which he never recovered : their deaths reminded many that, all too often, the schooldays of Academy pupils have been rudely intruded upon – by the death of a favourite teacher, by the tragically early passing of a fellow pupil, by the folly of war.

For most pupils, the final events of the Academy's 150th Year were, as usual at the end of a session, the Prize Givings. The Guest of Honour at the Senior Prize Giving was Lord Macfarlane of Bearsden whose presence served as a reminder of the close links – and the rivalry – that have long existed between the Academy and his own school, the High School of Glasgow. In 1878 the High School moved into premises vacated in Elmbank Street by the Academy; in 1976 the new independent High School was built on land which had once been the Academy's playing fields.

The day before Lord Macfarlane spoke in the Cargill Hall, the Junior Prize Giving was addressed by the Revd Fraser Macnaughton, then Chaplain of Dundee University, an Academical and a member of a long-established Academical family. Mr Macnaughton's theme was that it is more important to look forward than to look back and no one who heard him speak that morning could fail to have been persuaded of the truth of what he said.

Anniversaries, though, do encourage looking back and histories tend inevitably to celebrate the achievements and qualities of those who have gone before. The Glasgow Academy owes more than any book can convey to those who have kept faith with the vision of its founders – its Presidents and Chairmen, its Directors and Governors, its Rectors and its members of staff, teaching and non-teaching.

The men who met in the Star Hotel in 1845 shared their vision with the parents who sent their boys along to Renfield Street the following year, with the masters who taught in

the new classrooms of Elmbank Street in 1847, with the Directors who bought the site at Kelvinbridge in 1877, with the Academicals who founded the War Memorial Trust in 1919 and with the Governors who took the decision in 1990 that the Academy should become a co-educational school.

Part of that vision was that the Academy's pupils, enriched by whatever the school had had to offer them, would themselves enrich the life of the city and country in which they went on to take their places. Over the years, those aspirations have been fully realised. There can be few spheres of activity to which former pupils of the Academy have not made significant contributions.

The first President of the Academy, Henry Dunlop, had been Lord Provost of Glasgow : several boys from the school he helped to found were later to follow in his footsteps and others were to fill with distinction some of the many important offices of the city : Bailie, Senior Magistrate, Chairman of the Education Authority, Lord Dean of Guild and Deacon Convener of the Trades House. On several occasions Academicals have been honoured by the award of the St Mungo Prize. In the wider field of national government, there has scarcely been a time this century when the House of Commons has not had an Academical representative amongst its number : two Secretaries of State for Scotland and at least one 'shadow' Secretary of State have been educated at the Academy. Another Academical, Sir Louis Greig, was at one time Controller of the House-hold of the Duke of York, later to become His Majesty King George VI.

Many Academicals have served the Scottish Law with distinction. There was a time,

for example, just before the Second War, when three Academy boys were Judges of the Court of Session at the same time. At least one Solicitor-General for Scotland has also come from the Academy and one Master of the Supreme Court. The Dean of the Royal Faculty of Procurators has been an Academical. In England an Academical assumed the office of Master of the Rolls in 1996. Academicals have given their time and expertise to public bodies of every sort : the Crofters' Commission, the Scottish Milk Marketing Board, the Clyde Navigation Trust and the Royal Scottish National Orchestra would find a place in the lengthy list.

Academicals have served overseas in many different ways : one devoted his life to working as a medical missionary among the Kikuyu people of Kenya, another was Master of the Royal Mint in Ottawa, a third the Chief Police Magistrate in Fiji. In the days of Empire one former pupil became a member of the Council of the Viceroy of India and many others served in the administrations of the various dominions. In 1996 the British Ambassador in Washington and the Israeli Ambassador to the United Nations were both Academicals.

Church life has been much enriched by the contributions of Glasgow Academicals. George Matheson, author of the much-loved hymn *Oh love that wilt not let me go*, attended the Academy : so, too, did Moderators of the General Assemblies of the Church of Scotland, the United Free Church and the Presbyterian Church of England, several Bishops and a Lord High Commissioner to the General Assembly of the Church of Scotland. As well as Deans of the Thistle and of the Chapel Royal and Chaplains in Ordinary to the monarch there have been numerous parish ministers whose lives of service have been crucial to the well-being of those among whom they have lived. The Student Christian Movement and the World Student Christian Federation have each been led by an Academical.

So, too, in medicine. Whether it be in general practice or in hospital medicine, at home or abroad, Academicals have from the earliest days of the school devoted themselves to the care of the sick. The Medical Superintendents of at least two of Glasgow's great hospitals, the Western Infirmary and the Victoria Infirmary, have been Academicals. On one notable occasion, the University of Glasgow was able to establish four new chairs in medicine : three of them went to men who had been at the Academy. When the Chair of Pathology was founded, the first Professor was another Academy boy. At a time in the First World War when advances in antisepsis were of crucial importance an Academical produced flavine. Academicals have long been active in the British Medical Association and in the British Dental Association.

One Nobel Prize winner, the discoverer of argon, helium, xenon, krypton and neon, was educated at the Academy : scientists and academics in every discipline have been nurtured by the school and Academicals have held chairs in Universities all over the world – Sydney, Toronto, Columbia, Malaysia and Bombay are simply a selection – as well as in each of the ancient Scottish Universities and throughout the United Kingdom. The first Professor of Accountancy at Glasgow spent his schooldays at the Academy. Academicals have been found at the head of every sort of educational institution : Principal of Aberdeen University; Master of St John's College, Cambridge; Master of Balliol College, Oxford; High Master of Manchester Grammar School; Rector of Kelvinside Academy; Principal of George Watson's College.

Many Glasgow firms, household names in their day, were headed by Academy boys : Templeton's, the carpet manufacturer; Macfarlane Lang, makers of biscuits; Copland and Lye and the House of Fraser, department stores; and Bilsland's, the bakers, are just some examples. Other national firms owe much to the service of Academicals : Mavor and Coulson, with a world-wide reputation for mining and material-handling machinery, the North British Locomotive Company, Nobel's Explosives, ICI, British Petroleum, British Telecom. Shipbuilding was for many years part of Glasgow's lifeblood and from time to time the direction of several Clyde yards was in the hands of Academicals : Denny's; A & J Inglis (at the mouth of the Kelvin which flows past the Academy); Connell's; Fairfield; Lithgow's. An Academical was Chairman of P and O, the great shipping line, and another the Controller of Merchant Shipping during the Second World War.

At least two distinguished publishing families have Academy connections, Blackie and Hamish Hamilton, and Academicals have been editors of publications as diverse as the *Glasgow Herald*, the *Bulletin*, *Life and Work*, *GUM*, the Toronto *Globe and Mail* and the *Burlington Magazine*. The BBC and Channel Four television have both been under the direction of Academicals, as has the Royal Opera House, Covent Garden, while the Theatre Royal in Glasgow also owes much to an Academical. Television programmes as diverse as *Dixon of Dock Green* and *Monty Python's Flying Circus* have been directed or produced by Academicals.

One of the most notable of all Academicals, Lord Reith, returned to present the prizes in St Andrew's Hall in June 1950

There have been poets and playwrights and novelists of distinction – Maurice Lindsay was an honoured guest at the opening of the Turner Building – and in the world of art Academicals have had charge of the Tate Gallery, the Wallace Collection and the National Gallery in London. There have been Royal Academicians and one former pupil, George Pirie, was President of the Royal Scottish Academy.

Turn to other, very different, fields and everywhere there are to be found Glasgow Academicals who have distinguished themselves : Jack Buchanan starring in musical comedy, Jim Mollison making pioneering flights in the

history of aviation, Neil Campbell Duff designing many of Glasgow's distinctive picture houses and other familiar buildings, Harry Hodge acting as shorthand writer at the trial of Oscar Slater.

The Academy has produced distinguished soldiers, including the Director of Military Operations at the War Office just before the outbreak of the First World War. There has been just one Test cricketer – but there have been rugby internationalists galore, including the scorer of the winning goal in the very first match against England. At one time the Presidents of the Scottish Rugby Union and the

Scottish Cricket Union were both Academicals. Herbert Waddell, President of the Academical Club in its Centenary Year, was created CBE in 1980 for his services to rugby – he was capped fifteen times for Scotland and was President of both the Scottish Rugby Union and the Barbarians. Mountaineering and hill-walking in Scotland were greatly influenced by men who as boys attended the Academy : one, Bill Murray, died during the sesquicentennial year but will be widely remembered for books like *Mountaineering in Scotland* and *The Companion Guide to the West Highlands of Scotland*. Academicals have presided over the Scottish Sports Council, the Scottish Lawn Tennis Association, the Scottish Badminton Association and the Royal Caledonian Curling Club.

At least three influential organisations for youth owed much at their inception to Academy boys – the Scottish Schoolboys' Club to William Boyd, the Boys' Brigade to Sir John Roxburgh and the 1st Glasgow Troop of Boy Scouts to Robert Young. Glasgow owes much to the memory of other benefactors who passed through the Academy : Lord Rowallan presented to the city both Rouken Glen Park and Mansion and the Ardgoil Estate at the head of Loch Goil and Sir James Macfarlane gifted the site of what is now Canniesburn Hospital, while Sir John Reid bought Erskine House and its grounds and presented them to the Princess Louise Scottish Hospital for Limbless Sailors and Soldiers, so close to the hearts of many Glasgow people.

The first words which David Comins addressed to the girls and boys of The Glasgow Academy on 1 September 1994 spoke of his vision for the school. 'I want The Academy to be a school in which effort counts no less than ability, in which every talent gains due recognition and in

David Comins with the Head Girl – Rosaria Crolla – and Head Boy – Euan Stubbs – in The Academy's 150th Year

which individuals flourish without becoming stifled by our corporate life together. I would like The Academy to be a school where trust, tolerance and openness flourish, where barriers between us are removed and where bridges between us are built. I hope the strong will look after the weak and I hope, too, that every member of The Academy will feel significant and valued.' As that vision helps to shape the life of The Academy in the next chapter of its history it will ensure that young people leave the school as well equipped as ever they have been to serve the community and to keep faith with the ideals of the men who founded their school in a very different age, in a very different Glasgow.

Some Notables

Presidents and Chairmen of The Glasgow Academy Company
Henry Dunlop (1845 - 1867)
Anderson Kirkwood (1867 - 1871)
William G Blackie (1871 - 1878)
Robert Young (1878 - 1888)
William Ker (1888 - 1912)
John W Arthur (1912 - 1921)

Chairmen of The Glasgow Academicals' War Memorial Trust
Sir Robert Mackenzie (1920 - 1944)
David E Brand (1944 - 1948)
Sir Tennant Sloan (1948 - 1957)
Thomas G Robinson (1957 - 1964)
W Maxwell Simmers (1964 - 1972)
William Leggat Smith (1972 - 1980)
Alastair D S Rolland (1980 - 1985)
J Forrest McLelland (1985 - 1990)
William M Mann (1990 -   )

Honorary Governors of The Glasgow Academicals' War Memorial Trust
Sir John A Roxburgh, Bart, VD, DL, LLD (1923 - 1937)
General Sir A Hunter, GCB, GCVO, DSO, TD (1924 - 1936)
Sir John M MacLeod, Bart, CA, LLD (1924 - 1933)
Sir D Y Cameron, Kt, RA, RSA, LLD (1924 - 1945)
The Very Revd G H Morrison, DD (1924 - 1927)
Charles Ker, CA, LLD (1924 - 1939)
The Rt Hon Walter E Elliot, PC, MC, LLD, MB, DSc, FRS (1924 - 1957)
Sir James Bell, Bart, CB, LLD (1925 - 1930)
D M Hannay (1925 - 1929)
Walter Macfarlane (1925 - 1928)
The Very Revd Sir George Adam Smith, DD, LLD (1925 - 1942)
Nicol Paton Brown, CBE (1926 - 1934)
The Right Hon The Lord Lindsay of Birker, CBE, MA, LLD (1928 - 1951)
Dr A A Young (1929 - 1939)
The Very Revd Charles L Warr, CVO, DD, LLD, HonRSA (1934 - 1969)
Sir James Lithgow, Bart, GBE, MC, TD, DL, JP (1941 - 1951)
The Rt Hon The Lord Reith of Stonehaven, PC, GCVO, GBE, CB, DCL, LLD,
MInstCE, HonFRIBA (1941 - 1971)
Rear-Admiral W S Chalmers, CBE, DSC (1941 - 1971)
Sir John T Cargill, Bart, LLD (1944 - 1968)
Sir Robert C Mackenzie, KBE, CB, DL, CA (1944 - 1945)
W A Cargill (1950 - 1962)
Major-General D A H Graham, CB, CBE, DSO, MC (1953 - 1971)
The Right Hon The Lord Sinclair of Cleeve, KCB, KBE (1953 - 1978)
Stanley Smith, OBE, MC (1953 - 1974)
Sir James M Wordie, CBE, MA, BSc, LLD (1953 - 1961)